STUDENT SOLUTIONS MANUAL

M&N Toscano

APPLIED STATISTICS

FOR ENGINEERS AND SCIENTISTS

Using Microsoft Excel® and MINITAB®

David M. Levine | Patricia P. Ramsey | Robert K. Smidt

Prentice
Hall

Upper Saddle River, NJ 07458

Executive Editor: Sally Yagan
Acquisitions Editor: Quincy McDonald
Supplement Editor: Joanne Wendelken
Special Projects Manager: Barbara A. Murray
Production Editor: Blake Cooper
Supplement Cover Manager: Paul Gourhan
Supplement Cover Designer: PM Workshop Inc.
Manufacturing Buyer: Lisa McDowell

Printed in the United States of America

10 9 8 7 6 5 4 3 2 1

ISBN 0-13-028681-8

Prentice-Hall International (UK) Limited, London
Prentice-Hall of Australia Pty. Limited, Sydney
Prentice-Hall Canada, Inc., Toronto
Prentice-Hall Hispanoamericana, S.A., Mexico
Prentice-Hall of India Private Limited, New Delhi
Pearson Education Asia Pte. Ltd., Singapore
Prentice-Hall of Japan, Inc., Tokyo
Editora Prentice-Hall do Brazil, Ltda., Rio de Janeiro

Contents

chapter 1

Introduction to Statistics and Quality Improvement

1. (a) discrete; however, if the question were the time it takes to read a page in this text; the answer would be continuous
   (b) discrete   (c) continuous   (d) discrete
   (e) discrete   (f) continuous

3. (a) Place of residence: Morristown, New Jersey—is not a continuous variable; nominal scale.
   (b) Type of residence: Single family home—is not a continuous variable; nominal scale.
   (c) Date of birth: August 13, 1966—is not a continuous variable; interval scale.
   (d) Projected monthly payments: $2,479—is a continuous variable (although, in practice, the exactness of measurements is limited by conventions of rounding monetary amounts to the nearest cent); ratio scale.
   (e) Occupation: Director of Food Chemistry— is not a continuous variable; nominal scale.
   (f) Employer: Venus Candy Company—is not a continuous variable; nominal scale.
   (g) Number of years at jobs: 10—is not a continuous variable; ratio scale.
   (h) Annual income: $140,000—is a continuous variable (see comment in part d); ratio scale.
   (i) Amount of mortgage requested: $220,000—is a continuous variable (see comment in part d); ratio scale.
   (j) Term of mortgage: 15 years—is a continuous variable; ratio scale. Note: If we were to assume that mortgages can be given only on a *whole* number of months or years, then it would not be a continuous variable.

5. (a) variables measure   (b) variables measure   (c) attribute measure
   (d) attribute measure   (e) variables measure   (f) attribute measure

7. Answers will vary.

9. (a) Sample without replacement: You need to select a two-digit number inside the range of 01 to 97 each time. Starting at row 12, column 1 the first ten 2 digit numbers obtained from Row 12 are:
   39 08 77 19 38 40 35 55 43 24.
   All two-digit numbers obtained from row 12 fall inside the range of 01 to 97 and are thus selected.
   (b) Sample with replacement: Because none of the numbers selected in Part A occur twice within the sample, this sample: 39, 08, 77, 19, 38, 40, 35, 55, 43, 24 is the answer to both (a) and (b).
   (c) The results are the same, because, in this series of numbers, no two digit numbers occurred more than once. Note: if you were asked to draw a sample of $n = 11$, then you would see a difference between the two results. The eleventh two-digit number is 08, which would be selected in (b) and would not be selected in (a) because 08 was the second selection.

11. (a) quality of design   (b) quality of conformance   (c) quality of design
    (d) quality of conformance   (e) quality of performance   (f) quality of performance
    (g) quality of design
    Note that (b) and (d) could also result in poor quality performance: the cake is burned—cannot be used or the bearings are too small or too large to fit into a wheel—cannot be used.

13. A *population* consists of *all* members of a class or category of interest. A *sample* is some portion or subset of a population.

15. *Discrete variables* are countable as there is a gap between each possible value.
Continuous variables can take any numerical value within a continuum or an interval.

17. *Attribute measures* either are nominal variables based on counts or involve proportions calculated from discrete data. *Variables measures* are any continuous variables measured on an interval or ratio scale.

19. A probability sampling is one in which the probability of selecting an element from a population for inclusion in the sample is known. In nonprobability sampling, this probability is not known.

21. Quality management views the management's role as managing the process; traditional managerial approach views management's role as the managing of people (i.e., motivating, disciplining and rewarding).

23. (a) It is a continuous numerical variable and represents a ratio scale. The distance between a supporting leg of one desk to the closest supporting leg of another desk measured in feet.
  (b) It is a categorical variable and represents an ordinal scale. Desks are categorized as small, medium, large and extra large as evaluated by the office supply catalog. Alternatively, if the size is understood to be, for example, the volume of the desk in square inches, then it is a continuous numerical variable and represents a ratio scale.
  (c) It is a categorical variable and represents a nominal scale. Gender is male or female, as self-reported by the office worker.
  (d) It is a continuous numerical variable and represents a ratio scale. Time in minutes measured from the time the worker leaves home to the time he/she enters the office.
  (e) It is a categorical variable and represents a nominal scale. Job classification, as defined in the office management bulletin.
  (f) It is a continuous numerical variable and represents an interval scale if the temperature is measured on either the Celsius or Fahrenheit scale or a ratio scale if the temperature is measured on the Kelvin scale.
  The answers will vary for all of the operational definitions.

25. (a) It is a continuous numerical variable and represents a ratio scale. Time in minutes measured from the time the student enters the bookstore until he/she passes through the exit door.
  (b) It is a categorical variable and represents a nominal scale. Gender is male or female, as self-reported by the student.
  (c) It is a categorical variable and represents an ordinal scale. Freshman, Sophomore, Junior, or Senior as defined in the school bulletin.
  (d) It is a categorical variable and represents a nominal scale. Academic major, as defined in the school bulletin.
  (e) It is a continuous numerical variable and represents an interval scale. Grade-point average as calculated by the registrar.
  (f) It is a categorical variable and represents a nominal scale. Payment; defined as currency, personal check, or credit card.
  (g) It is a discrete numerical variable and represents a ratio scale. Number of books, either paperback or hard-cover , as defined by the bookstore.
  The answers will vary for all of the operational definitions.

27. Answers will vary.

chapter 2

Tables and Charts

1. Both the cause-and-effect diagram (fishbone) and the process flow diagram help to provide a clearer understanding of a process or a problem. The process diagram is used to show the flow of steps in a process from its beginning to its termination, whereas the cause and effect diagram can help to organize ideas and identify cause-and-effect relationships. In other words, a cause-and-effect diagram helps to identify factors that may be causing variability in the process output, whereas a process flow diagram serves as a road map for locating and solving problems and improving quality.

3. Answers will vary.

5. Answers will vary.

7. (a) Time order plot using NOISE data table.

(b) The data appear to be relatively stable with no evidence of a pattern over time.

9. (a) Time order plot using RECWATER data table.

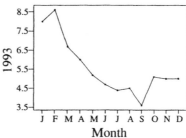

(b) The data are not relatively stable during the year. From these time-order plots a downward trend is evident in the monthly mean for the reclaimed water discharge.

11. Stem-and-leaf of C1, $N = 7$
Leaf Unit = 1.0

5	34
6	9
7	4
8	0
9	38

13. (a) and (b)

Manufacturer A:

Lengths of Life	Frequency
650–749	3
750–849	5
850–949	20
950–1049	9
1050–1149	3
1150–1249	0

Manufacturer B:

Lengths of Life	Frequency
650–749	0
750–849	2
850–949	8
950–1049	16
1050–1149	9
1150–1249	5

(c) Manufacturer A:

Lengths of Life	Frequency
650–699	2
700–749	1
750–799	1
800–849	4
850–899	9
900–949	11
950–999	5
1000–1049	4
1050–1099	3
1100–1149	0
1150–1199	0
1200–1249	0

Manufacturer B:

Lengths of Life	Frequency
650–699	0
700–749	0
750–799	0
800–849	2
850–899	2
900–949	6
950–999	6
1000–1049	10
1050–1099	6
1100–1149	3
1150–1199	4
1200–1249	1

(d) Manufacturer A:

Lengths of Life	Percentage
650–749	7.50%
750–849	12.50%
850–949	50.00%
950–1049	22.50%
1050–1149	7.50%
1150–1249	0.00%

Manufacturer B:

Lengths of Life	Percentage
650–749	0.00%
750–849	5.00%
850–949	20.00%
950–1049	40.00%
1050–1149	22.50%
1150–1249	12.50%

(e) Manufacturer A:

Manufacturer B:

(f)

(g) Manufacturer A:

Lengths of Life	Cumulative Frequency
650–749	3
750–849	8
850–949	28
950–1049	37
1050–1149	40
1150–1249	40

Manufacturer B:

Lengths of Life	Cumulative Frequency
650–749	0
750–849	2
850–949	10
950–1049	26
1050–1149	35
1150–1249	40

(h) Manufacturer A:

Lengths of Life	Cumulative %
650–749	7.50
750–849	20.00
850–949	70.00
950–1049	92.50
1050–1149	100.00
1150–1249	0.00

Manufacturer B:

Lengths of Life	Cumulative %
650–749	0.00
750–849	5.00
850–949	25.00
950–1049	65.00
1050–1149	87.50
1150–1249	100.00

(i)

(j) Manufacturer B bulbs have a longer life. From part (d) A-lamps are concentrated in the 950 hr to 1050 hr range. B-lamps are concentrated between the 1050 hr and 1150 hr range. There are no B-lamps with shorter life than 750 hr, whereas 7.5% of A-lamps live less than 750 hr. In addition, one can see from (I), that A-lamp ogive is drawn to the left of the B-lamp ogive.

15. (a)

dB	Frequency
66.0–67.9	2
68.0–69.9	0
70.0–71.9	1
72.0–73.9	4
74.0–75.9	10
76.0–77.9	10
78.0–79.9	8
80.0–81.9	4
82.0–83.9	1

(b)

dB	Frequency
66.0–67.9	5.00
68.0–69.9	0.00
70.0–71.9	2.50
72.0–73.9	10.00
74.0–75.9	25.00
76.0–77.9	25.00
78.0–79.9	20.00
80.0–81.9	10.00
82.0–83.9	2.50

(c)

dB	Cumulative %
66.0–67.9	5.00
68.0–69.9	5.00
70.0–71.9	7.50
72.0–73.9	17.50
74.0–75.9	42.50
76.0–77.9	67.50
78.0–79.9	87.50
80.0–81.9	97.50
82.0–83.9	100.00

(d)

(e)

(f)

Cumulative Percentage Polygon for Noise Level

(g) The noise level data are concentrated in the 74 dB and 80 dB range. There is no sound level lower than 66 dB or higher than 84 dB.

17. (a) The numbers of daily calls are stable over the 30 days.

Number of Daily Calls

(b) Stem-and-Leaf Display for Number of Calls

Stem unit:	100
26	9
27	
28	
29	
30	0 6 6 7 8 9
31	1 3 4 6 7 7 8 9 9
32	3 4 5 6 8 8
33	4 5 5 7 7
34	
35	
36	0 2
37	
38	1

(c)

Number	Frequency	Percentage
2500–2749	1	3.33
2750–2999	0	0.00
3000–3249	17	56.67
3250–3499	9	30.00
3500–3749	2	6.67
3750–3999	1	3.33
More	0	0.00

(d)

(e)
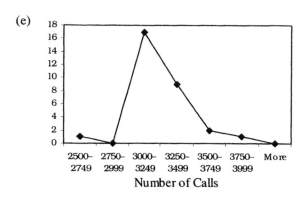
Number of Calls

(f)

Number	Cumulative %
2500–2749	3.33
2750–2999	3.33
3000–3249	60.00
3250–3499	90.00
3500–3749	96.67
3750–3999	100.00
More	100.00

(g)

Number of Daily Calls

(h) The number of daily calls is concentrated between 3000 and 3249 calls per day. Only 3.33% of daily calls are less than 3000 or more than 3250 calls per day.

19. (a) DMY Stem-and-Leaf Display

Stem unit: | 1

```
11 | 6 9
12 | 7
13 | 0 5 7
14 | 6 6 8
15 | 6 8
16 |
17 | 1 2 9
18 | 2 6 8
19 | 5
20 | 6 7 7
21 | 1
22 | 2
```

NC Stem-and-Leaf Display

Stem unit: | 1

```
11 | 8
12 | 2 7 7 7 8 9
13 | 1 1 3 4 4 6 6 7
14 | 0 1 7 8 8
15 | 1 3
16 | 0
```

(b) DMY

NC

(c) DMY

NC

(d) DMY

NC

(e) The dry matter yield data have two high points whereas the nitrogen concentration data have only one. DMY data are distributed over a wider range than NC data.

21. Answers will vary.   **23.** Answers will vary.   **25.** Answers will vary.

27. (a)

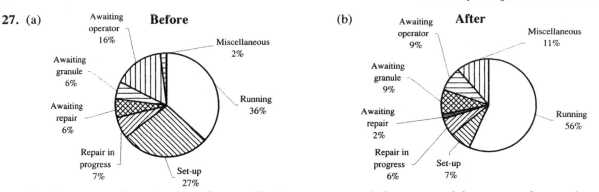

(c) The percent of running time after a quality improvement study increases and the percent of set-up time decreases.

(d)

(e)

(f) The percent of running time after a quality improvement study greatly exceeds the percent of time the machine expends on other activities, whereas before the improvement study it was comparable with set-up time percent.

(g)

(h)

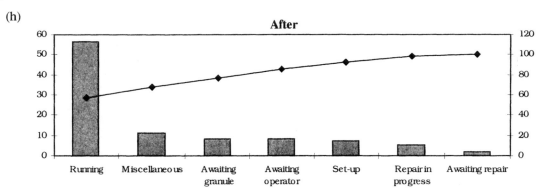

After

(i) After the quality improvement study the amount of running time greatly exceeds the amount of time the machine spent on other activities, while before the improvement study it was comparable with the amount of time spent for set-up. Pareto chart shows that before the improvement had been made the first two categories accounted for about 60% of all the time, while after the improvement the first category alone takes about 60% of the time.

29. (a) One-Way Summary Table
Count of Variable

Variable	Total
C	2
D	9
G	4
H	1
I	2
P	1
R	3
S	16
U	12
Grand Total	50

Variable	Frequency	Percentage	Cumulative Pct.
H	1	2.00	2.00
P	1	2.00	4.00
C	2	4.00	8.00
I	2	4.00	12.00
R	3	6.00	18.00
G	4	8.00	26.00
D	9	18.00	44.00
U	12	24.00	68.00
S	16	32.00	100.00

(b)

(c)

(d)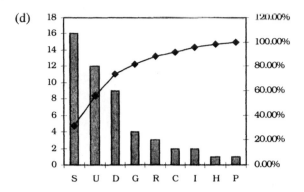

(e) The operator manager should focus on unsealed box top (32%), unreadable label (24%) and dirty carton (18%) as these categories combined account for about 70% of all the errors.

31. (a)

(b)

(c)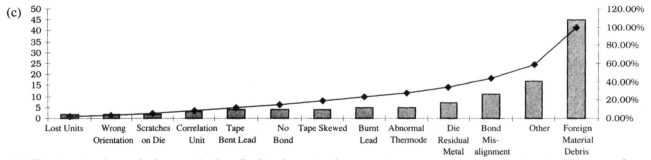

(d) The pie chart is not the best method to display these data because there are too many categories. It can be seen from the Pareto chart that foreign material debris comprises about 40% of the rejects. The Pareto diagram represents the categories in the descending rank order of their frequencies and makes it easier to determine which types of rejects are more important.

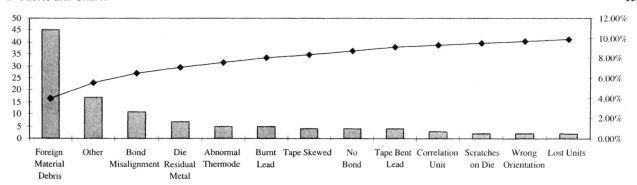

33. (a) Rows: Gender   Columns: Major

	No	Yes	All
Ns	28	16	44
S	10	22	32
All	38	38	76

(b)

	No	Yes	All
Ns	36.84	21.05	57.89
S	13.16	28.95	42.11
All	50.00	50.00	100.00

(c)

	No	Yes	All
Ns	63.64	36.36	100.00
S	31.25	68.75	100.00
All	50.00	50.00	100.00

(d)

	No	Yes	All
Ns	73.68	42.11	57.89
S	26.32	57.89	42.11
All	100.00	100.00	100.00

(e)

▨ No signs of osteoporosis
☐ Have signs of osteoporosis

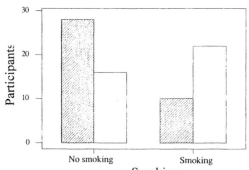

(f) Women who smoked displayed signs of osteoporosis more often compared to women who did not smoke.

35. (a) Rows: Age   Columns: Side

	Left	Right	Symmetrical	All
Adult	86	82	108	276
Juvenile	61	14	21	96
Pup	11	3	1	15
All	158	99	130	387

(b)

	Left	Right	Symmetrical	All
Adult	22.22	21.19	27.91	71.32
Juvenile	15.76	3.62	5.43	24.81
Pup	2.84	0.78	0.26	3.88
All	40.83	25.58	33.59	100.00

(c)

	Left	Right	Symmetrical	All
Adult	31.16	29.71	39.13	100.00
Juvenile	63.54	14.58	21.88	100.00
Pup	73.33	20.00	6.67	100.00
All	40.83	25.58	33.59	100.00

(d)

	Left	Right	Symmetrical	All
Adult	54.43	82.83	83.08	71.32
Juvenile	38.61	14.14	16.15	24.81
Pup	6.96	3.03	0.77	3.88
All	100.00	100.00	100.00	100.00

(e)

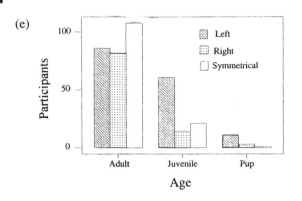

(f) Most of the juvenile and pups displayed saggital crest defects on the left side, whereas most adults had it symmetrically.

37. (a) Rows: Lab test Performed   Columns: Shift

	Day	Evening	All
Conforming	68.13	31.88	100.00
Nonconforming	40.00	60.00	100.00
All	67.00	33.00	100.00

(b)

	Day	Evening	All
Conforming	97.61	92.73	96.00
Nonconforming	2.39	7.27	4.00
All	100.00	100.00	100.00

(c)

	Day	Evening	All
Conforming	65.40	30.60	96.00
Nonconforming	1.60	2.40	4.00
All	67.00	33.00	100.00

(d) A table of row percentages is more informative because it shows the percentage of conforming and nonconforming tests that correspond to the morning or evening shift. The row percentages allow us to block the effect of disproportionate group size and show us that the pattern for day and evening tests among the nonconforming group is very different from the pattern for day and evening tests among the conforming group. Where 40% of the nonconforming group was tested during the day, 68% of the conforming group was tested during the day.

(e)

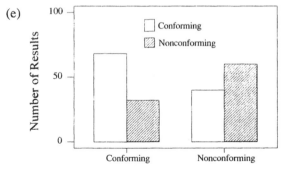

Lab Tests Performed

(f) Evening shift performed more nonconforming tests than the day shift did.

39. Answers will vary.

41. The process flow diagram is useful because it serves as a pictorial representation of a system and allows one to see the flow of steps in a process from its beginning to its termination.

43. A time-order plot helps to see whether the data are stable over the time periods involved. Until one can be reasonably certain that no patterns in the data exist over time, the use of any other method of analysis is premature and conclusions drawn from it may be misleading.

45. In a histogram the rectangular bars are constructed at the boundaries of each class whereas a polygon is formed by having the midpoint of each class represent the data in that class and then connecting the sequence of midpoints at their respective class percentages. Histograms cannot be constructed for more than one set of data, whereas polygons allow for such representations.

47. A bar chart should be used to directly compare the data variables.

49. A Pareto diagram is preferable when the categorical variables of interest are many.

51. A side-by-side bar chart is used for examination of the responses to two categorical variables simultaneously, whereas the bar chart is used for one categorical variable. A side-by-side bar chart is best suited to demonstrate the differences in magnitude rather than the percentage differences.

53. (a)

Liters	Frequency	Percentage
1.870–1.909	2	4.0
1.910–1.949	4	8.0
1.950–1.989	13	26.0
1.990–2.029	20	40.0
2.030–2.069	8	16.0
2.070–2.109	3	6.0
More	0	0.0

(b)

(c)

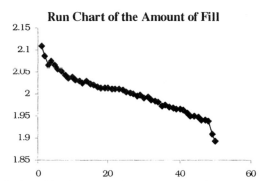

(d) From the run chart a downward trend appears evident in the process of filling two-liter bottles of soft drink.

(e) Using this histogram is premature and any conclusions drawn from it may be misleading.

55. (a)

(b)

(c)

(d) It might be useful when determining which filling and capping machines give the most nonconforming bottles.

(e) The Pareto diagram is more clear and straightforward in showing the relationship between different types of nonconforming bottles. As this is a subjective issue, different opinions are possible.

57. (a)

(b)

(c)

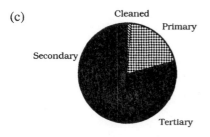

(d) The Pareto chart, because it shows that the secondary treatment has a higher percentage than the tertiary treatment, whereas it is not evident from the pie or bar charts.

(e) Secondary and tertiary treatments have almost the same percentage of waste, whereas the cleaned treatment has the smallest.

59. (a)

(b)

(c)

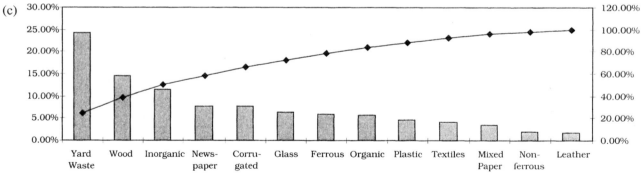

(d) A Pareto diagram is more preferable because the variable of interest contains many categories.

(e) Yard waste has the largest percent (about a quarter of all the waste profiled) whereas leather and nonferrous are the least.

61. (a) County A

	Cast Iron Pipe Break	Cast Iron Joint Break	Corroded Steel	Other	All
1989	43.44	1.56	41.56	13.44	100.00
1990	22.46	1.07	64.17	12.30	100.00
1991	20.75	0.47	68.87	9.91	100.00
All	31.29	1.11	55.49	12.10	100.00

County B

	Cast Iron Pipe Break	Cast Iron Joint Break	Corroded Steel	Other	All
1989	84.98	1.10	3.05	10.87	100.00
1990	79.81	1.24	1.86	17.08	100.00
1991	77.48	—	—	22.52	100.00
All	82.54	0.95	2.27	14.23	100.00

County C

	Cast Iron Pipe Break	Cast Iron Joint Break	Corroded Steel	Other	All
1989	72.53	8.58	8.15	10.73	100.00
1990	86.79	1.89	4.91	6.42	100.00
1991	77.55	2.86	3.67	15.92	100.00
All	79.27	4.31	5.52	10.90	100.00

County D

	Cast Iron Pipe Break	Cast Iron Joint Break	Corroded Steel	Other	All
1989	29.85	1.49	50.75	17.91	100.00
1990	22.46	0.72	51.45	25.36	100.00
1991	30.41	1.03	39.69	28.87	100.00
All	8.14	1.13	46.90	23.83	100.00

(b) County A

	Cast Iron Pipe Break	Cast Iron Joint Break	Corroded Steel	Other	All
1989	61.78	62.50	33.33	49.43	44.51
1990	18.67	25.00	30.08	26.44	26.01
1991	19.56	12.50	36.59	24.14	29.49
All	100.00	100.00	100.00	100.00	100.00

County B

	Cast Iron Pipe Break	Cast Iron Joint Break	Corroded Steel	Other	All
1989	61.87	69.23	80.65	45.88	60.09
1990	22.84	30.77	19.35	28.35	23.62
1991	15.29	—	—	25.77	16.29
All	100.00	100.00	100.00	100.00	100.00

County C

	Cast Iron Pipe Break	Cast Iron Joint Break	Corroded Steel	Other	All
1989	28.69	62.50	46.34	30.86	31.36
1990	39.05	15.63	31.71	20.99	35.67
1991	32.26	21.88	21.95	48.15	32.97
All	100.00	100.00	100.00	100.00	100.00

County D

	Cast Iron Pipe Break	Cast Iron Joint Break	Corroded Steel	Other	All
1989	40.00	50.00	40.80	28.35	37.71
1990	20.67	16.67	28.40	27.56	25.89
1991	39.33	33.33	30.80	44.09	36.40
All	100.00	100.00	100.00	100.00	100.00

(c) County A

	Cast Iron Pipe Break	Cast Iron Joint Break	Corroded Steel	Other	All
1989	19.33	0.70	18.50	5.98	44.51
1990	5.84	0.28	16.69	3.20	26.01
1991	6.12	0.14	20.31	2.92	29.49
All	31.29	1.11	55.49	12.10	100.00

County B

	Cast Iron Pipe Break	Cast Iron Joint Break	Corroded Steel	Other	All
1989	51.06	0.66	1.83	6.53	60.09
1990	18.86	0.29	0.44	4.04	23.62
1991	12.62	—	—	3.67	16.29
All	82.54	0.95	2.27	14.23	100.00

County C

	Cast Iron Pipe Break	Cast Iron Joint Break	Corroded Steel	Other	All
1989	22.75	2.69	2.56	3.36	31.36
1990	30.96	0.67	1.75	2.29	35.67
1991	25.57	0.94	1.21	5.25	32.97
All	79.27	4.31	5.52	10.90	100.00

County D

	Cast Iron Pipe Break	Cast Iron Joint Break	Corroded Steel	Other	All
1989	11.26	0.56	19.14	6.75	37.71
1990	5.82	0.19	13.32	6.57	25.89
1991	11.07	0.38	14.45	10.51	36.40
All	28.14	1.13	46.90	23.83	100.00

(d) A table of row percentages is more useful for determining the nature of the accidents, whereas a table of column percentages is more useful for showing the dynamics of change; causes of accidents for a range of years.

(e) County A
There were two almost equally frequent causes for leaks in 1989, but during the following years corroded steel became the main reason of the leak.

County B
The main reason of leaks was the cast iron joint break, but the percentage of leaks caused by the cast iron joint break decreased in the period from 1989 to 1991.
County C
The main reason of leaks was the cast iron joint break, and the percentage of leaks caused by the cast iron joint break was almost the same in the period from 1989 to 1991.
County D
The main reason of leaks was the corroded steel during 1989–1990, but the percentage of leaks caused by the corroded steel decreased while the percentage of leaks caused by the cast iron joint break and other reasons increased in 1991.

63. (a) Stem-and-Leaf Display for MPG

Stem unit: |10
```
1 |5 7 7 7 7 7 7 8 8 8 9 9 9 9 9 9
2 |0 0 0 0 0 0 0 0 0 0 0 0 1 1 1 1 1 1 1 1 1 2 2 2 2 2 2 2 2 2 2 2 3 3 3 3 3 3 4 4 4 4 4 4 5 5 6 6 6 6 6 6 6 7
  |8 8 8 8 9 9 9 9 9 9
3 |0 0 0 1 2 3 4 4 6
```

Stem-and-Leaf Display for Fuel Capacity   Stem-and-Leaf Display for Length

Stem unit: 1   Stem unit: 10
```
10 |0 6 6                                                14 |9
11 |9 9 9 9                                              15 |6
12 |5 5 8 8                                              16 |0 2 2 4 5
13 |2 2 2 2 2 2 2 3 5                                    17 |0 1 1 2 2 2 2 3 3 4 4 5 5 5 5 5 6 7 7 8 8
14 |5 5 5 5                                              18 |0 0 1 2 2 2 2 3 4 4 4 4 4 5 6 6 7 7 7 7 8 8 8
15 |2 2 4 5 5 5 5 5 6 9 9 9 9 9 9                            |8 8 9 9
16 |0 0 0 0 4 5 5 5 5 5 9                                19 |0 0 0 0 1 1 2 2 3 4 5 5 5 7 8
17 |0 0 1 1 2 2 4                                        20 |0 0 0 0 0 1 1 1 2 2 2 2 4 5 7 7
18 |0 0 0 0 0 0 0 0 0 0 5 5 5 5 5 5 5                    21 |2 2 4
19 |0 0 3
20 |0 0 0 0 0 0 6 8
21 |1
22 |5
23 |0
```

Stem-and-Leaf Display for Width

Stem unit: 1

```
63 | 0 0
64 | 0
65 | 0
66 | 0 0 0 0 0
67 | 0 0 0 0 0 0 0 0 0 0 0 0 0 0 0 0 0 0
68 | 0 0 0 0 0 0 0
69 | 0 0 0 0 0 0 0 0 0 0
70 | 0 0 0 0 0 0 0 0 0 0 0 0 0 0
71 | 0 0 0 0 0 0
72 | 0 0 0
73 | 0 0 0 0 0 0
74 | 0 0 0 0 0 0 0
75 | 0 0 0 0
76 | 0
77 |
78 | 0 0 0 0
```

Stem-and-Leaf Display for Weight

Stem unit: 100

```
18 | 5
19 |
20 | 7
21 | 4 7
22 | 9 9
23 | 9 9
24 | 1 2 4
25 | 0 1 4 4 7
26 | 0 0 3 4 7
27 | 2 7 7 9
28 | 6 7 7 7
29 | 0 1 1 6
30 | 3 5 7 9 10
31 | 0 0 1 5 5 8 8 8 10
32 | 3 5 6 8 8 9
33 | 2 5 7 10
34 | 0 1 2 2 4 5 5 5 6 9
35 | 2 4 4 5 5 5 6
36 | 7
37 | 1 1 1 3 7 7
38 | 1 4
39 | 4 10
40 | 1 1
41 |
```

Stem-and-Leaf Display for Wheelbase

Stem unit: 10

```
 9 | 3 3 4 4 5 7 7 7 7 8 8 8 8 8 9
10 | 0 0 0 0 0 1 1 1 2 2 3 3 3 3 3 3 3 3 3 3 3 3 4 4 4 4 4 4 4 5 5 5 6 6 6 6 6 6 7 7 7 7 7 8 8 8 8 8 8 8 8 9
   | 9 9 9 9
11 | 1 1 1 2 3 3 3 3 3 3 3 4 4 4 4 6
```

Stem-and-Leaf Display for Turning Circle

Stem unit: 1

```
34 | 0
35 | 0 0 0 0 0 0 0 0 0
36 | 0 0 0 0 0
37 | 0 0 0 0
38 | 0 0 0 0 0 0 0 0 0 0 0 0 0 0
39 | 0 0 0 0 0 0 0 0 0 0 0 0 0 0 0 0 0 0 0 0 0
40 | 0 0 0 0 0 0 0 0 0 0
41 | 0 0 0 0
42 | 0 0 0 0 0 0 0
43 | 0 0 0 0 0 0 0 0 0 0 0 0 0
44 | 0
45 | 0
```

Stem-and-Leaf Display for Luggage Capacity

Stem unit: 1

```
 8 | 0
 9 | 0 0
10 | 0 0 0 0 0 0
11 | 0 0 0 0
12 | 0 0 0 0 0 0 0 0 0 0 0 0 0
13 | 0 0 0 0 0 0 0 0 0 0 0
14 | 0 0 0 0 0 0 0 0 0 0 0 0 0 0 0 0 0 0 0
15 | 0 0 0 0 0 0 0 0
16 | 0 0 0 0 0 0 0 0 0 0 0
17 | 0 0 0 0 0
18 | 0
19 | 0 0 0 0
20 | 0
21 | 0 0
22 |
23 |
24 | 0 0
```

Stem-and-Leaf Display for Front Leg Room

Stem unit: 1

```
40 | 0 0 0 5 5 5 5 5
41 | 0 0 0 0 0 0 0 0 0 0 0 0 0 0 0 5 5 5 5
     5 5 5 5 5 5 5 5 5 5 5
42 | 0 0 0 0 0 0 0 0 0 0 0 0 0 0 0 0 0 0
     0 0 0 0 0 5 5 5 5 5 5 5 5 5 5 5
43 | 0 0 0 0 0 0 0 0 0 0 5 5

44 | 0 5
```

Stem-and-Leaf Display for Front Head Room

Stem unit: 1

```
1 | 0 5 5 5
2 | 0 0 0 0 0 0 5 5 5 5 5 5 5

3 | 0 0 0 0 0 0 0 0 0 0 0 0 0 0 0 0 0 0 5 5 5 5 5 5
    5 5 5 5 5 5 5 5 5 5
4 | 0 0 0 0 0 0 0 0 0 0 0 0 0 5 5 5 5 5 5 5 5 5 5 5
    5
5 | 0 0 0 0 0 0 0 0 0 5 5 5 5
6 | 0 5
```

(b)

mpg	Frequency	Percentage
10.0–14.0	0	0.00
15–19	16	17.98
20–24	44	49.44
25–29	20	22.47
30–34	8	8.99
35–39	1	1.12
More	0	0.00

Fuel Capacity	Frequency	Percentage
9.01–11.00	3	3.37
11.01–13.00	8	8.99
13.01–15.00	13	14.61
15.01–17.00	28	31.46
17.01–19.00	24	26.97
19.01–21.00	10	11.24
21.01–23.00	3	3.37
More	0	0.00

Length	Frequency	Percentage
151–160	3	3.37
161–170	5	5.62
171–180	22	24.72
181–190	29	32.58
191–200	16	17.98
201–210	11	12.36
211–220	3	3.37
More	0	0.00

Width	Frequency	Percentage
62.1–64.0	3	3.37
64.1–66.0	6	6.74
66.1–68.0	24	26.97
68.1–70.0	25	28.09
70.1–72.0	9	10.11
72.1–74.0	13	14.61
74.1–76.0	5	5.62
76.1–78.0	4	4.49
More	0	0.00

Weight	Frequency	Percentage
1499–2000	1	1.12
2001–2500	11	12.36
2501–3000	21	23.60
3001–3500	34	38.20
3501–4000	18	20.22
4001–4500	4	4.49
More	0	0.00

Wheel Base	Frequency	Percentage
91–95	5	5.62
96–100	15	16.85
101–105	27	30.34
106–110	26	29.21
111–115	15	16.85
116–120	1	1.12
More	0	0.00

Turning Circle	Frequency	Percentage
33.1–35.0	11	12.36
35.1–37.0	9	10.11
37.1–39.0	33	37.08
39.1–41.0	14	15.73
41.1–43.0	20	22.47
43.1–45.0	2	2.25
More	0	0.00

Luggage Capacity	Frequency	Percentage
7.1–10.0	9	10.11
10.1–13.0	28	31.46
13.1–16.0	37	41.57
16.1–19.0	10	11.24
19.1–22.0	3	3.37
22.1–25.0	2	2.25
More	0	0.00

Front Leg Room	Frequency	Percentage
39.9–40.0	3	3.37
40.1–41.0	19	21.35
41.1–42.0	40	44.94
42.1–43.0	23	25.84
43.1–44.0	3	3.37
44.1–45.0	1	1.12
More	0	0.00

Front Head Room	Frequency	Percentage
0.1–1.0	1	1.12
1.1–2.0	9	10.11
2.1–3.0	24	26.97
3.1–4.0	28	31.46
4.1–5.0	21	23.60
5.1–6.0	5	5.62
6.1–7.0	1	1.12
More	0	0.00

(c)

(d)

(e)

mpg	Frequency	Cumulative %
10.0–14.0	0	.00
15–19	16	17.98
20–24	44	67.42
25–29	20	89.89
30–34	8	98.88
35–39	1	100.00
More	0	100.00

Length	Frequency	Cumulative %
151–160	3	3.37
161–170	5	8.99
171–180	22	33.71
181–190	29	66.29
191–200	16	84.27
201–210	11	96.63
211–220	3	100.00
More	0	100.00

Weight	Frequency	Cumulative %
1499–2000	1	1.12
2001–2500	11	13.48
2501–3000	21	37.08
3001–3500	34	75.28
3501–4000	18	95.51
4001–4500	4	100.00
More	0	100.00

Turning Circle	Frequency	Cumulative %
33.1–35.0	11	12.36
35.1–37.0	9	22.47
37.1–39.0	33	59.55
39.1–41.0	14	75.28
41.1–43.0	20	97.75
43.1–45.0	2	100.00
More	0	100.00

Front Leg Room	Frequency	Cumulative %
39.9–40.0	3	3.37
40.1–41.0	19	24.72
41.1–42.0	40	69.66
42.1–43.0	23	95.51
43.1–44.0	3	98.88
44.1–45.0	1	100.00
More	0	100.00

Fuel Capacity	Frequency	Cumulative %
9.01–11.00	3	3.37
11.01–13.00	8	12.36
13.01–15.00	13	26.97
15.01–17.00	28	58.43
17.01–19.00	24	85.39
19.01–21.00	10	96.63
21.01–23.00	3	100.00
More	0	100.00

Width	Frequency	Cumulative %
62.1–64.0	3	3.37
64.1–66.0	6	10.11
66.1–68.0	24	37.08
68.1–70.0	25	65.17
70.1–72.0	9	75.28
72.1–74.0	13	89.89
74.1–76.0	5	95.51
76.1–78.0	4	100.00
More	0	100.00

Wheel Base	Frequency	Cumulative %
91–95	5	5.62
96–100	15	22.47
101–105	27	52.81
106–110	26	82.02
111–115	15	98.88
116–120	1	100.00
More	0	100.00

Luggage Capacity	Frequency	Cumulative %
7.1–10.0	9	10.11
10.1–13.0	28	41.57
13.1–16.0	37	83.15
16.1–19.0	10	94.38
19.1–22.0	3	97.75
22.1–25.0	2	100.00
More	0	100.00

Front Head Room	Frequency	Cumulative %
0.1–1.0	1	1.12
1.1–2.0	9	11.24
2.1–3.0	24	38.20
3.1–4.0	28	69.66
4.1–5.0	21	93.26
5.1–6.0	5	98.88
6.1–7.0	1	100.00
More	0	100.00

(f)

Length

Fuel Capacity

(g) Answers will vary.

(h)

mpg	Frequency	Percentage	Cumulative %
10.0–14.0	0	0.00	.00
15 –19	9	52.94	52.94
20–24	8	47.06	100.00
25–29	0	0.00	100.00
30–34	0	0.00	100.00
35–39	0	0.00	100.00
More	0	0.00	100.00

MPG

MPG

mpg	Frequency	Percentage	Cumulative %
10.0–14.0	0	0.00	.00
15–19	7	9.72	9.72
20–24	36	50.00	59.72
25–29	20	27.78	87.50
30–34	8	11.11	98.61
35–39	1	1.39	100.00
More	0	0.00	100.00

Fuel Capacity	Frequency	Percentage	Cumulative %
9.01–11.00	0	0.00	.00
11.01–13.00	0	0.00	.00
13.01–15.00	0	0.00	.00
15.01–17.00	5	29.41	29.41
17.01–19.00	5	29.41	58.82
19.01–21.00	4	23.53	82.35
21.01–23.00	3	17.65	100.00
More	0	0.00	100.00

Fuel Capacity	Frequency	Percentage	Cumulative %
9.01–11.00	3	4.17	4.17
11.01–13.00	8	11.11	15.28
13.01–15.00	13	18.06	33.33
15.01–17.00	23	31.94	65.28
17.01–19.00	19	26.39	91.67
19.01–21.00	6	8.33	100.00
21.01–23.00	0	0.00	100.00
More	0	0.00	100.00

Length	Frequency	Percentage	Cumulative %
151–160	0	0.00	.00
161–170	0	0.00	.00
171–180	3	17.65	17.65
181–190	1	5.88	23.53
191–200	9	52.94	76.47
201–210	1	5.88	82.35
211–220	3	17.65	100.00
More	0	0.00	100.00

Length	Frequency	Percentage	Cumulative %
151–160	3	4.17	4.17
161–170	5	6.94	11.11
171–180	19	26.39	37.50
181–190	28	38.89	76.39
191–200	7	9.72	86.11
201–210	10	13.89	100.00
211–220	0	0.00	100.00
More	0	0.00	100.00

Width	Frequency	Percentage	Cumulative %
62.1–64.0	0	0.00	.00
64.1–66.0	0	0.00	.00
66.1–68.0	2	11.76	11.76
68.1–70.0	2	11.76	23.53
70.1–72.0	4	23.53	47.06
72.1–74.0	3	17.65	64.71
74.1–76.0	2	11.76	76.47
76.1–78.0	4	23.53	100.00
More	0	0.00	100.00

Width	Frequency	Percentage	Cumulative %
62.1–64.0	3	4.17	4.17
64.1–66.0	6	8.33	12.50
66.1–68.0	22	30.56	43.06
68.1–70.0	23	31.94	75.00
70.1–72.0	5	6.94	81.94
72.1–74.0	10	13.89	95.83
74.1–76.0	3	4.17	100.00
76.1–78.0	0	0.00	100.00
More	0	0.00	100.00

Weight	Frequency	Percentage	Cumulative %
1499–2000	0	0.00	.00
2001–2500	0	0.00	.00
2501–3000	0	0.00	.00
3001–3500	5	29.41	29.41
3501–4000	8	47.06	76.47
4001–4500	4	23.53	100.00
More	0	0.00	100.00

Weight	Frequency	Percentage	Cumulative %
1499–2000	1	1.39	1.39
2001–2500	11	15.28	16.67
2501–3000	21	29.17	45.83
3001–3500	29	40.28	86.11
3501–4000	10	13.89	100.00
4001–4500	0	0.00	100.00
More	0	0.00	100.00

Wheel Base	Frequency	Percentage	Cumulative %
91–95	0	0.00	.00
96–100	1	5.88	5.88
101–105	3	17.65	23.53
106–110	6	35.29	58.82
111–115	6	35.29	94.12
116–120	1	5.88	100.00
More	0	0.00	100.00

Wheel Base	Frequency	Percentage	Cumulative %
91–95	5	6.94	6.94
96–100	14	19.44	26.39
101–105	24	33.33	59.72
106–110	20	27.78	87.50
111–115	9	12.50	100.00
116–120	0	0.00	100.00
More	0	0.00	100.00

Turning Circle	Frequency	Percentage	Cumulative %
33.1–35.0	1	5.88	5.88
35.1–37.0	2	11.76	17.65
37.1–39.0	5	29.41	47.06
39.1–41.0	3	17.65	64.71
41.1–43.0	5	29.41	94.12
43.1–45.0	1	5.88	100.00
More	0	0.00	100.00

Turning Circle	Frequency	Percentage	Cumulative %
33.1–35.0	10	13.89	13.89
35.1–37.0	7	9.72	23.61
37.1–39.0	28	38.89	62.50
39.1–41.0	11	15.28	77.78
41.1–43.0	15	20.83	98.61
43.1–45.0	1	1.39	100.00
More	0	0.00	100.00

Luggage Capacity	Frequency	Percentage	Cumulative %
7.1–10.0	5	29.41	29.41
10.1–13.0	4	23.53	52.94
13.1–16.0	5	29.41	82.35
16.1–19.0	0	0.00	82.35
19.1–22.0	3	17.65	100.00
22.1–25.0	0	0.00	100.00
More	0	0.00	100.00

Luggage Capacity	Frequency	Percentage	Cumulative %
7.1–10.0	4	5.56	5.56
10.1–13.0	24	33.33	38.89
13.1–16.0	32	44.44	83.33
16.1–19.0	10	13.89	97.22
19.1–22.0	0	0.00	97.22
22.1–25.0	2	2.78	100.00
More	0	0.00	100.00

Front Leg Room	Frequency	Percentage	Cumulative %
39.9–40.0	0	0.00	.00
40.1–41.0	1	5.88	5.88
41.1–42.0	6	35.29	41.18
42.1–43.0	8	47.06	88.24
43.1–44.0	2	11.76	100.00
44.1–45.0	0	0.00	100.00
More	0	0.00	100.00

Front Leg Room 1	Frequency	Percentage	Cumulative %
39.9–40.0	3	4.17	4.17
40.1–41.0	18	25.00	29.17
41.1–42.0	34	47.22	76.39
42.1–43.0	15	20.83	97.22
43.1–44.0	1	1.39	98.61
44.1–45.0	1	1.39	100.00
More	0	0.00	100.00

Front Head Room	Frequency	Percentage	Cumulative %
0.1–1.0	0	0.00	.00
1.1–2.0	2	11.76	11.76
2.1–3.0	6	35.29	47.06
3.1–4.0	5	29.41	76.47
4.1–5.0	4	23.53	100.00
5.1–6.0	0	0.00	100.00
6.1–7.0	0	0.00	100.00
More	0	0.00	100.00

Front Head Room 1	Frequency	Percentage	Cumulative %
0.1–1.0	1	1.39	1.39
1.1–2.0	7	9.72	11.11
2.1–3.0	18	25.00	36.11
3.1–4.0	23	31.94	68.06
4.1–5.0	17	23.61	91.67
5.1–6.0	5	6.94	98.61
6.1–7.0	1	1.39	100.00
More	0	0.00	100.00

The front-wheel-drive cars have greater mpg and smaller fuel capacity, length, width, weight, wheel base, slightly more luggage capacity and front leg room, and almost the same front head room as the rear-wheel-drive cars.

(i) Rows: Drive   Columns: Fuel

	0	1	All
0	9	8	17
1	16	56	72
All	25	64	89

(j)

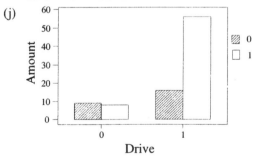

(k) It docs not matter what type of gasoline is used for rear-wheel cars, but it seems that most of front-wheel cars used the first type of gasoline.

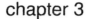
chapter 3

Describing and Summarizing Data

1. (a)

	Grade X	**Grade Y**
(1) Mean	575	575.4
(2) Median	575	575
(3) Standard Deviation	6.40	2.07

(b) If quality is measured by the average inner diameter, Grade X tires provide a better quality, because its mean and median are both equal to the expected value of 575 mm. If, however, quality is measured by consistency, Grade Y provides better quality, because its standard deviation is much smaller. The range in values for Grade Y is 5 mm compared to the range in values for Grade X, which is equal to 16 mm.

(c)

	Grade X	**Grade Y**
(1) Mean	575	577.4
(2) Median	575	575
(3) Standard Deviation	6.40	6.11

In the event that the fifth Y tire measures 588 mm rather than 578 mm, the Grade Y average inner diameter becomes 577.4 mm, which is much larger than Grade X average inner diameter. Also, the Grade Y standard deviation swells from 2.07 mm to 6.11 mm. Therefore, Grade X provides better quality in terms of the average inner diameter and has only slightly more variation than Grade Y. The range in values for Grade Y is now 15 mm, which is only slightly less than the range in values for Grade X.

3. (a)
  (1) Arithmetic Mean   25.677
  (2) Median   25
  (3) Mode   22
  (4) Midrange $(40+17)/2 = 28.5$
  (5) Quartiles $Q_1 = 21$, $Q_3 = 30$
  (6) Midhinge $(30 + 21)/2 = 25.5$
  (7) Range $40 - 17 = 23$
  (8) Interquartile Range $30 - 21 = 9$
  (9) Variance   37.959
  (10) Standard Deviation   6.1611

(b) Mean $= 25.677 >$ median $= 25$. The distribution is positive or right-skewed, because the mean is pulled upward in the direction of positive values.

(c)

$X_{smallest}$	Q_1	**Median**	Q_3	$X_{largest}$
17	21	25	30	40

(1) The distance from $X_{smallest}$ to $Q_1 = 4$, the distance from Q_3 to $X_{largest} = 10$.

(2) Median $= 25 <$ midhinge $= 25.5 <$ midrange $= 28.5$, therefore we may conclude that the distribution is right-skewed.

5. (a) (1) Arithmetic Mean   70.73
       (2) Median   70
       (3) Mode   70
       (4) Midrange $(56+86)/2 = 71$
       (5) Quartiles $Q_1 = 69.5$, $Q_3 = 72$
       (6) Midhinge $(69.5+72)/2 = 70.75$
       (7) Range $86-56 = 30$
       (8) Interquartile Range $72-69.5 = 2.5$
       (9) Variance   21.93
       (10) Standard Deviation   4.6827

   (b) Mean = 70.73 > median = 70. The distribution is slightly right-skewed, because the mean is pulled upward in the direction of positive values.

   (c)

$X_{smallest}$	Q_1	Median	Q_3	$X_{largest}$
56	69.5	70	72	86

   (1) The distance from $X_{smallest}$ to Q_1 is 13.5 and the distance from Q_3 to $X_{largest}$ is 14.

   (2) The distance from Q_1 to the median is 0.5 and the distance from the median to Q_3 is 2.

   (3) Median = 70 < midhinge = 70.75 < midrange = 71.

   Therefore we may conclude that the distribution is slightly right-skewed.

7. (a)

	Plant A	Plant B
(1) Arithmetic Mean	9.382	11.354
(2) Median	8.515	11.96
(3) Midrange	$(4.42+21.62)/2 = 13.02$	$(2.33+25.75)/2 = 14.04$
(4) First Quartile	7.29	6.25
(5) Third Quartile	11.42	14.25
(6) Midhinge	$(11.42+7.29)/2 = 9.355$	$(6.25 + 14.25)/2 = 10.25$
(7) Range	$21.62-4.42 = 17.2$	$25.75-2.33 = 23.42$
(8) Interquartile Range	$11.42-7.29 = 4.13$	$14.25-6.25 = 8$
(9) Variance	15.981	26.277
(10) Standard Deviation	3.998	5.126
(11) Coefficient of Variation	42.61%	45.15%

   (b)

	$X_{smallest}$	Q_1	Median	Q_3	$X_{largest}$
Plant A	4.42	7.29	8.515	11.42	21.62
Plant B	2.33	6.25	11.96	14.25	25.75

   (c) (1) For both distributions the distance from Q_3 to $X_{largest}$ greatly exceeds the distance from $X_{smallest}$ to Q_1.

      (2) Plant A: median = 8.515 < midhinge = 9.355 < midrange = 13.02
         Plant B: midhinge = 10.25 < midrange = 14.04 > median = 11.96
      Both the distributions are right-skewed. The data for Plant B requires a closer analysis because the mean of this data is less than the median, and the median is greater than the midhinge. This is typical of left skewed data. By constructing a chart similar to Figure 3.4 one can demonstrate more clearly that the data is slightly right skewed.

   (d) Plant B has a greater range of processing times, much more dispersion among data values, a higher median, a higher value for the third quartile, and a greater extreme value than Plant A.

9. (a)

		Carnes 3-Way Diffusers	Krueger 4-Way Diffusers
(1)	Arithmetic Mean	247.5	244.3
(2)	Median	250	245
(3)	Midrange	$(160+310)/2 = 235$	$(190+300)/2 = 245$
(4)	First Quartile	215	225
(5)	Third Quartile	285	265
(6)	Midhinge	$(215+285)/2 = 250$	$(225+265)/2 = 245$
(7)	Range	$310-160 = 150$	$300-190 = 110$
(8)	Interquartile Range	$285-215 = 70$	$265-225 = 40$
(9)	Variance	1557.407	732.677
(10)	Standard Deviation	39.464	27.068

(b)

	$X_{smallest}$	Q_1	Median	Q_3	$X_{largest}$
Carnes 3-Way Diffusers	160	215	250	285	310
Krueger 4-Way Diffusers	190	225	245	265	300

(c) For Krueger 4-Way Diffusers

(1) The distance from $X_{smallest}$ to Q_1 is equal the distance from Q_3 to $X_{largest} = 35$.

(2) The distance from Q_1 to the median is equal the distance from the median to $Q_3 = 20$.

(3) Median = midrange = midhinge = 245 so the data are perfectly symmetrical.

For Carnes 3-Way Diffusers

(1) The distance from $X_{smallest}$ to $Q_1 = 55$ and the distance from Q_3 to $X_{largest} = 25$.

Midrange = 235 < midhinge = 250 so the distribution is left-skewed.

(d) The Carnes 3-Way Diffusers have a greater range, more dispersion among data values, a slightly higher mean and median, and a higher value for the third quartile than Krueger diffusers.

11. (a)

Box-and-Whisker Plot

(b) The center of the distribution is asymmetric, with the median located a little closer to Q_1 than to Q_3. In addition, the upper tail appears to be substantially longer than the lower tail. Therefore, the distribution of temperature is right-skewed.

13. (a)

Noise Levels

(b) The center of the distribution is asymmetric, with the median located much closer to Q_1 than to Q_3. Therefore, the distribution is slightly right-skewed.

15. (a)

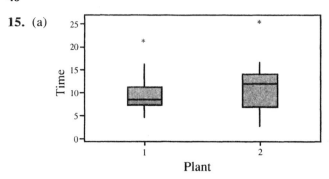

(b) The centers of the distributions are asymmetric. For plant A, the median is located much closer to Q_1 than to Q_3. For plant B, the median is located closer to Q_3 than to Q_1. In addition, the upper tails of distributions appear to be longer than the lower tails, so the distributions are right-skewed.

Note that estimating whether a distribution is right-or left-skewed is rather subjective (especially when graphical methods are employed). Thus, for verification Skewers provided by MINIT can be used for ambiguous cases (such as the Plant B case in the current problem).

17. Central tendency, variability, skewness, and kurtosis are useful for describing a set of numerical data.

19. The **arithmetic mean** acts as a balancing point. It is the only measure of location based on all of the observations, and is greatly affected by extreme values.

The **median** is the middle value in an ordered sequence of data, dividing a distribution into two equal parts. Using the median may be more appropriate than the mean when extreme observations are present, because the median is not affected by a change in value of an observation if the order of the observations remain the same.

The **mode** is the most frequently occurring value in a data set. It is not useful if each value occurs only once or if there are several differing modes of different values.

Midrange shows the geometrical center of the data set. Because it involves only the smallest and largest observations in the data set, the midrange is greatly affected by an extreme value or values.

Midhinge represents the mean of the first and third quartiles and is not affected by extreme values in the data.

21. The **range** measures the total spread in a set of data. It is an easily computed measure of variation, but takes into account only the largest and smallest values and fails to account for how the values are distributed between these two extremes. Unlike the range, **interquartile range** is not affected by extreme values and represents the range of the middle half of the data set. Unfortunately, like the range the interquartile range does not account for the distribution of the values in the set. **Variance** and **standard deviation** evaluate the spread or dispersion of data around the mean. The advantage of the standard deviation over the variance is that it has the same units as the original data.

23. Skewness represents the asymmetry of the distribution whereas kurtosis relates to the relative concentration of values in the center of the distribution as compared to the tails.

25. The box-and-whisker plot provides a graphical representation of the data through the five-number summary. This gives a more thorough understanding of the distribution of the data set than could be obtained from studying the mean, median, and standard deviation alone. The box-and-whisker plot is also a useful tool for comparing two or more groups graphically.

27. (a)

		Rainfall Depth	Runoff Depth
(1)	Arithmetic Mean	18.59	1.710
(2)	Median	14.55	1.515
(3)	Mode	No unique mode	No unique mode
(4)	Midrange	$(7.2 + 41.2)/2 = 24.2$	$(4.05 + 0.07)/2 = 2.06$
(5)	Quartiles	$Q_1 = 11.5$, $Q_3 = 27.3$	$Q_1 = 0.87$, $Q_3 = 2.49$
(6)	Midhinge	$(11.5 + 27.3)/2 = 19.4$	$(0.87 + 2.49)/1.68$
(7)	Range	$41.2 - 7.2 = 34$	$4.05 - 0.07 = 3.98$
(8)	Interquartile Range	$27.3 - 11.5 = 15.8$	$2.49 - 0.87 = 1.62$
(9)	Variance	109.782	1.22777
(10)	Standard Deviation	10.4777	1.10805

(b) **Rainfall Depth:** Mean = 18.59 > median = 14.55. The distribution is positive or right-skewed, because the mean is pulled upward in the direction of positive values.

Runoff Depth: Mean = 1.71 > median = 1.515. The distribution is positive or right-skewed, because the mean is pulled upward in the direction of positive values.

(c)

	X_{smallest}	Q_1	**Median**	Q_3	X_{largest}
Rainfall Depth	7.2	11.5	14.55	27.3	41.2
Runoff Depth	0.07	0.87	1.515	2.49	4.05

Rainfall Depth

(1) The distance from X_{smallest} to $Q_1 = 4.3$; the distance from Q_3 to $X_{\text{largest}} = 13.9$.

(2) Median = 14.55 < midhinge = 19.4 < midrange = 24.2, therefore we may conclude that the distribution is right-skewed.

Runoff Depth

(1) The distance from X_{smallest} to $Q_1 = 0.8$; the distance from Q_3 to $X_{\text{largest}} = 1.56$.

(2) Median = 1.515 < midhinge = 1.68 < midrange = 2.06, therefore we may conclude that the distribution is right-skewed.

(d)

Rainfall Depth

Runoff Depth

The center of the distribution is asymmetric, with the median located closer to Q_1 than to Q_3. In addition, the upper tail appears to be substantially longer than the lower tail, showing that the distribution is right-skewed.

The center of the distribution is asymmetric, with the median located a little closer to Q_1 than to Q_3. In addition, the upper tail appears to be longer than the lower tail, showing that the distribution is right-skewed.

(e) As the median of the Rainfall Depth distribution is located closer to Q_1 the distribution of Rainfall Depth is more right-skewed than in Runoff Depth.

29. (a)

		DMY	**NC**
(1)	Arithmetic Mean	16.713	13.643
(2)	Median	17.1	13.4
(3)	Mode	14.6, 20.7	12.7
(4)	Midrange	$(11.6 + 22.2)/2 = 16.9$	$(11.8 + 16.0)/2 = 13.9$
(5)	Quartiles	$Q_1 = 13.7$, $Q_3 = 19.5$	$Q_1 = 12.8$, $Q_3 = 14.7$
(6)	Midhinge	$(13.7 + 19.5)/2 = 16.6$	$(12.8 + 14.7)/2 = 13.75$
(7)	Range	$22.2 - 11.6 = 10.6$	$16.0 - 11.8 = 4.2$
(8)	Interquartile Range	$19.5 - 13.7 = 5.8$	$14.7 - 12.8 = 1.9$
(9)	Variance	10.4185	1.12711
(10)	Standard Deviation	3.22776	1.06166

(b) **DMY** Mean = 16.713 < median = 17.1 so the distribution is left-skewed.

NC Mean = 13.643 < median = 13.4 so the distribution is left-skewed.

(c)

	X_{smallest}	Q_1	**Median**	Q_3	X_{largest}
DMY	11.6	13.7	17.1	19.5	22.2

(1) The distance from X_{smallest} to $Q_1 = 2.1$; the distance from Q_3 to $X_{\text{largest}} = 2.7$.

(2) Median = 17.1 < midhinge = 16.6 < midrange = 16.9, therefore we may conclude that the distribution is slightly right-skewed.

	X_{smallest}	Q_1	**Median**	Q_3	X_{largest}
NC	11.8	12.8	13.4	14.7	16.0

(1) The distance from X_{smallest} to $Q_1 = 1.0$; the distance from Q_3 to $X_{\text{largest}} = 1.3$.

(2) Median = 13.4 < midhinge = 13.75 < midrange = 13.9, therefore we may conclude that the distribution is slightly right-skewed.

(d) In terms of location, the median, the first and third quartiles, and the minimum values are larger for the DMY data than for the NC data. In terms of dispersion, the range and the interquartile range are larger for the DMY data than for the NC data. Both distributions appear to be slightly right-skewed.

(e)

DMY

NC

The center of the distribution is asymmetric, with the median located a little closer to Q_3 than to Q_1. But the upper tail appears to be a little longer than the lower tail. Therefore we can conclude that this distribution is approximately symmetrical.

The center of the distribution is asymmetric, with the median located closer to Q_1 than to Q_3. In addition, the upper tail appears to be a little longer than the lower tail. Therefore, the distribution is right-skewed.

(f) Both box-and-whisker plots have similar tails (the upper tail appears to be a little longer than the lower one), but the median for DMY distribution is shifted to the right and the median for DMY distribution is shifted to the left. In addition, the NC distribution is right-skewed, and the DMY distribution may be symmetrical.

31. (a)

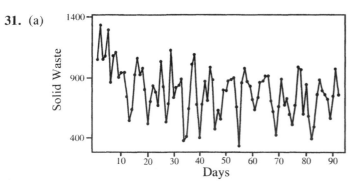

The data appear to be relatively stable with no evidence of a pattern over time.

(b) (1) Arithmetic Mean   787.9
    (2) Median   796.5
    (3) Mode   712, 859, 928
    (4) Midrange $(333 + 1334)/2 = 833.5$
    (5) Quartiles $Q_1 = 657$, $Q_3 = 913$
    (6) Midhinge $(913 + 657)/2 = 785$
    (7) Range $1334 - 333 = 1001$
    (8) Interquartile Range $913 - 657 = 256$
    (9) Variance   40861.4
    (10) Standard Deviation   202.142

(c)

$X_{smallest}$	Q_1	**Median**	Q_3	$X_{largest}$
333.0	657.0	796.5	913.0	1334.0

(d)

Solid Waste

(e) (1) The distance from $X_{smallest}$ to $Q_1 = 324$; the distance from Q_3 to $X_{largest} = 421$.

(2) Median $= 796.5 <$ midrange $= 833.5$, therefore we may conclude that the distribution is slightly right-skewed.

From the box-and-whisker plot we can see that the center of the distribution is slightly asymmetric, with the median located a little closer to Q_3 than to Q_1.

On the other hand, the upper tail appears to be longer than the lower tail, therefore, the distribution may be slightly right-skewed.

The data appear to be relatively stable with no evidence of a pattern over time.

(f)

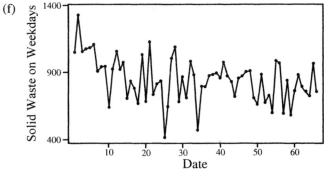

(1) Arithmetic Mean   848.8
(2) Median   864.0
(3) Mode   712, 859, 928
(4) Midrange $(1334.0 + 414.0)/2 = 874$
(5) Quartiles $Q_1 = 726$, $Q_3 = 970$
(6) Midhinge $(970 + 726)/2 = 848$
(7) Range $1334.0 - 414.0 = 920$
(8) Interquartile Range $970 - 726 = 244$
(9) Variance   27817.6
(10) Standard Deviation   166.786

$X_{smallest}$	Q_1	**Median**	Q_3	$X_{largest}$
414.0	726	864.0	970	1334.0

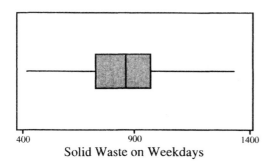

Solid Waste on Weekdays

(1) The distance from $X_{smallest}$ to $Q_1 = 312$; the distance from Q_3 to $X_{largest} = 364$.

(2) Median = 864 < midrange = 874, therefore we may conclude that the distribution is slightly right-skewed.
From the box-and-whisker plot we can see that the center of the distribution is slightly asymmetric, with the median located a little closer to Q_3 than to Q_1. On the other hand, the upper tail appears to be longer than the lower tail, therefore, the distribution may be slightly right-skewed.

The data appear to be relatively stable with no evidence of a pattern over time.

(g)

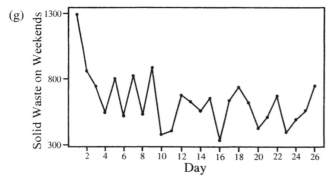

(1)	Arithmetic Mean	633.3
(2)	Median	626.0
(3)	Mode	No unique mode
(4)	Midrange	$(333+1294)/2 = 813.5$
(5)	Quartiles	$Q_1 = 511$, $Q_3 = 747$
(6)	Midhinge	$(511+747)/2 = 629$
(7)	Range	$1294 - 333 = 961$
(8)	Interquartile Range	$747 - 511 = 236$
(9)	Variance	41748.1
(10)	Standard Deviation	204.324

$X_{smallest}$	Q_1	**Median**	Q_3	$X_{largest}$
333.0	511	626.0	747	1294.0

Solid Waste on Weekends

(1) The distance from $X_{smallest}$ to $Q_1 = 178$; the distance from Q_3 to $X_{largest} = 547$.

(2) Median = 626 < midhinge = 629 < midrange = 813.5, therefore we may conclude that the distribution is right-skewed.
From the box-and-whisker plot it can be seen that the center of the distribution is symmetric. On the other hand, the upper tail appears to be substantially longer than the lower tail, therefore, the distribution is right-skewed.

(h) All measures of location are larger for the weekday distribution than for the weekend distribution. Both distributions have approximately equal ranges and interquartile ranges. Both distributions are only slightly asymmetrical (The weekend distribution is more right-skewed due to an extreme value in the data set).

33. (a)

Jobs	Frequency	Percentage	Cumulative %
0–24	66	59.46%	59.46%
25–49	16	14.41%	73.87%
50–74	9	8.11%	81.98%
75–99	5	4.50%	86.48%
100–124	2	1.80%	88.28%
125–149	7	6.31%	94.59%
150–174	3	2.70%	97.29%
175–199	1	0.90%	98.19%
200–224	1	0.90%	99.09%
225–249	1	0.90%	99.99%

(b) **Stem-and-Leaf Display for Data Cartridges**

Stem unit: 10

```
 0 | 1 1 1 1 1 1 2 2 2 2 2 3 3 3 3 3 4 4 4 4 4 4 5 5 5 5 5 5 6 6 6 7 7 7 7 8 8 8 8 9
 1 | 0 0 0 0 0 1 2 2 3 4 4 5 7 8 8 8 8 9
 2 | 0 0 0 0 1 2 3 4 8 8 9
 3 | 0 0 0 0 1 2 3 5 7
 4 | 0 0 2 3
 5 | 0 2 5 6 9
 6 | 0 0 7
 7 | 4
 8 | 0 6
 9 | 1 4 6
10 | 0
11 | 1
12 | 6 7
13 | 1 7
14 | 0 4 7
15 |
16 | 4 6
17 | 0
18 | 2
19 |
20 |
21 | 2
22 |
23 | 7
```

(1) Arithmetic Mean	39.6847
(2) Median	18
(3) Mode	5
(4) Midrange	$(1+237)/2 = 119$
(5) Quartiles	$Q_1 = 5$, $Q_3 = 52$
(6) Midhinge	$(5+52)/2 = 28.5$
(7) Range	$237 - 1 = 236$
(8) Interquartile Range	$52 - 5 = 47$
(9) Variance	2671.40
(10) Standard Deviation	51.6856

Data Cartridges

(c) The number of data cartridges required during a given day is distributed between 1 and 237. About 60% of all jobs are small and require only from 1 to 24 data cartridges. The most frequent requirement is 5 data cartridges. The "central half" of the data includes 5 to 52 data cartridges, with the median located much closer to the first quartile than to the third.

35. (a)

		Mpg	Fuel Capacity	Length	Width
(1)	Arithmetic Mean	23.292	16.354	185.76	69.944
(2)	Median	22	16.5	187	70
(3)	Mode	20	18	175, 184, 188, 200	67
(4)	Midrange	25.5	16.5	181.5	70.5
(5)	Quartiles	$Q_1 = 20$, $Q_3 = 26$	$Q_1 = 14.5$, $Q_3 = 18.25$	$Q_1 = 175$, $Q_3 = 195$	$Q_1 = 67$, $Q_3 = 72.5$
(6)	Midhinge	23	16.375	185	69.75
(7)	Range	21	13	65	15
(8)	Interquartile Range	6	3.75	20	5.5
(9)	Variance	20.5728	7.65342	176.705	11.4400
(10)	Standard Deviation	4.53572	2.76648	13.293	3.382

		Weight	Wheel base	Turning circle capacity
(1)	Arithmetic Mean	3131.4	104.88	39.225
(2)	Median	3175	105	39
(3)	Mode	2865	103	39
(4)	Midrange	3047.5	104.5	39.5
(5)	Quartiles	$Q_1 = 2742.5$, $Q_3 = 3500.5$	$Q_1 = 101$, $Q_3 = 108$	$Q_1 = 38$, $Q_3 = 41$
(6)	Midhinge	3121.5	104.5	39.75
(7)	Range	2405	23	11
(8)	Interquartile Range	758	7	3.5
(9)	Variance	273498	30.1096	6.97165
(10)	Standard Deviation	522.970	5.48722	2.64039

		Luggage capacity	Front leg room	Front head room
(1)	Arithmetic Mean	14.247	41.871	3.635
(2)	Median	14	42	3.5
(3)	Mode	14	42	3
(4)	Midrange	16	42.25	3.75
(5)	Quartiles	$Q_1 = 12$, $Q_3 = 16$	$Q_1 = 41.25$, $Q_3 = 42.5$	$Q_1 = 3$, $Q_3 = 4$
(6)	Midhinge	14	41.875	3.75
(7)	Range	16	4.5	5.5
(8)	Interquartile Range	4	1.25	1.5
(9)	Variance	9.39275	0.781	1.226
(10)	Standard Deviation	3.06476	0.884	1.107

(b)

	X_{smallest}	Q_1	Median	Q_3	X_{largest}
Mpg	15	20	22	26	36
Fuel Capacity	10	14.5	16.5	18.25	23
Length	149	175	187	195	214
Width	63	67	70	72.5	78
Weight	1845	2742.5	3175	3500.5	4250
Wheel base	93	101	105	108.	116
Turning Circle Capacity	34	38	39	41.5	45
Luggage Capacity	8	12	14	16	24
Front leg Room	40	41.25	42	42.5	44.5
Front head Room	1	3	3.5	4.5	6.5

(c)

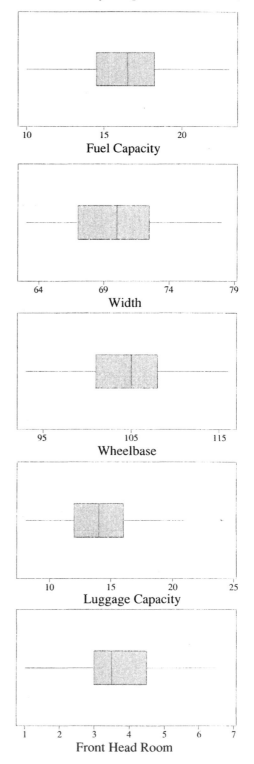

(d) The data for highway miles per gallon are right-skewed.
The data for fuel tank capacity are left-skewed.
The data for length are left-skewed.
The data for width are right-skewed.
The data for weight are left-skewed.
The data for wheel base are left skewed.
The data for turning circle capacity are right-skewed.
The data for luggage capacity are right-skewed.
The data for front leg room are right-skewed.
The data for front head room are right-skewed.

chapter 4

Probability and Discrete Probability Distributions

1. (a) Classical (b) Empirical, if the appropriate data are available; otherwise subjective
   (c) Classical (d) Subjective

3. (a) The test diagnosis is positive.
   (b) The test diagnosis is positive and the person has the disease.
   (c) Three probabilities are given:

   P(the test diagnosis is positive) = 0.04
   P(the patient has the disease | the test diagnosis is positive) = 0.95
   P(the patient does not have the disease | the test diagnosis is negative) = 0.99

   (1) P(the test diagnosis is negative) = $1 - P$(the test diagnosis is positive) = $1 - 0.04 = 0.96$
   (2) P(the test diagnosis is negative *and* the patient does not have the disease)
      = P(the patient does not have the disease | the test diagnosis is negative) $\times P$(the test diagnosis is negative)
      = $0.99 \times 0.96 = 0.9504$
   (3) P(the test diagnosis is positive *and* the patient has the disease)
      = P(the patient has the disease | the test diagnosis is positive) $\times P$(the test diagnosis is positive)
      = $0.95 \times 0.04 = 0.0380$
   (4) Step 1:
      P(the test diagnosis is negative *and* the patient has the disease)
      = P(the test diagnosis is negative) $- P$(the test diagnosis is negative *and* the patient does not have the disease)
      = $0.96 - 0.9504 = 0.0096$
      Step 2:
      P(the disease is present) = P(the test diagnosis is negative *and* the patient has the disease)
      $+ P$(the test diagnosis is positive *and* the patient has the disease) = $0.0096 + 0.0380 = 0.0476$
   (5) P(the test diagnosis is positive *or* the patient has the disease) = P(the test diagnosis is positive)
      $+ P$(the patient has the disease) $- P$(the test diagnosis is positive *and* the patient has the disease)
      = $0.04 + 0.0476 - 0.0380 = 0.0496$

   (d) P(the test diagnosis is positive | the patient has the disease)
   $= \dfrac{P(\text{the test diagnosis is positive } and \text{ the patient has the disease})}{P(\text{the patient has the disease})} = \dfrac{0.038}{0.0476} = 0.798$

   (e) P(the patient has the disease | the test diagnosis is positive) = 0.95. This probability is GIVEN.
   Note that it could be computed using the following formula:
   P(the patient has the disease | the test diagnosis is positive)
   $= \dfrac{P(\text{the test diagnosis is positive } and \text{ the patient has the disease})}{P(\text{the test diagnosis is positive})} = \dfrac{0.038}{0.04} = 0.95$

   (f) These answers are different because the probability that "the test diagnosis is positive" and the probability that "the patient has the disease" are not equal.

A 2×2 cross-classification table for this problem takes the following form:

	Disease	No disease	Total
Positive	0.0380	0.0020	0.04
Negative	0.0096	0.9504	0.96
Total	0.0476	0.9524	1

5. (a) P(both cards are red) = P(the first card is red *and* the second card is red) = P(the 1st card is red) × P(the 2nd card is red), as the two events are independent. Further, P(the 1st card is red) = 26/52, because 26 of 52 cards are red. The event probabilities are multiplied because the cards are selected *without replacement*; the number of cards remaining after the first selection is 51, and the number of red cards is 25. Therefore, P(the second card is red) = 25/51 and P(both cards are red) = $26/52 \times 25/51 = 0.2451$.

   (b) P(the first card is an ace *and* the second card is ten *or* jack *or* queen *or* king) = P(the first card is an ace) × P(the second card is ten *or* jack *or* queen *or* king). The individual event probabilities are multiplied because the two events are independent. Further, P(the first card is an ace) = 4/52, because there are 4 aces in a standard deck of playing cards.

   P(the second card is ten *or* jack *or* queen *or* king) = P(the second card is ten) + P(the second card is jack) + P(the second card is queen) + P(the second card is king). The individual event probabilities are added because these events are mutually exclusive . Because the cards are selected *without replacement*, the number of cards remaining after the first selection is 51, and the number of tens, jacks, queens or kings is 4. Therefore, P(the second card is ten *or* jack *or* queen *or* king) = $4/51 + 4/51 + 4/51 + 4/51 = 16/51$ and P(the first card is an ace *and* the second card is ten *or* jack *or* queen *or* king) = $4/52 \times 16/51 = 0.0241$.

   (c) For Part (a): P(both cards are red) = P(the first card is red *and* the second card is red) = P(the first card is red) × P(the second card is red). The individual probabilities are multiplied because the two events are independent. Further, P(the first card is red) = 26/52, because 26 of 52 cards are red. The cards are selected *with replacement*, the second selection is the same as the first one. Therefore, P(the second card is red) = 26/52 and P(both cards are red) = $26/52 \times 26/52 = 0.250$.

   P(the first card is an ace *and* the second card is a ten *or* jack *or* queen *or* king) = P(the first card is an ace) × P(the second card is ten *or* jack *or* queen *or* king). The individual probabilities are multiplied because the two events are independent. Further P(the first card is an ace) = 4/52, because there are 4 aces in a standard deck of playing cards. In addition, P(the second card is ten *or* jack *or* queen *or* king) = P(the second card is ten) + P(the second card is jack) + P(the second card is queen) + P(the second card is king). The individual event probabilities are added because these events are mutually exclusive . The cards are selected *with replacement*, so the number of cards used in the second selection is 52, and the number of tens, jacks, queens or kings is 4. Therefore, P(the second card is ten *or* jack *or* queen *or* king) = $4/52 + 4/52 + 4/52 + 4/52 = 16/52$ and P(the first card is an ace *and* the second card is ten *or* jack *or* queen *or* king) = $4/52 \times 16/52 = 0.0237$.

7. (a) P(both computers are intact) = P(the first computer is intact) × P(the second computer is intact). This is because these events are independent. Further, P(the first computer is intact) = 40/50, because 40 of 50 computers are intact. The computers are selected *without* replacement, so the number of computers remaining after the first selection is 49, and the number of intact computers is 39. Therefore, P(the second computer is intact) = 39/49 and P(both computers are intact) = $40/50 \times 39/49 = 0.6367$.

   (b) P(both computers are damaged but operative) = P(the first computer is damaged but operative) × P(the second computer is damaged but operative). The individual events are multiplied because these events are independent. Further, P(the first computer is damaged but operative) = 8/50, because 8 of 50 computers are damaged, but operative. The computers are selected *without* replacement, so the number of computers remaining after the first selection is 49, and the number of damaged, but operative computers is 7. Therefore, P(the second computer is damaged, but operative) = 7/49 and P(both computers are damaged but operative) = $8/50 \times 7/49 = 0.0229$.

(c) For Part (a): P(both computers are intact) = P(the first computer is intact) $\times$ P(the second computer is intact). This is because these events are independent. Further, P(the first computer is intact) = $40/50$, because 40 of 50 computers are intact. The computers are selected *with* replacement, so the number of computers in the second set remains 50, and the number of intact computers is 40. Therefore, P(the second computer is intact) = $40/50$ and P(both computers are intact) = $40/50 \times 40/50 = 0.640$.

For Part (b): P(both computers are damaged but operative) = P(the first computer is damaged but operative) $\times$ P(the second computer is damaged but operative). The individual events are multiplied because these events are independent. Further, P(the first computer is damaged, but operative) = $8/50$, because 8 of 50 computers are damaged, but operative. The computers are selected, *with* replacement, so the number of computers in the second set remains 50, and the number of damaged, but operative computers is 8. Therefore, P(the second computer is damaged but operative) = $8/50$ and P(both computers are damaged but operative) = $8/50 \times 8/50 = 0.0256$.

(d) P(three computers are damaged but operative) = P(the first computer is damaged but operative) $\times$ P(the second computer is damaged but operative) $\times$ P(the 3rd computer is damaged but operative). The individual events are multiplied because these events are independent. Further, P(the first computer is damaged but operative) = $8/50$, because 8 of 50 computers are damaged but operative. The computers are selected *without* replacement, the number of computers remaining after the first selection is 49, and the number of damaged but operative computers is 7. Therefore, P(the second computer is damaged but operative) = $7/49$. The number of computers remaining after the second selection is 48, and the number of damaged but operative computers is 6. Therefore, P(the 3rd computer is damaged but operative) = $6/48$, and P(all three computers are damaged but operative) = $8/50 \times 7/49 \times 6/48 = 0.002857$.

(e) P(three computers are damaged, but operative) = P(the first computer is damaged but operative) $\times$ P(the second computer is damaged, but operative) $\times$ P(the 3rd computer is damaged, but operative). The individual events are multiplied because these events are independent. Further, P(the first computer is damaged but operative) = $8/50$, because 8 of 50 computers are damaged, but operative. The computers are selected *with* replacement, so the number of computers in the second and in the 3rd events remains 50, and the number of damaged but operative computers remains 8. Therefore, P(the second computer is damaged but operative) = P(the 3rd computer is damaged but operative) = $8/50$, and P(all three computers are damaged but operative) = $8/50 \times 8/50 \times 8/50 = 0.004096$.

9. (a) Distribution A: Distribution B:

       $\mu = 0(0.25) + 1(0.25) + 2(0.25) + 3(0.25) = 1.5$ $\mu = 0(0.2) + 1(0.4) + 2(0.4) + 3(0.2) = 1.8$

(b) Distribution A:

$$\sigma_x^2 = (0-1.5)^2(0.25) + (1-1.5)^2(0.25) + (2-1.5)^2(0.25) + (3-1.5)^2(0.25) = 1.25$$

$$\sigma_x = \sqrt{\sigma_x^2} = \sqrt{1.25} = 1.118$$

Distribution B:

$$\sigma_x^2 = (0-1.8)^2(0.2) + (1-1.8)^2(0.4) + (2-1.8)^2(0.4) + (3-1.8)^2(0.2) = 1.208$$

$$\sigma_x = \sqrt{\sigma_x^2} = \sqrt{1.208} = 1.099$$

(c) The expected value for Distribution B is greater than the expected value for Distribution A. The standard deviation for Distribution A is larger than the standard deviation for Distribution B.

11. (a) $\mu = 0(0.10) + 1(0.20) + 2(0.45) + 3(0.15) + 4(0.05) + 5(0.05) = 2.0$

(b) $\sigma_x^2 = (0-2)^2(0.1) + (1-2)^2(0.2) + (2-2)^2(0.45) + (3-2)^2(0.15) + (4-2)^2(0.05) + (5-2)^2(0.05) = 1.4$

$$\sigma_x = \sqrt{\sigma_x^2} = \sqrt{1.4} = 1.183$$

(c) Average value of the traffic accidents is 2 per day. Probability range is 2.0 ± 1.183

13. (a) $P(X=1|n=4,\ p=0.20) = \dfrac{4!}{1!(4-1)!}0.2^1(1-0.2)^{4-1} = 0.4096$

(b) $P(X=3|n=4,\ p=0.80) = \dfrac{4!}{3!(4-3)!}0.8^3(1-0.8)^{4-3} = 0.4096$

(c) $P(X \le 1|n=5,\ p=0.30) = P(X=0|n=5,\ p=0.30) + P(X=1|n=5,\ p=0.30) = \dfrac{5!}{0!(5-0)!}0.3^0(1-0.3)^{5-0}$

$+ \dfrac{5!}{1!(5-1)!}0.3^1(1-0.3)^{5-1} = 0.16807 + 0.36015 = 0.52822$

(d) $P(X > 1|n=6,\ p=0.40) = 1 - P(X \le 1|n=6,\ p=0.40) = 1 - P(X=0|n=6,\ p=0.40) - P(X=1|n=6,\ p=0.40)$

$= 1 - \dfrac{6!}{0!(6-0)!}0.4^0(1-0.4)^{6-0} - \dfrac{6!}{1!(6-1)!}0.4^1(1-0.4)^{6-1} = 1 - 0.046656 - 0.186624 = 0.76672$

(e) $P(X < 2|n=3,\ p=0.10) = P(X=0|n=3,\ p=0.10) + P(X=1|n=3,\ p=0.10)$

$= \dfrac{3!}{0!(3-0)!}0.1^0(1-0.1)^{3-0} + \dfrac{3!}{1!(3-1)!}0.1^1(1-0.1)^{3-1} = 0.729 + 0.243 = 0.972$

15. (a) $p=0.25,\ n=5$

1. $P(X=5|5,\ 0.25) = \dfrac{5!}{5!(5-5)!}0.25^5(1-0.25)^{5-5} = 0.001$

2. $P(X \ge 4|5,\ 0.25) = P(X=4|5,\ 0.25) + P(X=5|5,\ 0.25) = \dfrac{5!}{4!(5-4)!}0.25^4(1-0.25)^{5-4}$

$+ \dfrac{5!}{5!(5-5)!}0.25^5(1-0.25)^{5-5} = 0.015 + 0.001 = 0.016$

3. $P(X=0|5,\ 0.25) = \dfrac{5!}{0!(5-0)!}0.25^0(1-0.25)^{5-0} = 0.237$

4. $P(X \le 2|5,\ 0.25) = P(X=0|5,\ 0.25) + P(X=2|5,\ 0.25) = \dfrac{5!}{0!(5-0)!}0.25^0(1-0.25)^{5-0}$

$+ \dfrac{5!}{1!(5-1)!}0.25^2(1-0.25)^{5-1} + \dfrac{5!}{2!(5-2)!}0.25^2(1-0.25)^{5-2} = 0.896$

(b) Two assumptions are necessary: (1) The probabilities of selecting any given ball are all equal. (The probability of selecting a particular ball is $1/4 = 0.25$.) (2) The outcome on a particular trial (a particular ball is selected) is independent of the outcome of any other trial (some other ball was selected).

(c) $\mu = np = 5 \times 0.25 = 1.25$, $\sigma = \sqrt{np(1-p)} = \sqrt{5 \times 0.25(1-0.25)} = 0.9682$

17. (a) $p=0.05,\ n=6$

1. $P(X=0|5,\ 0.05) = \dfrac{6!}{0!(6-0)!}0.05^0(1-0.05)^{6-0} = 0.735092$

2. $P(X < 2|6,\ 0.05) = P(X=0|6,\ 0.05) + P(X=1|6,\ 0.05) = \dfrac{6!}{0!(6-0)!}0.05^0(1-0.05)^{6-0}$

$+ \dfrac{6!}{1!(6-1)!}0.05^1(1-0.05)^{6-1} = 0.735092 + 0.232134 = 0.967226$

3. $P(X \ge 1|6,\ 0.05) = 1 - P(X=0|6,\ 0.05) = 1 - \dfrac{6!}{0!(6-0)!}0.05^0(1-0.05)^{6-0} = 1 - 0.735092 = 0.264908$

(b) Four assumptions are necessary. (1) All discharges are independent; and are possible (2) Only two outcomes are possible; an appliance is either discharging or it is not, (3) Discharge happens on a brief time interval, (4) The probability of an outcome p is the same for all the appliances and is constant from trial to trial.

(c) $\mu = np = 6 \times 0.05 = 0.3$, and $\sigma = \sqrt{np(1-p)} = \sqrt{6 \times 0.05(1-0.05)} = 0.534$

19. (a) $n = 4$, $p = 0.9$

   1. $P(X = 4 | 4, \ 0.9) = \dfrac{4!}{4!(4-4)!} 0.9^4 (1 - 0.9)^{4-4} = 0.6561$

   2. $P(X = 0 | 4, \ 0.9) = \dfrac{4!}{0!(4-0)!} 0.9^0 (1 - 0.9)^{4-0} = 0.0001$

   3. $P(X \geq 3 | 4, \ 0.9) = P(X = 3 | 4, \ 0.9) + P(X = 4 | 4, \ 0.9) = \dfrac{4!}{3!(4-3)!} 0.9^3 (1 - 0.15)^{4-3} + \dfrac{4!}{4!(4-4)!} 0.9^4 (1 - 0.15)^{4-4}$
      $= 0.2916 + 0.6561 = 0.9477$

   4. $P(X < 2 | 4, \ 0.9) = P(X = 1 | 4, \ 0.9) + P(X = 0 | 4, \ 0.9) = \dfrac{4!}{1!(4-1)!} 0.9^1 (1 - 0.9)^{4-1} + \dfrac{4!}{0!(4-0)!} 0.9^0 (1 - 0.9)^{4-0}$
      $= 0.0036 + 0.0001 = 0.0037$

   (b) Three assumptions are necessary: (1) All test results are independent, (2) Only two outcomes are possible; passing the first test or not, and (3) the probability of the passing the first test, p, is constant from trial to trial and is equal to the probability that a CD player passes the first test as evaluated from previous data. This probability, p, is 0.9.

   (c) $\mu = np = 4 \times 0.9 = 3.6$, $\sigma = \sqrt{np(1 - p)} = \sqrt{4 \times 0.9(1 - 0.9)} = 0.6$

   (d) $n = 4$, $p = 0.99$

   1. $P(X = 4 | 4, \ 0.99) = \dfrac{4!}{4!(4-4)!} 0.99^4 (1 - 0.99)^{4-4} = 0.9605$

   2. $P(X = 4 | 4, \ 0.99) = \dfrac{4!}{0!(4-0)!} 0.99^0 (1 - 0.99)^{4-0} = 0.00000001$

   3. $P(X \geq 3 | 4, \ 0.99) = P(X = 3 | 4, \ 0.99) + P(X = 4 | 4, \ 0.99) = \dfrac{4!}{3!(4-3)!} 0.99^3 (1 - 0.99)^{4-3}$
      $+ \dfrac{4!}{4!(4-4)!} 0.99^4 (1 - 0.99)^{4-4} = 0.0388 + 0.9601 = 0.999$

   4. $P(X < 2 | 4, \ 0.99) = P(X = 1 | 4, \ 0.99) + P(X = 0 | 4, \ 0.99) = \dfrac{4!}{1!(4-1)!} 0.99^1 (1 - 0.99)^{4-1}$
      $+ \dfrac{4!}{0!(4-0)!} 0.99^0 (1 - 0.99)^{4-0} = 0.00000396 + 0.00000001 = 0.00000397$

21. $n = 10$, $p = 0.10$

   (a) $P(X > 4 | 10, \ 0.10) = 1 - P(X = 0 | 10, \ 0.10) - P(X = 1 | 10, \ 0.10) - P(X = 2 | 10, \ 0.10) - P(X = 3 | 10, \ 0.10)$
      $- P(X = 4 | 10, \ 0.10) = 1 - \dfrac{10!}{0!(10-0)!} 0.1^0 (1 - 0.1)^{10-0} - \dfrac{10!}{1!(10-1)!} 0.1^1 (1 - 0.1)^{10-1} - \dfrac{10!}{2!(10-2)!} 0.1^2 (1 - 0.1)^{10-2}$
      $- \dfrac{10!}{3!(10-3)!} 0.1^3 (1 - 0.1)^{10-3} - \dfrac{10!}{4!(10-4)!} 0.1^4 (1 - 0.1)^{10-4} = 1 - 0.349 - 0.387 - 0.194 - 0.0574 - 0.0112$
      $= 0.00163$

   (b) $P(2 \leq X \leq 5 | 10, \ 0.10) = P(X = 2 | 10, \ 0.10) + P(X = 3 | 10, \ 0.10) + P(X = 4 | 10, \ 0.10) + P(X = 5 | 10, \ 0.10)$
      $= \dfrac{10!}{2!(10-2)!} 0.1^2 (1 - 0.1)^{10-2} + \dfrac{10!}{3!(10-3)!} 0.1^3 (1 - 0.1)^{10-3} + \dfrac{10!}{4!(10-4)!} 0.1^4 (1 - 0.1)^{10-4}$
      $+ \dfrac{10!}{5!(10-5)!} 0.1^5 (1 - 0.1)^{10-5} = 0.194 + 0.0574 + 0.0112 + 0.00149 = 0.264$

   (c) $n = 8$, $p = 0.10$
      $P(X > 4 | 8, \ 0.10) = 1 - P(X = 0 | 8, \ 0.10) - P(X = 1 | 8, \ 0.10) - P(X = 2 | 8, \ 0.10) - P(X = 3 | 8, \ 0.10)$
      $- P(X = 4 | 8, \ 0.10) = 1 - \dfrac{8!}{0!(8-0)!} 0.1^0 (1 - 0.1)^{10-0} - \dfrac{8!}{1!(8-1)!} 0.1^1 (1 - 0.1)^{10-1} - \dfrac{8!}{2!(8-2)!} 0.1^2 (1 - 0.1)^{10-2}$
      $- \dfrac{8!}{4!(8-4)!} 0.1^4 (1 - 0.1)^{10-4} = 1 - 0.4305 - 0.383 - 0.149 - 0.0331 - 0.0045 = 0.000432$

$P(2 \leq X \leq 5|8, \ 0.10) = P(X = 2|8, \ 0.10) + P(X = 3|8, \ 0.10) + P(X = 4|8, \ 0.10) + P(X = 5|8, \ 0.10)$

$= \dfrac{8!}{2!(8-2)!}0.1^2(1-0.1)^{10-2} + \dfrac{8!}{3!(8-3)!}0.1^3(1-0.1)^{10-3} + \dfrac{8!}{4!(8-4)!}0.1^4(1-0.1)^{10-4}$

$+ \dfrac{8!}{5!(8-5)!}0.1^5(1-0.1)^{10-5} = 0.1489 + 0.0331 + 0.00459 + 0.000408 = 0.187$

23. (a) $P(X = 4|n = 5, \ N = 52, \ A = 26) = \dfrac{\dbinom{26}{4}\dbinom{52-26}{5-4}}{\dbinom{52}{5}} = \dfrac{\dfrac{26!}{4!22!} \times \dfrac{26!}{1!25!}}{\dfrac{52!}{5!47!}} = 0.150$

(b) $P(X = 2|n = 5, \ N = 52, \ A = 4) = \dfrac{\dbinom{4}{2}\dbinom{52-4}{5-2}}{\dbinom{52}{5}} = \dfrac{\dfrac{4!}{2!2!} \times \dfrac{48!}{3!45!}}{\dfrac{52!}{5!47!}} = 0.0399298$

(c) $P(X = 0|n = 5, \ N = 52, \ A = 13) = \dfrac{\dbinom{13}{0}\dbinom{52-13}{5-0}}{\dbinom{52}{5}} = \dfrac{\dfrac{13!}{0!13!} \times \dfrac{39!}{5!34!}}{\dfrac{52!}{5!47!}} = 0.2215336$

(d) There are only 4 aces in a standard deck of playing cards. $P(X = 5|n = 5, \ N = 52, \ A = 4) = 0$

25. (a) $P(X = 1|n = 4, \ N = 15, \ A = 5) = \dfrac{\dbinom{5}{1}\dbinom{15-5}{4-1}}{\dbinom{15}{4}} = \dfrac{\dfrac{5!}{1!4!} \times \dfrac{10!}{3!7!}}{\dfrac{15!}{4!11!}} = 0.440$

(b) $P(X \geq 1|n = 4, \ N = 15, \ A = 5) = 1 - P(X = 0|n = 4, \ N = 15, \ A = 5) = 1 - \dfrac{\dbinom{5}{0}\dbinom{15-5}{4-0}}{\dbinom{15}{4}} = 1 - \dfrac{\dfrac{5!}{0!5!} \times \dfrac{10!}{4!6!}}{\dfrac{15!}{4!11!}}$

$= 1 - 0.154 = 0.846$

(c) $P(X \leq 2|n = 4, \ N = 15, \ A = 5) = P(X = 0|n = 4, \ N = 15, \ A = 5) + P(X = 1|n = 4, \ N = 15, \ A = 5)$

$+ P(X = 2|n = 4, \ N = 15, \ A = 5) = \dfrac{\dbinom{5}{0}\dbinom{15-5}{4-0}}{\dbinom{15}{4}} + \dfrac{\dbinom{5}{1}\dbinom{15-5}{4-1}}{\dbinom{15}{4}} + \dfrac{\dbinom{5}{2}\dbinom{15-5}{4-2}}{\dbinom{15}{4}} = \dfrac{\dfrac{5!}{0!5!} \times \dfrac{10!}{4!6!}}{\dfrac{15!}{4!11!}} + \dfrac{\dfrac{5!}{1!4!} \times \dfrac{10!}{3!7!}}{\dfrac{15!}{4!11!}}$

$+ \dfrac{\dfrac{5!}{2!3!} \times \dfrac{10!}{2!8!}}{\dfrac{15!}{4!11!}} = 0.154 + 0.440 + 0.330 = 0.923$

(d) $\mu = \dfrac{nA}{N} = \dfrac{4 \times 5}{15} = 1.33$

27. (a) $P(X = 6|n = 6, \ N = 54, \ A = 6) = \dfrac{\dbinom{6}{6}\dbinom{54-6}{6-6}}{\dbinom{54}{6}} = \dfrac{\dfrac{6!}{6!0!} \times \dfrac{48!}{0!48!}}{\dfrac{54!}{6!48!}} = 3.87 \times 10^{-8}$

(b) $P(X = 5 | n = 6, N = 54, A = 6) = \dfrac{\binom{6}{5}\binom{54-6}{6-5}}{\binom{54}{6}} = \dfrac{\frac{6!}{5!1!} \times \frac{48!}{1!47!}}{\frac{54!}{6!48!}} = 1.12 \times 10^{-5}$

(c) $P(X = 4 | n = 6, N = 54, A = 6) = \dfrac{\binom{6}{4}\binom{54-6}{6-4}}{\binom{54}{6}} = \dfrac{\frac{6!}{4!2!} \times \frac{48!}{2!46!}}{\frac{54!}{6!48!}} = 0.000655$

(d) $P(X = 0 | n = 6, N = 54, A = 6) = \dfrac{\binom{6}{0}\binom{54-6}{6-0}}{\binom{54}{6}} = \dfrac{\frac{6!}{0!6!} \times \frac{48!}{6!42!}}{\frac{54!}{6!48!}} = 0.475$

(e) $\mu = \dfrac{nA}{N} = \dfrac{6 \times 6}{54} = 0.667$

(f) $P(X = 6 | n = 6, N = 40, A = 6) = \dfrac{\binom{6}{6}\binom{40-6}{6-6}}{\binom{40}{6}} = \dfrac{\frac{6!}{6!0!} \times \frac{34!}{0!34!}}{\frac{40!}{6!34!}} = 2.61 \times 10^{-7}$

$P(X = 5 | n = 6, N = 40, A = 6) = \dfrac{\binom{6}{5}\binom{40-6}{6-5}}{\binom{40}{6}} = \dfrac{\frac{6!}{5!1!} \times \frac{34!}{1!33!}}{\frac{40!}{6!34!}} = 5.31 \times 10^{-5}$

$P(X - 4 | n = 6, N = 40, A = 6) = \dfrac{\binom{6}{4}\binom{40-6}{6-4}}{\binom{40}{6}} = \dfrac{\frac{6!}{4!2!} \times \frac{34!}{2!32!}}{\frac{40!}{6!34!}} = 0.00219$

$P(X = 0 | n = 6, N = 40, A = 6) = \dfrac{\binom{6}{0}\binom{40-6}{6-0}}{\binom{40}{6}} = \dfrac{\frac{6!}{0!6!} \times \frac{34!}{6!28!}}{\frac{40!}{6!34!}} = 0.350383$

$\mu = \dfrac{nA}{N} = \dfrac{6 \times 6}{40} = 0.9$

29. (a) $p = 0.35, X = 2$

    (1) $P(n = 2) = \binom{2-1}{2-1} 0.35^2 (1 - 0.35)^{2-2} = 0.123$ (2) $P(n = 5) = \binom{5-1}{2-1} 0.35^2 (1 - 0.35)^{5-2} = 0.135$

    (3) $P(n = 10) = \binom{10-1}{2-1} 0.35^2 (1 - 0.35)^{10-2} = 0.0351$

  (b) $\mu = 2/0.35 = 5.714286, \ \sigma = \sqrt{\dfrac{2(1 - 0.35)}{0.35^2}} = 3.258$

31. (a) $p = 0.05, X = 1$

    (1) $P(n = 1) = \binom{1-1}{1-1} 0.05^1 (1 - 0.05)^{1-1} = 0.05$ (2) $P(n = 5) = \binom{5-1}{1-1} 0.05^1 (1 - 0.05)^{1-1} = 0.040725$

    (3) $P(n = 10) = \binom{10-1}{1-1} 0.05^1 (1 - 0.05)^{10-1} = 0.031512$

(b) $\mu = \dfrac{2}{0.05} = 40$, $\sigma = \sqrt{\dfrac{2(1-0.05)}{0.05^2}} = 27.5681$

(c) $p = 0.02$, $X = 1$

    (1) $P(n=1) = \dbinom{1-1}{1-1} 0.02^1(1-0.02)^{1-1} = 0.2$

    (2) $P(n=5) = \dbinom{5-1}{1-1} 0.02^1(1-0.02)^{5-1} = 0.0819$

    (3) $P(n=10) = \dbinom{10-1}{1-1} 0.02^1(1-0.02)^{10-1} = 0.0268$, $\mu = \dfrac{2}{0.2} = 10$, $\sigma = \sqrt{\dfrac{2(1-0.2)}{0.2^2}} = 6.325$

33. (a) $p = 0.6$, $X = 3$

    (1) $P(n=3) = \dbinom{3-1}{3-1} 0.6^3(1-0.6)^{3-3} = 0.216$

    (2) $P(n=5) = \dbinom{5-1}{3-1} 0.6^3(1-0.6)^{5-3} = 0.2073$

    (3) $P(n=10) = \dbinom{10-1}{3-1} 0.6^3(1-0.6)^{10-3} = 0.0127$

(b) $\mu = \dfrac{3}{0.6} = 5$, $\sigma = \sqrt{\dfrac{3(1-0.6)}{0.6^2}} = 1.83$

(c) $p = 0.6$, $X = 1$

    (1) $P(n=3) = \dbinom{3-1}{1-1} 0.6^1(1-0.6)^{3-1} = 0.096$

    (2) $P(n=5) = \dbinom{5-1}{1-1} 0.6^1(1-0.6)^{5-1} = 0.0154$

    (3) $P(n=10) = \dbinom{10-1}{1-1} 0.6^1(1-0.6)^{10-1} = 0.000157$

(d) $\mu = \dfrac{1}{0.6} = 1.667$, $\sigma = \sqrt{\dfrac{1(1-0.6)}{0.6^2}} = 1.054$

35. (a) $P(X=0|\lambda=3.5) = \dfrac{e^{-3.5}3.5^0}{0!} = 0.0302$

    (b) $P(X=3|\lambda=5.0) = \dfrac{e^{-5.0}5.0^0}{3!} = 0.1403$

(c) $P(X \geq 2|\lambda=0.5) = 1 - P(X=0|\lambda=0.5) - P(X=1|\lambda=0.5) = 1 - \dfrac{e^{-0.5}0.5^0}{0!} - \dfrac{e^{-0.5}0.5^1}{1!} = 1 - 0.607 - 0.303 = 0.0902$

(d) $P(X < 0|\lambda=10) = 0.000000$

(e) $P(X = 12 \text{ or } 13 \text{ or } 14) = P(X=12|\lambda=15) + P(X=13|\lambda=15) + P(X=14|\lambda=15)$

    $P(X=12|\lambda=15) = \dfrac{e^{-15}15^{12}}{12!} = 0.0829$

    $P(X=13|\lambda=15) = \dfrac{e^{-15}15^{13}}{13!} = 0.0956$

    $P(X=14|\lambda=15) = \dfrac{e^{-15}15^{14}}{14!} = 0.1024$

    $P(X = 12 \text{ or } 13 \text{ or } 14) = 0.281$

37. (a) $P(X=0|\lambda=2.5) = \dfrac{e^{-2.5}2.5^2}{2!} = 0.0821$

    (b) $P(X=2|\lambda=2.5) = \dfrac{e^{-2.5}2.5^2}{2!} = 0.257$

(c) $P(X \geq 1|\lambda=2.5) = 1 - P(X=0|\lambda=2.5) = \dfrac{e^{-2.5}2.5^0}{0!} = 1 - 0.0821 = 0.918$

(d) $P(X \leq 1|\lambda=2.5) = P(X=0|\lambda=2.5) + P(X=0|\lambda=2.5) = \dfrac{e^{-2.5}2.5^0}{0!} + \dfrac{e^{-2.5}2.5^1}{1!} = 0.082085 + 0.20521 = 0.287$

39. (a) $P(X=8|\lambda=10.0) = \dfrac{e^{10}10^8}{8!} = 0.113$

(b) $P(X = 8 \text{ or } X = 9|\lambda=10.0) = P(X=8|\lambda=10.0) + P(X=9|\lambda=10.0) = \dfrac{e^{-10}10^8}{8!} + \dfrac{e^{-10}10^9}{9!} = 0.113 + 0.125110 = 0.238$

(c) $P(X=0|\lambda=10.0) = \dfrac{e^{10}10^0}{0!} = 0.0000450$

41. (a) $P\left(X \ge 1 \middle| \lambda = \dfrac{12}{5}\right) = 1 - P(X = 0 | \lambda = 2.4) = 1 - \dfrac{e^{-2.4}2.4^0}{0!} = 1 - 0.090718 = 0.909282$

(b) $P(X = 5 | \lambda = 10) + P(X = 6 | \lambda = 10) + \ldots + P(X = 15 | \lambda = 10) = \dfrac{e^{-10}10^5}{5!} + \ldots + \dfrac{e^{-10}10^8}{8!} + \dfrac{e^{-10}10^9}{9!} + \ldots + \dfrac{e^{-10}10^{15}}{15!}$

$= 0.0378 + 0.0631 + 0.0901 + 0.113 + 0.125 + 0.125 + 0.114 + 0.0948 + 0.0729 + 0.0521 + 0.0347 = 0.922$

43. A simple event is defined by one characteristic whereas a joint event is defined by two or more characteristics.

45. Events are mutually exclusive if they cannot occur at the same time. Events are collectively exhaustive if one of them must occur.

47. If two events are independent, then the probability of both events occurring is equal to the product of their respective probabilities. If two events are not independent, then the probability of both events occurring is the product of the probability of the first event and the conditional probability of the second event given that the first event has already occurred.

49. (a) Each elementary event is classified into one of two mutually exclusive and collectively exhaustive categories.
(b) The probabilities of an outcome are constant from trial to trial.
(c) The outcome of a particular trial is independent of the outcome on any other trial.

51. The binomial distribution is used in situations in which the probability of success remains constant from trial to trial. This is true when the data are selected *with replacement* or when the data are selected from a very large population. The fact that an object was selected does not change the probabilities of other objects being selected. The hypergeometric distribution is used in situations in which the probability of success changes from trial to trial because the data are selected *without replacement* from a finite (small) population.

53. The negative binomial distribution is used to determine the probability that x^{th} success occurs on the nth trial whereas the geometric distribution is used to determine the probability that the first success occurs on the nth trial. Thus, the geometric distribution is a special case of the negative binomial distribution.

55. The binomial distribution analyzes the number of nonconforming items in a sample of n units; the Poisson distribution analyzes the number of nonconformities per sampled continuum (or per area opportunity).

57. (a) Consider a binomial distribution, $n = 5$, $p = 0.6$

(1) $P(X = 3 | n = 5, \ p = 0.6) = \dfrac{5!}{3!(5-3)!}0.6^3(1-0.6)^{5-3} = 0.346$

(2) $P(X \ge 3 | n = 5, \ p = 0.6) = P(X = 3 | n = 5, \ p = 0.6) + P(X = 4 | n = 5, \ p = 0.6) + P(X = 5 | n = 5, \ p = 0.6)$

$= \dfrac{5!}{3!(5-3)!}0.6^3(1-0.6)^{5-3} + \dfrac{5!}{4!(5-4)!}0.6^4(1-0.6)^{5-4} + \dfrac{5!}{5!(5-5)!}0.6^5(1-0.6)^{5-5} = 0.346 + 0.259 + 0.078 = 0.683$

(3) $P(X = 5 | n = 5, \ p = 0.6) = \dfrac{5!}{5!(5-5)!}0.6^5(1-0.6)^{5-5} = 0.0778$

(4) $P(X = 0 | n = 5, \ p = 0.6) = \dfrac{5!}{0!(5-0)!}0.6^0(1-0.6)^{5-0} = 0.0102$

(b) $\mu = np = 5 \times 0.60 = 3$, $\sigma = \sqrt{np(1-p)} = \sqrt{5 \times 0.6(1-0.6)} = 1.0954$

(c) Consider a binomial distribution, $n = 10$, $p = 0.6$

(1) $P(X = 3 | n = 10, \ p = 0.6) = \dfrac{10!}{3!(10-3)!}0.6^3(1-0.6)^{10-3} = 0.0425$

(2) $P(X \geq 3 | n = 10, \ p = 0.6) = 1 - P(X = 0 | n = 10, \ p = 0.6) - P(X = 1 | n = 10, \ p = 0.6) - P(X = 2 | n = 10, \ p = 0.6)$

$= 1 - \dfrac{10!}{0!(10-0)!} 0.6^0 (1-0.6)^{10-0} - \dfrac{10!}{1!(10-1)!} 0.6^1 (1-0.6)^{10-1} - \dfrac{10!}{2!(10-2)!} 0.6^2 (1-0.6)^{10-2}$

$= 1 - 0.00010 - 0.00157 - 0.01062 = 0.9878$

(3) $P(X = 5 | n = 10, \ p = 0.6) = \dfrac{10!}{5!(10-5)!} 0.6^5 (1-0.6)^{10-5} = 0.201$

(4) $P(X = 0 | n = 10, \ p = 0.6) = \dfrac{10!}{0!(10-0)!} 0.6^0 (1-0.6)^{10-0} = 0.000105$, $\mu = np = 10 \times 0.60 = 6$

$\sigma = \sqrt{np(1-p)} = \sqrt{10 \times 0.6(1-0.6)} = 1.55$

(d) Consider a binomial distribution, $n = 5$, $p = 0.7$

(1) $P(X = 3 | n = 5, \ p = 0.7) = \dfrac{5!}{3!(5-3)!} 0.7^3 (1-0.7)^{5-3} = 0.3087$

(2) $P(X \geq 3 | n = 5, \ p = 0.7) = P(X = 3 | n = 5, \ p = 0.7) + P(X = 4 | n = 5, \ p = 0.7) + P(X = 5 | n = 5, \ p = 0.7)$

$= \dfrac{5!}{3!(5-3)!} 0.7^3 (1-0.7)^{5-3} + \dfrac{5!}{4!(5-4)!} 0.7^4 (1-0.7)^{5-4} + \dfrac{5!}{5!(5-5)!} 0.7^5 (1-0.7)^{5-5}$

$= 0.30870 + 0.36015 + 0.16807 = 0.83692$

(3) $P(X = 5 | n = 5, \ p = 0.7) = \dfrac{5!}{5!(5-5)!} 0.7^5 (1-0.7)^{5-5} = 0.168$

(4) $P(X = 0 | n = 5, \ p = 0.7) = \dfrac{5!}{0!(5-0)!} 0.7^0 (1-0.7)^{5-0} = 0.00243$, $\mu = np = 5 \times 0.70 = 3.5$

$\sigma = \sqrt{np(1-p)} = \sqrt{5 \times 0.7(1-0.7)} = 1.024695$

59. (a) Binomial distribution: $n = 5$, $p = 0.0002$

(1) $\mu = 5 \times 0.0002 = 0.001$

(2) $P(X \geq 1 | n = 5, \ p = 0.0002) = 1 - P(X = 0 | n = 5, \ p = 0.0002) = 1 - \dfrac{5!}{0!(5-0)!} 0.0002^0 (1-0.0002)^{5-0}$

$= 1 - 0.999 = 0.001$

(b) Binomial distribution: $n = 10,000$, $p = 0.0002$

(1) $P(X \geq 1 | n = 10,000, \ p = 0.0002) = 1 - P(X = 0 | n = 10,000, \ p = 0.0002)$

$= 1 - \dfrac{10,000!}{0!(10,000-0)!} 0.0002^0 (1-0.0002)^{10,000-0} = 1 - 0.135 = 0.865$

(2) $\mu = 10,000 \times 0.0002 = 2$

61. (a) The hypergeometrical distribution:

(1) $P(X = 0 | N = 20, \ A = 8, \ n = 5) = \dfrac{\dbinom{8}{0}\dbinom{20-8}{5-0}}{\dbinom{20}{5}} = \dfrac{\dfrac{8!}{0!8!} \times \dfrac{12!}{5!7!}}{\dfrac{20!}{5!15!}} = 0.0511$

(2) $P(X \geq 1 | N = 20, \ A = 8, \ n = 5) = 1 - P(X = 0 | N = 20, \ A = 8, \ n = 5) = 1 - \dfrac{\dbinom{8}{0}\dbinom{20-8}{5-0}}{\dbinom{20}{5}} = 1 - \dfrac{\dfrac{8!}{0!8!} \times \dfrac{12!}{5!7!}}{\dfrac{20!}{5!15!}}$

$= 1 - 0.0511 = 0.949$

(3) $P(X = 5 | N = 20, \ A = 8, \ n = 5) = \dfrac{\dbinom{8}{5}\dbinom{20-8}{5-5}}{\dbinom{20}{5}} = \dfrac{\dfrac{8!}{5!3!} \times \dfrac{12!}{0!12!}}{\dfrac{20!}{5!15!}} = 0.00361$

(b) $\mu = \dfrac{nA}{N} = \dfrac{5 \times 8}{20} = 2$, $\sigma_x = \sqrt{\dfrac{nA(N-A)}{N^2}}\sqrt{\dfrac{N-n}{N-1}} = \sqrt{\dfrac{5*8(20-8)}{20^2}}\sqrt{\dfrac{20-5}{20-1}} = 0.9733$

(c) The binomial distribution:

(1) $P(X = 0 | p = 0.40, n = 5) = \dfrac{5!}{0!(5-0)!}0.4^0(1-0.4)^{5-0} = 0.0778$

(2) $P(X \geq 1 | p = 0.40, n = 5) = 1 - P(X = 0 | p = 0.40, n = 5) = 1 - \dfrac{5!}{0!(5-0)!}0.4^0(1-0.4)^{5-0} = 1 - 0.0778 = 0.922$

(3) $P(X = 5 | p = 0.40, n = 5) = \dfrac{5!}{5!(5-5)!}0.4^5(1-0.4)^{5-5} = 0.0102$

(d) $\mu = np = 5 \times 0.40 = 2$, $\sigma = \sqrt{np(1-p)} = \sqrt{5 \times 0.4(1-0.4)} = 1.095445$

(e) The answers are close, but different due to the difference between the binomial and hypergeometrical distributions; see problem 4.51 above. Indeed, in the situation described in (a) and (b), the probability of success does not remain constant from trial to trial. Conversely, in part (c) we assume that the probability of success is the same for all trials, because the sample size is less than 5% of the population size (i.e., the population is large).

63. (a) $P(X = 0 | \lambda = 4) = \dfrac{e^{-4}4^0}{0!} = 0.018316$

(b) $P(X \geq 1 | \lambda = 4) = 1 - P(X = 0 | \lambda = 4) = 1 - \dfrac{e^{-4}4^0}{0!} = 1 - 0.0183 = 0.982$

(c) $P(X > 4 | \lambda = 4) = 1 - P(X \leq 4 | \lambda = 4) = 1 - P(X = 1 | \lambda = 4) - P(X = 2 | \lambda = 4) - P(X = 3 | \lambda = 4) - P(X = 4 | \lambda = 4)$

$= 1 - \dfrac{e^{-4}4^0}{0!} - \dfrac{e^{-4}4^1}{1!} - \dfrac{e^{-4}4^2}{2!} - \dfrac{e^{-4}4^3}{3!} - \dfrac{e^{-4}4^4}{4!} = 1 - 0.0183 - 0.0733 - 0.147 - 0.195 - 0.195 = 0.371$

65. (a) $P(X = 1 | \lambda = 1) = \dfrac{e^{-1}1^1}{1!} = 0.368$

(b) $P(X \geq 1 | \lambda = 1) = 1 - P(X = 0 | \lambda = 1) = 1 - \dfrac{e^{-1}1^0}{0!} = 1 - 0.368 = 0.632$

(c) $P(X = 5 | \lambda = 5) = \dfrac{e^{-5}5^5}{5!} = 0.175$

(d) $P(X \geq 5 | \lambda = 5) = 1 - P(X = 0 | \lambda = 5) - P(X = 1 | \lambda = 5) - P(X = 2 | \lambda = 5) - P(X = 3 | \lambda = 5) - P(X = 4 | \lambda = 5)$

$= 1 - \dfrac{e^{-5}5^0}{0!} - \dfrac{e^{-5}5^1}{1!} - \dfrac{e^{-5}5^2}{2!} - \dfrac{e^{-5}5^3}{3!} - \dfrac{e^{-5}5^4}{4!} = 1 - 0.00674 - 0.0337 - 0.084224 - 0.140374 - 0.175 = 0.560$

(e) As the area of opportunity increases by a factor of 5, the average number of successes per area of opportunity increases 5 times as well (assuming that the average number of successes per unit area does not change). Note, however, that the increase in the number of all the combinations that lead to successes is *less* than the increase in the number of all of the combinations that do not result in successes.

chapter 5

Continuous Probability Distributions and Sampling Distributions

1. (a) $f(x) = \dfrac{1}{b-a} = \dfrac{1}{10-0} = 0.1$

    (1) $P(5 < x < 7) = 0.1 \times (7-5) = 0.1 \times 2 = 0.2$
    (2) $P(2 < x < 3) = 0.1 \times (3-2) = 0.1 \times 1 = 0.1$

  (b) $\mu = \dfrac{a+b}{2} = \dfrac{10+0}{2} = \dfrac{10}{2} = 5.0$

  (c) $\sigma^2 = \dfrac{(b-a)^2}{12} = \dfrac{10^2}{12} = 8.33$, $\sigma = \sqrt{8.33} = 2.887$

3. (a) $f(x) = \dfrac{1}{25-10} = \dfrac{1}{15}$

    (1) $P(x < 20) = \dfrac{1}{15} \times (20-10) = \dfrac{1}{15} \times 10 = 0.667$
    (2) $P(20 < x < 22) = \dfrac{1}{15} \times (22-20) = \dfrac{1}{15} \times 2 = 0.133$

  (b) $P(x > 18) = \dfrac{1}{15} \times (25-18) = \dfrac{1}{15} \times 7 = 0.467$

  (c) $\mu = \dfrac{a+b}{2} = \dfrac{25+10}{2} = \dfrac{35}{2} = 17.5$

  (d) $\sigma^2 = \dfrac{(b-a)^2}{12} = \dfrac{15^2}{12} = 18.75$, $\sigma = \sqrt{18.75} = 4.33$

5. 24-hours $= 24 \times 60 = 1{,}440$ min, therefore $f(x) = \dfrac{1}{1440} = 6.94 \times 10^{-4}$

  (a) 5:55 A.M. $= 5 \times 60 + 55 = 355$ min
     7:38 P.M. $= 19 \times 60 + 38 = 1178$ min

    $P(355 < x < 1{,}178) = \dfrac{1}{1{,}440} \times (1178 - 355) = \dfrac{1}{1{,}440} \times 823 = 0.5715$

  (b) 10 P.M. $= 22 \times 60 = 1{,}320$ min
     5 A.M $= 5 \times 60 = 300$ min
     $P(10\ \text{P.M} < x < 5\ \text{A.M.}) = P(10\ \text{P.M.} < x < 12\ \text{P.M.}) + P(0\ \text{A.M.} < x < 5\ \text{A.M.}) = P(1{,}320 < x < 1440) + P(0 < x < 300)$

     $= \dfrac{1}{1{,}440} \times 120 + \dfrac{1}{1{,}440} \times 300 = 0.0833 + 0.208 = 0.291$

  (c) P (a failure will be detected within 10 minutes of its occurrence)
     $= P(50 < x < 60) + P(110 < x < 120) + P(170 < x < 180) + \ldots + P(1{,}430 < x < 1{,}440)$

     $= \dfrac{1}{1{,}440} \times 10 + \dfrac{1}{1{,}440} \times 10 + \dfrac{1}{1{,}440} \times 10 + \ldots + \dfrac{1}{1{,}440} \times 10$

     $= 24 \times \dfrac{1}{1{,}440} \times 10 = 0.167$

  (d) P(it will take at least 40 minutes to detect that a failure has occurred)
     $= P(0 < x < 20) + P(60 < x < 80) + P(120 < x < 140) + \ldots + P(1380 < x < 1400)$

     $= \dfrac{1}{1{,}440} \times 20 + \dfrac{1}{1{,}440} \times 20 + \dfrac{1}{1{,}440} \times 20 + \ldots + \dfrac{1}{1{,}440} \times 20 = 24 \times \dfrac{1}{1{,}440} \times 20 = 0.333$

7. (a) (1) $P(-2 < Z < 0) = P(0 < Z < 2) = 0.4772$

      (2) $P(-1.25 < Z < 2.25) = P(-1.25 < Z < 0) + P(0 < Z < 2.25) = 0.3944 + 0.4878 = 0.8822$

      (3) $P(-1.75 < Z < 1.75) = P(-1.75 < Z < 0) + P(0 < Z < 1.75) = 0.4599 + 0.4599 = 0.9198$

      (4) $P(Z < -1.50) = P(Z < 0) - P(-1.50 < Z < 0) = 0.5 - 0.4332 = 0.0668$

      (5) $P(Z > -1.50) = P(Z > 0) + P(-1.50 < Z < 0) = 0.5 + 0.4332 = 0.9332$

      (6) $P(Z < -1.0 \text{ or } Z > 1.50) = P(Z < -1.0) + P(Z > 1.5) = P(Z < 0) - P(-1.0 < Z < 0) + P(Z > 0) - P(0 < Z < 1.5)$

$$= 0.5 - 0.3413 + 0.5 - 0.4332 = 0.2255$$

      (7) $P(Z < -3.0 \text{ or } Z > 3.0) = P(Z < -3.0) + P(Z > 3.0) = P(Z < 0) - P(-3.0 < Z < 0) + P(Z > 0) - P(0 < Z < 3.0)$

$$= 0.5 - 0.49865 + 0.5 - 0.49865 = 0.0027$$

(b) 90% of the values exceed Z, 10% are less than Z; therefore Z is negative. If 10% of the values are below Z then 40% of all the values must fall between Z and 0; therefore the area between Z and 0 is 0.40, and $Z = -1.28$.

(c) Only 1% of the values exceed Z, therefore Z is positive. If 1% of the values are above Z then 49% of all the values must fall between Z and 0; subsequently the area between Z and 0 is 0.49, and $Z = 2.33$.

(d) The values of Z are symmetrically distributed around the mean, so 49.5% of all values fall between −Z and 0 and 49.5% of all values fall between 0 and +Z. Therefore $Z^{\text{Lower}} = -2.58$, $Z^{\text{Upper}} = 2.58$.

9.   Mean   4.7 ounces

      Standard Deviation   0.4 ounces

    (a) (1) $Z = \dfrac{X - \mu_x}{\sigma_x} = \dfrac{5.00 - 4.70}{0.40} = 0.75$, $P(4.7 < X < 5) = 0.2734$

      (2) $Z = \dfrac{X - \mu_x}{\sigma_x} = \dfrac{5.00 - 4.70}{0.40} = 0.75$, $P(X < 5) = P(X < 4.7) + P(4.7 < X < 5) = 0.5 + 0.2734 = 0.7734$,

           $Z = \dfrac{X - \mu_x}{\sigma_x} = \dfrac{5.50 - 4.70}{0.40} = 2$, $P(X < 5.5) = P(X < 4.7) + P(4.7 < X < 5.5) = 0.5 + 0.4772 = 0.9772$,

           $P(5 < X < 5.5) = P(X < 5.5) - P(X < 5) = 0.9772 - 0.7734 = 0.2038$

      (3) $Z = \dfrac{X - \mu_x}{\sigma_x} = \dfrac{4.00 - 4.70}{0.40} = -1.75$, $P(X < 4) = P(X < 4.7) - P(4 < X < 4.7) = 0.5 - 0.4599 = 0.0401$,

           $Z = \dfrac{X - \mu_x}{\sigma_x} = \dfrac{5.00 - 4.70}{0.40} = 0.75$, $P(X < 5) = P(X < 4.7) + P(4.7 < X < 5) = 0.5 + 0.2734 = 0.7734$,

           $P(4 < X < 5) = P(X < 5) - P(X < 4) = 0.7734 - 0.0401 = 0.7333$

      (4) $Z = \dfrac{X - \mu_x}{\sigma_x} = \dfrac{4.00 - 4.70}{0.40} = -1.75$, $P(X > 4) = P(4 < X < 4.7) + P(X > 4.7) = 0.4599 + 0.5 = 0.9599$

      (5) $Z = \dfrac{X - \mu_x}{\sigma_x} = \dfrac{5.00 - 4.70}{0.40} = 0.75$, $P(X > 5) = P(X > 4.7) - P(4.7 < X < 5) = 0.5 - 0.2734 = 0.2266$

(b) 77% of all the values exceed X, therefore X is below the mean and Z is negative. If 23% of the values are below X, then 27% of all the values must fall between X and the mean; subsequently, the area between the mean and X is 0.27, and $Z = -0.74$. $X = \mu_x + z\sigma_x = 4.7 - 0.74 \times 0.40 = 4.404$

(c) The values of X are symmetrically distributed around the mean, so 45% of all values fall between X_L and the mean and 45% of all values fall between the mean and X_U. Therefore $Z_{\text{Lower}} = 1.65$, $Z_{\text{Upper}} = 1.65$.

      $X_L = 4.70 - 1.65 \times 0.40 = 4.04$, $X_U = 4.70 + 1.65 \times 0.40 = 5.36$

11. (a) Mean   575 mm

           Standard Deviation   5 mm

      (1) $Z = \dfrac{X - \mu_x}{\sigma_x} = \dfrac{579 - 575}{5} = 0.8$, $P(575 < X < 579) = 0.2881$

(2) $Z = \dfrac{X - \mu_x}{\sigma_x} = \dfrac{572 - 575}{5} = -0.6$, $P(X < 572) = P(X < 575)$ $P(572 < X < 575) = 0.5 - 0.2257 = 0.2743$,

$\quad Z = \dfrac{X - \mu_x}{\sigma_x} = \dfrac{580 - 575}{5} = 1$, $P(X < 580) = P(X < 575) + P(575 < X < 580) = 0.5 + 0.3413 = 0.8413$,

$\quad P(572 < X < 580) = P(X < 580) - P(X < 572) = 0.8413 - 0.2743 = 0.5670$

(3) $Z = \dfrac{X - \mu_x}{\sigma_x} = \dfrac{570 - 575}{5} = -1$, $P(X > 570) = P(570 < X < 575) + P(X > 575) = 0.3413 + 0.5 = 0.8413$

(4) $Z = \dfrac{X - \mu_x}{\sigma_x} = \dfrac{580 - 575}{5} = 1$, $P(X < 580) = P(X < 575) + P(575 < X < 580) = 0.5 + 0.3413 = 0.8413$

(b) 80% of all the values exceed X, therefore X is below the mean and Z is negative. If 20% of the values are below X then 30% of all the values must fall between the mean and X; subsequently the area between the mean and X is 0.30, and $Z = -0.84$. $X = \mu_x + Z\sigma_x = 575 - 0.84 \times 5 = 570.8$

(c) The values of X are symmetrically distributed around the mean, so 40% of all the values fall between X_L and mean and 40% of all values fall between the mean and X_U. Therefore $Z_{\text{Lower}} = -1.28$ and $Z_{\text{Upper}} = 1.28$.

$\quad X_L = 575 - 1.28 \times 5 = 568.6$, $X_U = 575 + 1.28 \times 5 = 581.4$

(d) The cumulative distribution function in part (b) calculated a value of X such that the area under the curve between it and the largest possible value of X equals 0.8. However in part (c) we are looking for the value of X such that the area under the curve between $-X$ and $+X$ equals 0.8.

(e) Mean   575
     Standard Deviation   0.04

     (a) Using PHStat we obtain:

(1) Z Value for 575	0	
Z Value for 579	100	
$P(X \le 575)$	0.5	
$P(X \le 579)$	1	
$P(575 \le X \le 579)$	0.5	
(2) Z Value for 572	−75	
Z Value for 580	125	
$P(X \le 572)$	0	
$P(X \le 580)$	1	
$P(572 \le X \le 580)$	1	
(3) Z Value	−125	
$P(X > 570)$	1	
(4) Z Value	125	
$P(X \le 580)$	1	

(b) 80% of all the values exceed X, therefore X is below the mean and Z is negative. If 20% of the values are below X then 30% of all the values must fall between the mean and X; subsequently the area between the mean and X is 0.30, and $Z = -0.84$. $X = \mu_x + Z\sigma_x = 575 - 0.84 \times 0.04 = 574.9664$.

(c) The values of X are symmetrically distributed around the mean, so 40% of all the values fall between X_L and the mean and 40% of all values fall between the mean and X_U. Therefore $Z_{\text{Lower}} = -1.28$ and $Z_{\text{Upper}} = 1.28$.

$\quad X_L = 575 - 1.28 \times 0.04 = 574.9488$, $X_U = 575 + 1.28 \times 0.04 = 575.0512$. The cumulative distribution function in part (b) calculated a value of X such that the area under the curve between it and the largest possible value of X equals 0.8. However in part (c) we are looking for the value of X such that the area under the curve between $-X$ and $+X$ equals 0.8.

Mean   575
Standard Deviation   4

    (1) Z Value for 575   0
            Z Value for 579   1
            $P(X \leq 575)$ 0.5
            $P(X \leq 579)$ 0.841
            $P(575 \leq X \leq 579)$ 0.341

    (2) Z Value for 572   −0.75
            Z Value for 580   1.25
            $P(X \leq 572)$ 0.2266
            $P(X \leq 580)$ 0.8943
            $P(572 \leq X \leq 580)$ 0.6677

    (3) Z Value   −1.25
            $P(X > 570)$ 0.8943

    (4) Z Value   1.25
            $P(X \leq 580)$ 0.8943

(d) 80% of all the values exceed X, therefore X is below the mean and Z is negative. If 20% of the values are below X then 30% of all the values must fall between the mean and X; subsequently the area between the mean and X is 0.30, and $Z = -0.84$. $X = \mu_x + Z\sigma_x = 575 - 0.84 \times 4 = 571.64$

(e) The values of X are symmetrically distributed around the mean, so 40% of all the values fall between X_L and mean and 40% of all the values fall between the mean and X_U. Therefore $Z_{\text{Lower}} = -1.28$ and $Z_{\text{Upper}} = 1.28$.
$X_L = 575 - 1.28 \times 4 = 569.88$, $X_U = 575 + 1.28 \times 4 = 580.12$

13. Mean   80
     Standard Deviation   20

(a) $Z = \dfrac{X - \mu_x}{\sigma_x} = \dfrac{77 - 80}{20} = -0.15$, $P(X < 77) = P(X < 80) - P(77 < X < 80) = 0.5 - 0.0596 = 0.4404$

(b) $Z = \dfrac{X - \mu_x}{\sigma_x} = \dfrac{74 - 80}{20} = -0.3$, $P(X < 74) = P(X < 80) = P(74 < X < 80) = 0.5 - 0.1179 = 0.3821$

$Z = \dfrac{X - \mu_x}{\sigma_x} = \dfrac{84 - 80}{20} = 0.2$

$P(X < 84) = P(X < 80) + P(80 < X < 84) = 0.5 + 0.0792 = 0.5793$

$P(74 < X < 84) = P(X < 84) - P(X < 74) = 0.5793 - 0.3821 = 0.1972$

(c) 25% of the values exceed X, therefore X is above the mean and Z is positive. If 25% of the values are above X then 25% of all the values must fall between X and the mean; subsequently the area between X and the mean is 0.25, and $Z = 0.67$.
$X = \mu_x + Z\sigma_x = 80 + 0.67 \times 20 = 93.4$.

15. $\mu_x = 500 \times 0.04 = 20$, $\sigma_x^2 = np(1-p) = 500 \times 0.04(1 - 0.04) = 19.2$

Because the variance is greater than 10, the normal distribution can be used to approximate the binomial distribution.

(a) $Z = \dfrac{X - np}{\sqrt{np(1-p)}} = \dfrac{10 - 500 \times 0.04}{\sqrt{500 \times 0.04(1 - 0.04)}} = -2.28$, $P(X < 10) = P(X < 20) - P(10 < X < 20) = 0.5 - 0.4887 = 0.0113$

(b) $Z = \dfrac{X - np}{\sqrt{np(1-p)}} = \dfrac{15 - 500 \cdot 0.04}{\sqrt{500 \cdot 0.04(1 - 0.04)}} = -1.14$, $P(X < 15) = P(X < 20) - P(15 < X < 20) = 0.5 - 0.3729 = 0.1271$

$Z = \dfrac{X - np}{\sqrt{np(1-p)}} = \dfrac{25 - 500 \times 0.04}{\sqrt{500 \times 0.04(1 - 0.04)}} = 1.14$

$P(X < 25) = P(X < 20) + P(20 < X < 25) = 0.5 + 0.3729 = 0.8729$

$P(15 < X < 25) = P(X < 25) - P(X < 15) = 0.8729 - 0.1271 = 0.7458$

(c) $Z = \dfrac{X - np}{\sqrt{np(1-p)}} = \dfrac{15 - 500 \cdot 0.04}{\sqrt{500 \cdot 0.04(1 - 0.04)}} = -1.14$, $P(X > 15) = P(15 < X < 20) + P(X < 20) = 0.3729 + 0.5 = 0.8729$

17. $\mu_x = 50 \times 0.7 = 35$, $\sigma_x^2 = np(1-p) = 50 \times 0.7(1 - 0.7) = 10.5$

Because the variance is greater than 10, the normal distribution can be used to approximate the binomial distribution.

(a) $Z = \dfrac{X - np}{\sqrt{np(1-p)}} = \dfrac{25 - 50 \cdot 0.70}{\sqrt{50 \cdot 0.70(1 - 0.70)}} = -3.08$, $P(X > 25) = P(25 < X < 35) + P(X > 35) = 0.49897 + 0.5 = 0.99897$

(b) $Z = \dfrac{X - np}{\sqrt{np(1-p)}} = \dfrac{40 - 50 \cdot 0.70}{\sqrt{50 \cdot 0.70(1 - 0.70)}} = 1.54$, $P(X > 40) = P(X > 35) - P(35 < X < 40) = 0.5 - 0.4382 = 0.0618$

(c) $Z = \dfrac{X - np}{\sqrt{np(1-p)}} = \dfrac{30 - 50 \cdot 0.70}{\sqrt{50 \cdot 0.70(1 - 0.70)}} = -1.54$, $P(X < 30) = P(X < 35) - P(30 < X < 35) = 0.5 - 0.4382 = 0.0618$

19. $\mu_x = \lambda = 50$

Because λ is greater than 5, the normal distribution can be used to approximate the Poisson distribution.

(a) $Z = \dfrac{X - \lambda}{\sqrt{\lambda}} = \dfrac{35 - 50}{\sqrt{50}} = -2.12$, $P(X > 35) = P(35 < X < 50) + P(X > 50) = 0.4830 + 0.5 = 0.9830$

(b) $Z = \dfrac{X - \lambda}{\sqrt{\lambda}} = \dfrac{50 - 50}{\sqrt{50}} = 0$, $P(X > 50) = 0.5$

(c) $Z = \dfrac{X - \lambda}{\sqrt{\lambda}} = \dfrac{40 - 50}{\sqrt{50}} = -1.41$, $P(X < 40) = P(X < 50) - P(40 < X < 50) = 0.50 - 0.4207 = 0.0793$

$Z = \dfrac{X - \lambda}{\sqrt{\lambda}} = \dfrac{60 - 50}{\sqrt{50}} = 1.41$

$P(X < 60) = P(X < 50) + P(50 < X < 60) = 0.5 + 0.4207 = 0.9207$

$P(40 < X < 50) = P(X < 50) - P(X < 40) = 0.9207 - 0.0793 = 0.8414$

21. The length of paper is 50 feet; therefore $\lambda = 1 \times 10 = 10$. Because λ is greater than 5, the normal distribution can be used to approximate the Poisson distribution.

(a) $Z = \dfrac{X - \lambda}{\sqrt{\lambda}} = \dfrac{5 - 10}{\sqrt{10}} = -1.58$, $P(X > 5) = P(5 < X < 10) + P(X > 10) = 0.4429 + 0.5 = 0.9429$

(b) $Z = \dfrac{X - \lambda}{\sqrt{\lambda}} = \dfrac{5 - 10}{\sqrt{10}} = -1.58$, $P(X < 5) = P(X < 10) - P(5 < X < 10) = 0.5 - 0.4429 = 0.0571$

(c) $Z = \dfrac{X - \lambda}{\sqrt{\lambda}} = \dfrac{15 - 10}{\sqrt{10}} = 1.58$

$P(X < 15) = P(X < 10) + P(10 < X < 15) = 0.5 + 0.4429 = 0.9429$

$P(5 < X < 15) = P(X < 15) - P(X < 5) = 0.9429 - 0.0571 = 0.8858$

23. (a)

Normal Probability Plot of the Mean Tensile Strength

(b) The plot seems to approximately follow a straight line. The mean tensile strength appears to be normally distributed.

25. (a)

Normal Probability Plot of the Amount of Chromium

(b) This curve rises more slowly at first, and then the rate of increase grows rapidly. By examining the normal probability plot, it follows that the distribution of the amount of chromium is right-skewed.

27. (a)

Normal Probability Plot of the Weight of the Rubber Edges

(b) The plot seems to approximately follow a straight line. The weights of the rubber edges appear to be approximately normally distributed.

29. (a) $\mu_x = e^{\mu_{\ln(x)} + \sigma^2_{\ln(x)}/2} = e^{3.1 + (1.2)^2/2} = e^{3.82} = 45.60421$

(b) $\sigma_x = \sqrt{e^{2(3.1) + (1.2)^2} \cdot \left(e^{(1.2)^2} - 1\right)} = \sqrt{e^{7.64} \cdot (e^{1.44} - 1)} = \sqrt{6698.222} = 81.84267$

(c) (1) $Z = \dfrac{\ln(X) - \mu_{\ln(x)}}{\sigma_{\ln(x)}} = \dfrac{\ln(5) - 3.1}{1.2} = -1.24$, $P(X < 5) = 0.5 - 0.3925 = 0.1075$

(2) $Z = \dfrac{\ln(X) - \mu_{\ln(x)}}{\sigma_{\ln(x)}} = \dfrac{\ln(10) - 3.1}{1.2} = -0.66$, $P(X > 10) = 0.5 + 0.2454 = 0.7454$

(3) $Z = \dfrac{\ln(X) - \mu_{\ln(x)}}{\sigma_{\ln(x)}} = \dfrac{\ln(5) - 3.1}{1.2} = -1.24$, $P(X < 5) = 0.5 - 0.3925 = 0.1075$

$Z = \dfrac{\ln(X) - \mu_{\ln(x)}}{\sigma_{\ln(x)}} = \dfrac{\ln(15) - 3.1}{1.2} = -0.33$

$P(X < 15) = 0.5 - 0.1293 = 0.3707$

$P(5 < X < 15) = P(X < 15) - P(X < 5) = 0.3707 - 0.1075 = 0.2632$

31. (a) $\mu_x = e^{\mu_{\ln(x)} + \sigma^2_{\ln(x)}/2} = e^{2.5 + (0.5)^2/2} = e^{2.625} = 13.80457$

(b) $\sigma_x = \sqrt{e^{2(2.5) + (0.5)^2} \cdot \left(e^{(0.5)^2} - 1\right)} = \sqrt{e^{5.25} \cdot (e^{0.25} - 1)} = \sqrt{54.12566} = 7.357015$

(c) (1) $Z = \dfrac{\ln(X) - \mu_{\ln(x)}}{\sigma_{\ln(x)}} = \dfrac{\ln(15) - 2.5}{0.5} = 0.42$, $P(X < 15) = 0.1628 + 0.5 = 0.6628$

$Z = \dfrac{\ln(X) - \mu_{\ln(x)}}{\sigma_{\ln(x)}} = \dfrac{\ln(20) - 2.5}{0.5} = 0.99$, $P(X > 20) = 0.5 - 0.3389 = 0.1611$

(3) $Z = \dfrac{\ln(X) - \mu_{\ln(x)}}{\sigma_{\ln(x)}} = \dfrac{\ln(15) - 2.5}{0.5} = 0.42, \; P(X < 15) = 0.1628 + 0.5 = 0.6628$

$Z = \dfrac{\ln(X) - \mu_{\ln(x)}}{\sigma_{\ln(x)}} = \dfrac{\ln(30) - 2.5}{0.5} = 1.8$

$P(X < 30) = 0.5 + 0.4641 = 0.9641$

$P(15 < X < 30) = P(X < 30) - P(X < 15) = 0.9641 - 0.6628 = 0.3013$

33. $\lambda = 50$

(a) $P(\text{arrival time} < 0.05) = 1 - e^{-50(0.05)} = 0.917915$ 　　(b) $P(\text{arrival time} < 0.0167) = 1 - e^{-50(0.0167)} = 0.566126$

(c) $\mu = \dfrac{1}{\lambda} = \dfrac{1}{50} = 0.02$ minute 　　　　　　　　(d) $\sigma = \dfrac{1}{\lambda} = \dfrac{1}{50} = 0.02$ minute

(e) $\lambda = 60$

$P(\text{arrival time} < 0.05) = 1 - e^{-60(0.05)} = 0.950213$ 　　　$P(\text{arrival time} < 0.0167) = 1 - e^{-60(0.0167)} = 0.632856$

$\mu = \dfrac{1}{\lambda} = \dfrac{1}{60} = 0.0167$ minute $= 1$ second 　　　$\sigma = \dfrac{1}{\lambda} = \dfrac{1}{60} = 0.0167$ minute $= 1$ second

(f) $\lambda = 30$

$P(\text{arrival time} < 0.05) = 1 - e^{-30(0.05)} = 0.77687$ 　　　$P(\text{arrival time} < 0.0167) = 1 - e^{-30(0.0167)} = 0.394076$

$\mu = \dfrac{1}{\lambda} = \dfrac{1}{30} = 0.0333$ minute $= 2$ seconds 　　$\sigma = \dfrac{1}{\lambda} = \dfrac{1}{30} = 0.0333$ minute $= 2$ seconds

35. $\lambda = 8$

(a) $P(\text{arrival time} < 0.25) = 1 - e^{-8(0.25)} = 0.864665$ 　　(b) $P(\text{arrival time} < 0.05) = 1 - e^{-8(0.05)} = 0.32968$

(c) $\lambda = 15$

$P(\text{arrival time} < 0.25) = 1 - e^{-15(0.25)} = 0.976482$ 　　　$P(\text{arrival time} < 0.05) = 1 - e^{-15(0.25)} = 0.527633$

37. $\alpha = 2.5$, $\beta = 10$

(a) $P(X < 5) = 1 - e^{-(x/\beta)^\alpha} = 1 - e^{-(5/10)^{2.5}} = 1 - e^{-0.1767} = 0.162033$

(b) $P(X < 10) = 1 - e^{-(x/\beta)^\alpha} = 1 - e^{-(10/10)^{2.5}} = 0.632121$ 　　(c) $P(X < 20) = 1 - e^{-(x/\beta)^\alpha} = 1 - e^{-(20/10)^{2.5}} = 0.996507$

39. $\alpha = 3$, $\beta = 10$

(a) $P(X < 5) = 1 - e^{-(x/\beta)^\alpha} = 1 - e^{-(5/10)^3} = 0.117503$

(b) $P(X \geq 2) = 1 - P(X < 2) = 1 - 1 + e^{-(x/\beta)^\alpha} = e^{-(2/10)^3} = 0.992031915$

(c) $P(X < 6) = 1 - e^{-(x/\beta)^\alpha} = 1 - e^{-(6/10)^3} = 0.194265$

$P(X < 15) = 1 - e^{-(x/\beta)^\alpha} = 1 - e^{-(15/10)^3} = 0.965782$

$P(6 < X < 15) = P(X < 15) - P(X < 6) = 0.965782 - 0.194265 = 0.771517$

(d) $\alpha = 5$, $\beta = 10$

$P(X < 5) = 1 - e^{-(x/\beta)^\alpha} = 1 - e^{-(5/10)^5} = 0.030767$

$P(X \geq 2) = 1 - P(X < 2) = 1 - 1 + e^{-(x/\beta)^\alpha} = e^{-(2/10)^5} = 0.999680051$

$P(X < 6) = 1 - e^{-(x/\beta)^\alpha} = 1 - e^{-(6/10)^5} = 0.074814$

$P(X < 15) = 1 - e^{-(x/\beta)^\alpha} = 1 - e^{-(15/10)^5} = 0.999496$

$P(6 < X < 15) = P(X < 15) - P(X < 6) = 0.999496 - 0.074814 = 0.924682$

41. $\alpha = 1.5$, $\beta = 10$

(a) $P(X < 10) = 1 - e^{-(x/\beta)^\alpha} = 1 - e^{-(10/10)^{1.5}} = 0.632121$

(b) $P(X \geq 5) = 1 - P(X < 5) = 1 - 1 + e^{-(x/\beta)^\alpha} = e^{-(5/10)^{1.5}} = 0.702188501$

(c) $P(5 < X < 10) = P(X < 10) - P(X < 5) = 1 - e^{-(10/10)^{1.5}} - 1 + e^{-(5/10)^{1.5}} = 0.33431$

(d) $\alpha = 1, \ \beta = 10$

$$P(X < 10) = 1 - e^{-(x/\beta)^\alpha} = 1 - e^{-(10/10)^1} = 0.632121$$

$$P(X \geq 5) = 1 - P(X < 5) = 1 - 1 + e^{-(x/\beta)^\alpha} = e^{-(5/10)^1} = 0.60653066$$

$$P(X < 5) = 1 - e^{-(x/\beta)^\alpha} = 1 - e^{-(5/10)^1} = 0.393469$$

$$P(5 < X < 10) = P(X < 10) - P(X < 5) = 0.632121 - 0.393469 = 0.238652$$

43. (a) $Z = \dfrac{\overline{X} - \mu_{\overline{x}}}{\sigma_x / \sqrt{n}} = \dfrac{14 - 14.1}{1.4 / \sqrt{49}} = -0.5, \ P(\overline{X} > 14) = P(14 < \overline{X} < 14.1) + P(\overline{X} > 14.1) = 0.1915 + 0.5 = 0.6915$

(b) Only 1% of all the sample means should be below $\overline{X}$, therefore $\overline{X}$ is below the mean and Z is negative. If 1% of the values is below $\overline{X}$ then 49% of all the values must fall between $\overline{X}$ and the mean; subsequently the area between $\overline{X}$ and the mean is 0.49, and $Z = -2.33$.

$$\overline{X} = \mu_x + Z \frac{\sigma_x}{\sqrt{n}} = 14.1 - 2.33 \frac{1.4}{\sqrt{49}} = 13.634$$

(c) The distribution of the sample mean must be normally distributed. This assumption is met because we are given a large enough sample.

(d) (a) $Z = \dfrac{\overline{X} - \mu_{\overline{x}}}{\sigma_x / \sqrt{n}} = \dfrac{14 - 14.1}{1.4 / \sqrt{64}} = -0.57, \ P(\overline{X} > 14) = P(14 < \overline{X} < 14.1) + P(\overline{X} > 14.1) = 0.2157 + 0.5 = 0.7157$

(b) Only 1% of all the sample mean should be below $\overline{X}$, therefore $\overline{X}$ is below the mean and Z is negative. If 1% of the values are below $\overline{X}$ then 49% of all the values must fall between $\overline{X}$ and the mean; subsequently the area between $\overline{X}$ and the mean is 0.49, and $Z = -2.33$.

$$\overline{X} = \mu_x + Z \frac{\sigma_x}{\sqrt{n}} = 14.1 - 2.33 \frac{1.4}{\sqrt{64}} = 13.69225$$

45. (a) $Z = \dfrac{\overline{X} - \mu_{\overline{x}}}{\sigma_x / \sqrt{n}} = \dfrac{4.60 - 4.70}{0.40 / \sqrt{25}} = -1.25, \ P(\overline{X} > 4.6) = P(4.6 < \overline{X} < 4.7) + P(\overline{X} > 4.7) = 0.3944 + 0.5 = 0.8944$

(b) The areas between the lower X and the mean and the area between the mean and the upper X should be equal to 0.35. Thus the Z values are -1.04 and 1.04.

$$\overline{X}_L = \mu_x - Z \frac{\sigma_x}{\sqrt{n}} = 4.7 - 1.04 \frac{0.4}{\sqrt{25}} = 4.6168$$

$$\overline{X}_U = \mu_x + Z \frac{\sigma_x}{\sqrt{n}} = 4.7 + 1.04 \frac{0.4}{\sqrt{25}} = 4.7832$$

(c) 23% of all the sample means should be below $\overline{X}$, therefore $\overline{X}$ is below the mean and Z is negative. If 23% of the values are below $\overline{X}$ then 27% of all the values must fall between $\overline{X}$ and the mean; subsequently the area between $\overline{X}$ and the mean is 0.27, and $Z = -0.74$.

$$\overline{X} = \mu_x + Z \frac{\sigma_x}{\sqrt{n}} = 4.7 - 0.74 \frac{0.4}{\sqrt{25}} = 4.6408$$

(d) In Problem 5.9(b), the X value = 4.404, whereas for this problem the X value = 4.6408. This is because the sampling distribution of the mean is less variable than the distribution of individual values.

47. (a) $Z = \dfrac{p - \pi}{\sqrt{\dfrac{\pi(1 - \pi)}{n}}} = \dfrac{0.25 - 0.20}{\sqrt{\dfrac{0.20(1 - 0.20)}{100}}} = 1.25, \ P(0.2 < p < 0.25) = 0.3944$

(b) $Z = \dfrac{p - \pi}{\sqrt{\dfrac{\pi(1-\pi)}{n}}} = \dfrac{0.25 - 0.20}{\sqrt{\dfrac{0.20(1-0.20)}{100}}} = 1.25$, $P(p < 0.25) = P(p < 0.2) + P(0.2 < p < 0.25) = 0.5 + 0.3944 = 0.8944$

$Z = \dfrac{p - \pi}{\sqrt{\dfrac{\pi(1-\pi)}{n}}} = \dfrac{0.30 - 0.20}{\sqrt{\dfrac{0.20(1-0.20)}{100}}} = 2.5$

$P(p < 0.30) = P(p < 0.2) + P(0.2 < p < 0.30) = 0.5 + 0.4938 = 0.9938$

$P(0.25 < p < 0.30) = P(p < 0.30) - P(p < 0.25) = 0.9938 - 0.8944 = 0.0994$

(c) $Z = \dfrac{p - \pi}{\sqrt{\dfrac{\pi(1-\pi)}{n}}} = \dfrac{0.25 - 0.20}{\sqrt{\dfrac{0.20(1-0.20)}{100}}} = 1.25$, $P(p < 0.25) = P(p < 0.2) + P(0.2 < p < 0.25) = 0.5 + 0.3944 = 0.8944$

(d) $\sigma_p = \sqrt{\dfrac{\pi(1-\pi)}{n}} = \sqrt{\dfrac{0.2(1-0.2)}{25}} = 0.08$

Using PHStat we obtain:

Z Value for 0.2	0	Z Value for 0.25	0.625
Z Value for 0.25	0.625	Z Value for 0.3	1.25
$P(p \le 0.2)$	0.5	$P(p \le 0.25)$	0.7340
$P(p \le 0.25)$	0.7340	$P(p \le 0.3)$	0.8944
$P(0.2 \le p \le 0.25)$	0.2340	$P(0.25 \le p \le 0.3)$	0.1603
Z Value	0.6250		
$P(p \le 0.25)$	0.7340		

49. (a) Mean 0.505

$Z = \dfrac{p - \pi}{\sqrt{\dfrac{\pi(1-\pi)}{n}}} = \dfrac{0.56 - 0.505}{\sqrt{\dfrac{0.505(1-0.505)}{100}}} = 1.10$

$P(p > 0.56) = P(p > 0.505) = P(0.505 < p < 0.56) = 0.5 - 0.3643 = 0.1357$

(b) Mean 0.6

$Z = \dfrac{p - \pi}{\sqrt{\dfrac{\pi(1-\pi)}{n}}} = \dfrac{0.56 - 0.6}{\sqrt{\dfrac{0.6(1-0.6)}{100}}} = -0.82$, $P(p > 0.56) = P(p < 0.60) + P(0.56 < p < 0.60) = 0.5 + 0.2939 = 0.7939$

(c) Mean 0.49

$Z = \dfrac{p - \pi}{\sqrt{\dfrac{\pi(1-\pi)}{n}}} = \dfrac{0.56 - 0.49}{\sqrt{\dfrac{0.49(1-0.49)}{100}}} = 1.4$, $P(p > 0.56) = P(p < 0.49) - P(0.49 < p < 0.56) = 0.5 - 0.4192 = 0.0808$

(d) (a) Mean 0.505

$Z = \dfrac{p - \pi}{\sqrt{\dfrac{\pi(1-\pi)}{n}}} = \dfrac{0.56 - 0.505}{\sqrt{\dfrac{0.505(1-0.505)}{400}}} = 2.20$

$P(p > 0.56) = P(p > 0.505) - P(0.505 < p < 0.56) = 0.5 - 0.4861 = 0.0139$

(b) Mean 0.6

$Z = \dfrac{p - \pi}{\sqrt{\dfrac{\pi(1-\pi)}{n}}} = \dfrac{0.56 - 0.6}{\sqrt{\dfrac{0.6(1-0.6)}{400}}} = -1.63$, $P(p > 0.56) = P(p < 0.60) + P(0.56 < p < 0.60) = 0.5 + 0.4484 = 0.9484$

(c) Mean   0.49

$$Z = \frac{p - \pi}{\sqrt{\dfrac{\pi(1-\pi)}{n}}} = \frac{0.56 - 0.49}{\sqrt{\dfrac{0.49(1-0.49)}{400}}} = 2.80,$$

$P(p > 0.56) = P(p > 0.49) - P(0.49 < p < 0.56) = 0.5 - 0.4974 = 0.0026$

51. (a) $Z = \dfrac{p - \pi}{\sqrt{\dfrac{\pi(1-\pi)}{n}}} = \dfrac{0.96 - 0.95}{\sqrt{\dfrac{0.95(1-0.95)}{1000}}} = 1.45,\ P(0.95 < p < 0.96) = 0.4265$

(b) $Z = \dfrac{p - \pi}{\sqrt{\dfrac{\pi(1-\pi)}{n}}} = \dfrac{0.94 - 0.95}{\sqrt{\dfrac{0.95(1-0.95)}{1000}}} = -1.45,\ P(p < 0.94) = P(p < 0.95) - P(0.94 < p < 0.95) = 0.5 - 0.4265 = 0.0735$

$Z = \dfrac{p - \pi}{\sqrt{\dfrac{\pi(1-\pi)}{n}}} = \dfrac{0.97 - 0.95}{\sqrt{\dfrac{0.95(1-0.95)}{1000}}} = 2.90$

$P(p < 0.97) = P(p < 0.95) + P(0.95 < p < 0.97) = 0.5 + 0.4981 = 0.9981$

$P(0.94 < p < 0.97) = P(p < 0.97) - P(p < 0.94) = 0.9981 - 0.0735 = 0.9246$

(c) $Z = \dfrac{p - \pi}{\sqrt{\dfrac{\pi(1-\pi)}{n}}} = \dfrac{0.93 - 0.95}{\sqrt{\dfrac{0.95(1-0.95)}{1000}}} = 2.90,\ P(p > 0.93) = P(0.93 < p < 0.95) + P(p > 0.95) = 0.4981 + 0.5 = 0.9981$

(d) $\sigma_p = \sqrt{\dfrac{\pi(1-\pi)}{n}} = \sqrt{\dfrac{0.95(1-0.95)}{1000}} = 0.01$

Using PHStat we obtain

Z Value for 0.95	0		Z Value for 0.94	−1
Z Value for 0.96	1		Z Value for 0.97	2
$P(X \le 0.95)$	0.5		$P(X \le 0.94)$	0.1587
$P(X \le 0.96)$	0.8413		$P(X \le 0.97)$	0.9772
$P(0.95 \le X \le 0.96)$	0.3413		$P(0.94 \le X \le 0.97)$	0.8186

Z Value	−2
$P(X > 0.93)$	0.9772

53. Any normally distributed variable X can be converted to its standardized form by using the transformation formula for Z. We can then determine the desired probabilities from the table for the standard normal distribution (Table A.2).

55. 1.   Sketch the normal curve, and then place the values for the means on the X and Z axes, respectively.
   2.   Determine whether X is above or below the mean.
   3.   Split the appropriate half of the normal curve into two parts—the portion from the desired X to the mean, and the portion from the desired X to the tail.
   4.   Shade the area of interest.
   5.   By using Table A.2 for the standardized normal distribution, determine the appropriate Z value corresponding to the area under the normal curve from the desired X to the mean μ_x.
   6.   Solve the equation $X = \mu_x + Z\sigma_x$ for X.

57. By standardizing the values, only one table for the probabilities of the standard normal distribution is needed.

59. The average time between arrivals is inversely proportional to the average number of arrivals per unit time.

61. The standard error of the mean decreases as the sample size increases, because the standard error of the mean is inversely proportional to the root of the sample size.

63. (a) (1) $Z = \dfrac{X - \mu_x}{\sigma_x} = \dfrac{1.00 - 0.72}{0.10} = 2.8$, $P(X > 1) = P(X > 0.72) - P(0.72 < X < 1) = 0.5 - 0.4974 = 0.0026$

      (2) $Z = \dfrac{X - \mu_x}{\sigma_x} = \dfrac{0.70 - 0.72}{0.10} = -0.2$, $P(X < 0.7) = P(X < 0.72) - P(0.7 < X < 0.72) = 0.5 - 0.0793 = 0.4207$

          $Z = \dfrac{X - \mu_x}{\sigma_x} = \dfrac{0.80 - 0.72}{0.10} = 0.8$

          $P(X < 0.80) = P(X < 0.72) + P(0.72 < X < 0.80) = 0.5 + 0.2881 = 0.7881$

           $P(0.70 < X < 0.80) = P(X < 0.80) - P(X < 0.70) = 0.7881 - 0.4207 = 0.3674$

  (b) 30% of all the values exceed X, therefore X is above the mean, and Z is positive. If 30% of the values are above X, then 20% of all the values must fall between X and the mean; subsequently the area between X and the mean is 0.20, and $Z = 0.52$.
     $X = \mu_x + Z\sigma_x = 0.72 + 0.52 \times 0.10 = 0.772$

  (c) 90% of all the values exceed X, therefore X is below the mean, and Z is negative. If 10% of the values are below X, then 40% of all the values fall between X and the mean; subsequently the area between X and the mean is 0.40, and $Z = -1.28$.
     $X = \mu_x + Z\sigma_x = 0.72 - 1.28 \times 0.10 = 0.60$

  (d) (1) $Z = \dfrac{\overline{X} - \mu_{\overline{x}}}{\sigma_x / \sqrt{n}} = \dfrac{0.7 - 0.72}{0.10 / \sqrt{16}} = -0.8$, $P(\overline{X} > 0.7) = P(0.7 < \overline{X} < 0.72) + P(\overline{X} > 0.72) = 0.2881 + 0.5 = 0.7881$

      (2) $Z = \dfrac{\overline{X} - \mu_{\overline{x}}}{\sigma_x / \sqrt{n}} = \dfrac{0.7 - 0.72}{0.10 / \sqrt{16}} = -0.8$, $P(\overline{X} < 0.7) = P(\overline{X} < 0.72) - P(0.7 < \overline{X} < 0.72) = 0.5 - 0.2881 = 0.2119$

          $Z = \dfrac{\overline{X} - \mu_{\overline{x}}}{\sigma_x / \sqrt{n}} = \dfrac{0.8 - 0.72}{0.10 / \sqrt{16}} = 3.2$

          $P(\overline{X} < 0.8) = P(\overline{X} < 0.72) + P(0.72 < \overline{X} < 0.8) = 0.5 + 0.49931 = 0.99931$

           $P(0.7 < \overline{X} < 0.8) = P(\overline{X} < 0.8) - P(\overline{X} < 0.7) = 0.99931 - 0.2119 = 0.78741$

  (e) The areas between the lower $\overline{X}$ and the mean, and the area between the mean and the upper $\overline{X}$ should be equal to $0.9/2 = 0.45$. Thus the Z values are -1.65 and 1.65.

     $\overline{X}_L = \mu_x - Z\dfrac{\sigma_x}{\sqrt{n}} = 0.72 - 1.65\dfrac{0.1}{\sqrt{16}} = 0.67875$

     $\overline{X}_U = \mu_x + Z\dfrac{\sigma_x}{\sqrt{n}} = 0.72 + 1.65\dfrac{0.10}{\sqrt{16}} = 0.76125$

  (f) This difference appears because the sampling distribution of the mean is less variable than the distribution of individual values.

65. (a) (1) $Z = \dfrac{X - \mu_x}{\sigma_x} = \dfrac{60 - 70}{5} = -2.0$, $P(X < 60) = P(X < 70) - P(60 < X < 70) = 0.5 - 0.4772 = 0.0228$,

          $Z = \dfrac{X - \mu_x}{\sigma_x} = \dfrac{80 - 70}{5} = 2.0$, $P(X < 80) = P(X < 70) + P(70 < X < 80) = 0.5 + 0.4772 = 0.9772$,

          $P(60 < X < 80) = P(X < 80) - P(X < 60) = 0.9772 - 0.0228 = 0.9544$

      (2) $Z = \dfrac{X - \mu_x}{\sigma_x} = \dfrac{85 - 70}{5} = 3.0$, $P(X > 85) = P(X > 70) - P(70 < X < 85) = 0.5 - 0.49865 = 0.00135$,

          $Z = \dfrac{X - \mu_x}{\sigma_x} = \dfrac{60 - 70}{5} = -2.0$, $P(X \geq 60) = P(60 < X < 70) + P(X > 70) = 0.4772 + 0.5 = 0.9772$

(b) X exceeds 0.1% of the scuba divers, therefore X is below the mean and Z is negative. If 0.1% of the values is below X then 49.9% of all the values must fall between X and the mean; subsequently the area between X and the mean is 0.499, and $Z = -3.09$. $X = \mu_x + Z\sigma_x = 70 - 3.09 \times 5 = 54.55$

(c) 95% of all scuba divers exceed X, therefore X is below the mean and Z is negative. If 5% of the values are below X then 45% of all the values must fall between X and the mean; subsequently the area between X and the mean is 0.45, and $Z = -1.64$. $X = \mu_x + Z\sigma_x = 70 - 1.64 \times 5 = 61.8$

(d) (1) $Z = \dfrac{\overline{X} - \mu_{\bar{x}}}{\sigma_{\bar{x}}/\sqrt{n}} = \dfrac{65 - 70}{5/\sqrt{4}} = -2$, $P(\overline{X} > 65) = P(65 < \overline{X} < 70) + P(\overline{X} > 70) = 0.4772 + 0.5 = 0.9772$

(2) $Z = \dfrac{\overline{X} - \mu_{\bar{x}}}{\sigma_{\bar{x}}/\sqrt{n}} = \dfrac{65 - 70}{5/\sqrt{4}} = -2$, $P(\overline{X} < 65) = P(\overline{X} < 70) - P(65 < \overline{X} < 70) = 0.5 - 0.4772 = 0.0228$,

$Z = \dfrac{\overline{X} - \mu_{\bar{x}}}{\sigma_{\bar{x}}/\sqrt{n}} = \dfrac{75 - 70}{5/\sqrt{4}} = 2$, $P(\overline{X} < 75) = P(\overline{X} < 70) + P(70 < \overline{X} < 75) = 0.50 + .4772 = 0.9772$,

$P(65 < \overline{X} < 75) = 0.9772 - 0.0228 = 0.9544$

(e) The areas between the lower $\overline{X}$ and the mean and the area between the mean and the upper $\overline{X}$ should be equal to $\dfrac{0.9}{2} = 0.45$. Thus the Z values are -1.65 and 1.65. $\overline{X}_L = \mu_x - Z\dfrac{\sigma_x}{\sqrt{n}} = 70 - 1.65\dfrac{5}{\sqrt{4}} = 65.875$,

$\overline{X}_U = \mu_x + Z\dfrac{\sigma_x}{\sqrt{n}} = 70 + 1.65\dfrac{5}{\sqrt{4}} = 74.125$

67. (a) $\mu_x = e^{\mu_{\ln(x)} + \sigma_{\ln(x)}^2/2} = e^{4.5 + (1.3)^2/2} = e^{5.345} = 209.5579$

(b) $\sigma_x = \sqrt{e^{2(4.5)+(1.3)^2} \cdot \left(e^{(1.3)^2} - 1\right)} = \sqrt{e^{10.69} \cdot \left(e^{1.69} - 1\right)} = \sqrt{194079.316} = 440.544341$

(c) (1) $Z = \dfrac{\ln(X) - \mu_{\ln(x)}}{\sigma_{\ln(x)}} = \dfrac{\ln(100) - 4.5}{1.3} = 0.08$, $P(X < 100) = 0.5 + 0.0319 = 0.5319$

(2) $Z = \dfrac{\ln(X) - \mu_{\ln(x)}}{\sigma_{\ln(x)}} = \dfrac{\ln(200) - 4.5}{1.3} = 0.61$, $P(X < 200) = 0.5 + 0.2291 = 0.7291$

(3) $Z = \dfrac{\ln(X) - \mu_{\ln(x)}}{\sigma_{\ln(x)}} = \dfrac{\ln(100) - 4.5}{1.3} = 0.08$, $P(X < 100) = 0.5 + 0.0319 = 0.5319$,

$Z = \dfrac{\ln(X) - \mu_{\ln(x)}}{\sigma_{\ln(x)}} = \dfrac{\ln(200) - 4.5}{1.3} = 0.61$, $P(X < 200) = 0.5 + 0.2291 = 0.7291$,

$P(100 < X < 200) = P(X < 200) - P(X < 100) = 0.7291 - 0.5319 = 0.1972$

(d) $\mu_x = e^{\mu_{\ln(x)} + \sigma_{\ln(x)}^2/2} = e^{5 + (1.3)^2/2} = e^{5.845} = 345.5025$,

$\sigma_x = \sqrt{e^{2(5)+(1.3)^2} \cdot \left(e^{(1.3)^2} - 1\right)} = \sqrt{e^{11.69} \cdot \left(e^{1.69} - 1\right)} = \sqrt{527562.279} = 726.334826$

(1) $Z = \dfrac{\ln(X) - \mu_{\ln(x)}}{\sigma_{\ln(x)}} = \dfrac{\ln(100) - 5}{1.3} = -0.3$, $P(X < 100) = 0.5 - 0.1179 = 0.3821$

(2) $Z = \dfrac{\ln(X) - \mu_{\ln(x)}}{\sigma_{\ln(x)}} = \dfrac{\ln(200) - 5}{1.3} = 0.23$, $P(X < 200) = 0.5 + 0.0910 = 0.5910$

(3) $Z = \dfrac{\ln(X) - \mu_{\ln(x)}}{\sigma_{\ln(x)}} = \dfrac{\ln(100) - 5}{1.3} = -0.3$, $P(X < 100) = 0.5 - 0.1179 = 0.3821$,

$Z = \dfrac{\ln(X) - \mu_{\ln(x)}}{\sigma_{\ln(x)}} = \dfrac{\ln(200) - 5}{1.3} = 0.23$, $P(X < 200) = 0.5 + 0.0910 = 0.5910$,

$P(100 < X < 200) = P(X < 200) - P(X < 100) = 0.5910 - 0.3821 = 0.2089$

(e) $\mu_x = e^{\mu_{\ln(x)} + \sigma^2_{\ln(x)}/2} = e^{4.5 + (1.5)^2/2} = e^{5.625} = 277.2723$,

$\sigma_x = \sqrt{e^{2(4.5) + (1.5)^2} \cdot \left(e^{(1.5)^2} - 1\right)} = \sqrt{e^{11.25} \cdot \left(e^{2.25} - 1\right)} = \sqrt{652536.45} = 807.797283$

(1) $Z = \dfrac{\ln(X) - \mu_{\ln(x)}}{\sigma_{\ln(x)}} = \dfrac{\ln(100) - 4.5}{1.5} = 0.07$, $P(X < 100) = 0.5 + 0.0279 = 0.5279$

(2) $Z = \dfrac{\ln(X) - \mu_{\ln(x)}}{\sigma_{\ln(x)}} = \dfrac{\ln(200) - 4.5}{1.5} = 0.53$, $P(X < 200) = 0.5 + 0.2019 = 0.7019$

(3) $Z = \dfrac{\ln(X) - \mu_{\ln(x)}}{\sigma_{\ln(x)}} = \dfrac{\ln(100) - 4.5}{1.5} = 0.07$, $P(X < 100) = 0.5 + 0.0279 = 0.5279$,

$Z = \dfrac{\ln(X) - \mu_{\ln(x)}}{\sigma_{\ln(x)}} = \dfrac{\ln(200) - 4.5}{1.5} = 0.53$, $P(X < 200) = 0.5 + 0.2019 = 0.7019$,

$P(100 < X < 200) = P(X < 200) - P(X < 100) = 0.7019 - 0.5279 = 0.174$

69. (a)

The Normal Probability Plot of the ANC of All the Lakes

(b) The acid-neutralized capacities of all the lakes appear to be a right-skewed distribution, because the curve rises slowly at first, and then the rate of increase progresses rapidly.

(c)

The Normal Probability Plot of ANC of the Seepage Lakes

(d) The acid-neutralized capacities of the seepage lakes appear to belong to the right-skewed distribution, because the curve rises slowly at first, and then the rate of increase progresses rapidly.

(e) **The Normal Probability Plot of CAN of the Drainage Lakes**

(f) The acid-neutralized capacities of the drainage lakes appear to belong to the right-skewed distribution, because the curve rises slowly at first, and then the rate of increase progresses rapidly.

(g) **The Normal Probability Plot of All the Lakes.**

The Normal Probability Plot of the Seepage Lakes.

Except for several points at the lower and upper ends of the scale, the plot seems to approximately follow a straight line. Thus, it can be concluded that the data appears to be approximately normally distributed.

Except for several points at the lower and upper ends of the scale, the plot seems to approximately follow a straight line. Thus, it can be concluded that the data appears to be approximately normally distributed.

The acid-neutralized capacities of the drainage lakes appear to be left-skewed distribution, because the curve rises more rapidly at first, and then the rate of increase decreases.

(h) All distributions of (a)–(f) are right-skewed whereas the new variable consisting of the natural logarithm of the acid neutralizing capacity appears to be approximately normally distributed.

The Normal Probability Plot of the Drainage Lakes.

chapter 6

Statistical Process Control Charts I: Basic Concepts and Attributes Charts

1. (a) **NP Chart for Abandoned Calls**

(b) Yes, rules 1–5 provide that this process is in a state of statistical control.

(c) Rules 1–5 provide that this process is in a state of statistical control.

(d) **P Chart for Abandoned Calls**

(e) Yes, rules 1–5 provide that this process is in a state of statistical control.

(f) Rules 1–5 provide that this process is in a state of statistical control.

(g) The results are the same.

3. (a) **NP Chart for Nonconforming Tiles**

(b) Yes, rules 1–5 provide that this process is in a state of statistical control.

(c) Rules 1–5 provide that this process is in a state of statistical control.

(d)   **P Chart for Nonconforming Tiles**

(e) Yes, rules 1–5 provide that this process is in a state of statistical control.
(f) Rules 1–5 provide that this process is in a state of statistical control.
(g) The results are the same.

5.   (a)   **P Chart for Nonconforming Components**

(b) Due to rule 4 (8 points below the centerline), the process is out of control.
(c) The process is out of control, but there are no exceptional points for removing.

7.   (a)   **P Chart for Pending**

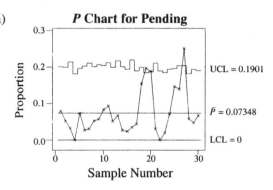

(b) There are points outside the control limits, so the process is out of control.
(c) It is necessary to determine the reason for the high proportions of unfocused, or pending samples on the 9th, 20th and 27th days.

9.   (a)   **c Chart for Imperfect Rolls**

(b) There is a point above UCL, so this process is out of control.

(c) After removing the out-of-control point, (28), the process control chart appears as shown to the right. The revised process is in a better state of statistical control.

c Chart for Imperfect Rolls

11. (a) **c Chart for Vehicle Accident Data**

(b) Yes, rules 1–5 provide that this process is in a state of statistical control.

(c) Rules 1–5 provide that this process is in a state of statistical control.

(d) **c Chart for Vehicle Accident Data (With Expanded Control Limits)**

The process is out of statistical control (8 points below center line).

(e) This course leads to the decrease in the number of accidents, and shifts away from the mean.

(f) Calculate control limits for further monitoring using only data of 1993–1995 years.

(g) **u Chart for Vehicle Accident Data**

(h) There is a small variability in sample sizes, so c and u charts lead to the same result.

13. (a)

u Chart for Code Errors

(b) There are points above UCL, so the process is out of control.

(c) After removing the 4 out-of-control points, the u chart appears as shown below.

u Chart for Code Errors
(Recalculated Without Out-Of-Control Points)

The revised process in in a state of statistical control.

15. (a)

c Chart for Cartridges Sent

(b) Due to rules 1 and 4, the process is out if control.

(c) After removing the out-of-control point, (19), the control chart appears as shown below.

c Chart for Cartridges Sent
(Recalculated Without Out-Of-Control Points)

Due to rule 4, the process is still out of control.

17. When only chance or common cause affect the system, the process is said to be stable (that is, in a state of statistical control).

19. Control charts can detect special causes. Special causes are then eliminated to reduce the process variability. This results in improved product quality.

21. One or more points plotted above the UCL or below the LCL indicate that the system is out of control. Should this occur, the process is interrupted and efforts are undertaken to identify the special cause that resulted in the signal.

23. Moment calculations in p and np charts are based on binomial distribution; the 3σ rule is derived from both the central limit theorem and from the normal distribution.

25. The assumptions are as follows:
(1) There are only two possible outcomes for an event. An item must be found to be either conforming or nonconforming. No intermediate values are possible.
(2) The probability of nonconforming items is constant.
(3) Successive items are independent.
(4) All samples contain the same number of items (p charts only).

27. In the United States, the upper control limit is usually placed three standard deviations above the mean, and the lower control limit is placed three standard deviations below the mean.

29. (a)

(b) There is one point above UCL, so this process is out of control. This day is probably the day after Labor Day (a holiday in the United States).

(c)

There is one point above UCL, so this process is out of control.

(d) The two charts differ only in their ordinates by the factor of 125. The shape of the plot and the relationship between the plotted values and the control limits are the same. Therefore, both charts convey the same information.

31. (a)

(b) There are two points above UCL, so this process is out of control.

(c) After removing the out-of-control points, (20, 25), the control chart appears as shown below.

The revised process is in a state of statistical control.

33. (a)

(b) Yes, rules 1–5 provide that this process is in a state of statistical control.

(c) Rules 1–5 provide that this process is in a state of statistical control.

35. (a)

p Chart for Problems

(b) Rules 1 and 2 provide that this process is out of control.

(c) After removing the out-of-control point, (4), the control chart appears as shown below.

p Chart for Problems

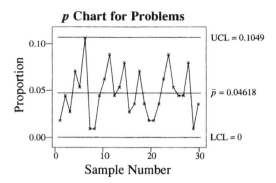

All points are inside the control limits, but due to rule 2 the process is out of control.

37. (a)

u Chart for Alerts

(b) Yes, rules 1–5 provide that this process is in a state of statistical control.

(c) Rules 1–5 provide that this process is in a state of statistical control.

39. (a)

c Chart for Deliveries

(b) There is one point above UCL, so this process is out of control.

(c) After removing the control point (20) is in the state of statistical control now.

c Chart for Deliveries

(d)

c Chart for Deliveries

The revised process is in a state of statistical control.

(e) Yes, because the revised process is stable.

All points are within the revised control limits.

41. (a) The LCL and UCL vary with sample size. When
$n = 100$, the LCL $= 0.0119$ and the UCL $= 0.2133$.
When $n = 112$, the LCL $= 0.0175$ and the
UCL $= 0.2077$. When $n = 126$, the LCL $= 0.0229$
and the UCL $= 0.2022$.

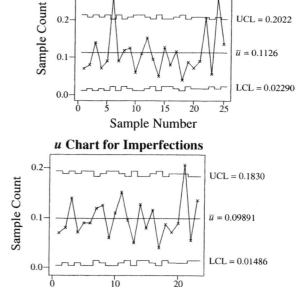

(b) There are two points representing roll 6 and roll 24
above the UCL, so the printing process is out of
control.

(c) After the elimination of points 6 and 24, the control
chart is shown below. The LCL and UCL vary with
sample size. When $n = 500$, the LCL $= 0.0046$ and
the UCL $= 0.1932$. When $n = 112$, the LCL $= 0.0098$
and the UCL $= 0.1880$. When $n = 126$, the
LCL $= 0.0149$ and the UCL 0.1829.

The process is still out of control.

43. Answers will vary.

chapter 7

Statistical Process Control Charts II: Variable Control Charts

1. The data is in stacked format. Before using PHStat compute the mean and range for each group.

(a)

Control Chart	
Sample/Subgroup Size	5
$\overline{R}$	274.867
R Chart	
D_3 Factor	0
D_4 Factor	2.114
Lower Control Limit	0
Center Line	274.867
Upper Control Limit	581.068

(b) There are no points outside of the control limits and there is no evidence of a pattern in the R chart. Therefore, we can conclude that the process is in a state of statistical control.

(c)

$\overline{X}$ Chart	
Average of Subgroup	197.887
A_2 Factor	0.577
Lower Control Limit	39.289
Center	197.887
Upper Control Limit	356.485

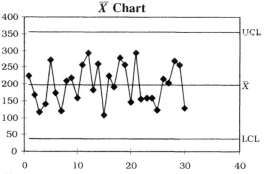

There are no points outside of the control limits, so the process is in a state of statistical control.

(d) There are no points outside of the control limits and there is no evidence of a pattern in the $\overline{X}$ chart. Therefore, we can conclude that the process is in a state of statistical control.

(e)

S Chart	
$\overline{S}$	108.771
B_3 factor	0
B_4 factor	2.089
Lower Control Limit	0
Center Line	108.771
Upper Control Limit	227.222

(f) There are no points outside of the control limits and there is no evidence of a pattern in the S chart. Therefore, we can conclude that the process is in a state of statistical control.

(g)

$\overline{X}$ Chart	
Average $\overline{X}$	197.887
A_3 factor	1.427
Lower Control Limit	42.671
Center Line	197.887
Upper Control Limit	353.103

There are no points outside of the control limits and there is no evidence of a pattern in the $\overline{X}$ chart. Therefore, we can conclude that the process is in a state of statistical control.

(h) Results of (a) and (d) and (e–f) are the same. Process is stable and in a state of statistical control.

(i) Process is stable and is in a state of statistical control.

3. (a)

Control Chart	
Sample/Subgroup Size	6
$\overline{R}$	11.917
R Chart	
D_3 Factor	0
D_4 Factor	2.004
Lower Control Limit	0
Center	11.9167
Upper Control Limit	23.881

(b) There are no points outside of the control limits and there is no evidence of a pattern in the R chart.

(c)

$\overline{X}$ Chart	
Average of Subgroup	40.660
A_2 Factor	0.483
Lower Control Limit	34.90
Center	40.660
Upper Control Limit	46.415

(d) The process is out of control. There is no evidence of a pattern in the $\overline{X}$ chart.

(e)

S Chart	
$\overline{S}$	4.625
B_3 factor	0.03
B_4 factor	1.97
Lower Control Limit	0.139
Center Line	4.625
Upper Control Limit	9.111

(f) There are no points outside the control limits and there is no evidence of a pattern in the S chart.

(g)

$\bar{X}$ Chart	
Average $\bar{X}$	40.656
A_3 factor	1.287
Lower Control Limit	34.708
Center Line	40.660
Upper Control Limit	46.612

(h) The results of (a) and (d) and (e–f) are the same. Process is stable and out of statistical control.

(i) Process is stable and out of statistical control.

5. (a)

Control Chart	
Sample/Subgroup Size	4
$\bar{R}$	2.354
R Chart	
D_3 Factor	0
D_4 Factor	2.282
Lower Control Limit	0
Center	2.354
Upper Control Limit	5.373

(b) The process is out of control. Data points 9 and 17 should be removed from the data set.

Control Chart	
Sample/Subgroup Size	4
$\bar{R}$	1.793
R Chart	
D_3 Factor	0
D_4 Factor	2.282
Lower Control Limit	0
Center	1.793
Upper Control Limit	4.091

The process is out of control. Data point 6 should be removed from the data set because it is above the upper control limit.

Control Chart	
Sample/Subgroup Size	4
$\bar{R}$	1.678
R Chart	
D_3 Factor	0
D_4 Factor	2.282
Lower Control Limit	0
Center	1.678
Upper Control Limit	3.830

The process is globally out of statistical control.

(c)

$\bar{X}$ Chart	
Average $\bar{X}$	24.758
A_3 factor	0.729
Lower Control Limit	23.041
Center Line	24.758
Upper Control Limit	26.474

The process is out of statistical control.

(d) The process is globally out of statistical control.

(e)

S Chart	
$\bar{S}$	0.971
B_3 factor	0
B_4 factor	2.266
Lower Control Limit	0
Center Line	0.971
Upper Control Limit	2.201

(f) The process is out of statistical control. Data points 9 and 17 should be removed fom the data set.

S Chart	
$\bar{S}$	0.720
B_3 factor	0
B_4 factor	2.266
Lower Control Limit	0
Center Line	0.720
Upper Control Limit	1.632

The process is out of statistical control.

(g)

$\overline{X}$ Chart	
Average $\overline{X}$	24.758
A_3 factor	1.628
Lower Control Limit	23.176
Center Line	24.758
Upper Control Limit	26.339

The process is out of statistical control.

(h)   Results of (a) and (d) and (e–f) are the same. The process is out of statistical control.

(i)   The process is out of statistical control.

7.   Before use PHStat compute the mean and range for each group.

(a)

Control Chart	
Sample/Subgroup Size	4
$\overline{R}$	0.042
R Chart	
D_3 Factor	0
D_4 Factor	2.282
Lower Control Limit	0
Center	0.042
Upper Control Limit	0.096

(b)   The *R* chart does not indicate that the process is out of statistical control.

(c)

$\overline{X}$ Chart	
Average of Subgroup	4.128
A_2 factor	0.729
Lower Control Limit	4.097
Center	4.128
Upper Control Limit	4.158

The process is out of statistical control. There is no evidence of a pattern in the $\overline{X}$-bar chart.

(d)   The process is out of statistical control. There is no evidence of a pattern in the $\overline{X}$-bar chart.

(e)

S Chart	
$\overline{S}$	0.018
B_3 factor	0
B_4 factor	2.266
Lower Control Limit	0
Center Line	0.018
Upper Control Limit	0.042

(f) The S chart does not indicate that the process is out of statistical control.

(g)

$\overline{X}$ Chart	
Average $\overline{X}$	4.128
A_3 factor	1.628
Lower Control Limit	4.097
Center Line	4.128
Upper Control Limit	4.158

The $\overline{X}$ chart indicates that the process is out of statistical control.

(h) The results of B, $\overline{X}$ and $\overline{\overline{X}}$ charts are the same.

(i) The process is out of statistical control.

9. (a)

(b) There are no points outside of the control limits and no evidence of a pattern in the Individual Value chart.

(c)

Individual Value Chart	
$\overline{X}$	0.475
S	1.123
C_4 factor	0.990
Lower Control Limit	−2.929
Center Line	0.475
Upper Control Limit	3.880

(d) The average flushness measurement has been reduced from 1.962 to 0.4752, the number of out-of-control points has been reduced from 32 to 12. Further work should provide an additional reduction of the average value and/or reduce the variability so that more points will be within the specification limits.

(e)

The average flushness measurement has been reduced from 1.962 to 0.4752. The number of control points has been reduced as well. Further work should provide additional reduction of these characteristics for a more stable process in which statistical control is more feasible.

11. (a)

Moving Range Chart	
$\overline{MR}$	2.081
D_3 factor	0.000
D_4 factor	3.267
Lower Control Limit	0.000
Center Line	2.081
Upper Control Limit	6.800

(b) The process is in a state of statistical control.

(c)

Individual Value Chart	
$\overline{X}$	255.620
E_2 factor	2.659
Lower Control Limit	250.084
Center Line	255.620
Upper Control Limit	261.155

(d)

Individual Value Chart	
$\overline{X}$	255.620
S	2.415
C_4 factor	0.990
Lower Control Limit	248.301
Center Line	255.620
Upper Control Limit	262.938

Moving Average Chart

The process is in a state of statistical control.

$\overline{X}$ Chart (Moving Range Method)

The process is in a state of statistical control.

$\overline{X}$ Chart (Standard Deviation Method)

(e) The process is in a state of statistical control.

(f) All of the results are the same for parts (a) through (e)—the process is in a state of statistical control.

13. (a)

Moving Range Chart	
$\overline{MR}$	1.702
D_3 factor	0.000
D_4 factor	3.267
Lower Control Limit	0.000
Center Line	1.702
Upper Control Limit	5.561

The process is out of statistical control.

(b) Data points 2 and 3 should be removed from the data set.

Moving Range Chart	
$\overline{MR}$	1.606
D_3 factor	0.000
D_4 factor	3.267
Lower Control Limit	0.000
Center Line	1.606
Upper Control Limit	5.248

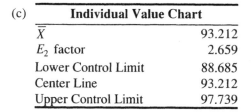

The revised process is in a state of statistical control.

(c)

Individual Value Chart	
$\overline{X}$	93.212
E_2 factor	2.659
Lower Control Limit	88.685
Center Line	93.212
Upper Control Limit	97.739

The process is out of statistical control.

(d)

Individual Value Chart	
$\overline{X}$	93.212
S	1.808
C_4 factor	0.990
Lower Control Limit	87.730
Center Line	93.212
Upper Control Limit	98.694

$\overline{X}$ **Chart (Standard Deviation Method)**

(e) The process is in a state of statistical control.

(f) The standard deviation method is the most efficient procedure and results in a controllable process; therefore, one should choose this method for the percent purity data.

15. (a)

Moving Range Chart	
$\overline{MR}$	578.566
D_3 factor	0.000
D_4 factor	3.267
Lower Control Limit	0.000
Center Line	578.566
Upper Control Limit	1890.177

Moving Range Chart

The process is in a state of statistical control.

(b) The process is in a state of statistical control.

(c)

Individual Value Chart	
$\overline{X}$	11756.23
E_2 factor	2.659
Lower Control Limit	10217.82
Center Line	11756.23
Upper Control Limit	13294.64

$\overline{X}$ **Chart (Moving Range Method)**

The process is in a state of statistical control.

(d)

Individual Value Chart	
$\overline{X}$	12038.880
S	494.047
C_4 factor	0.990
Lower Control Limit	10541.770
Center Line	12038.880
Upper Control Limit	13536.000

$\overline{X}$ **Chart (Standard Deviation Method)**

(e) The process is in a state of statistical control.

(f) The results are the same for all of the parts.

17. (a) CUSUM Chart

Container	Average	Standard Deviation	Z_i	S_{H_i}	S_{L_i}
1	10.550	0.311	−1.096	0.000	0.596
2	10.525	0.287	−1.267	0.000	1.363
3	10.625	0.275	−0.581	0.000	1.443
4	10.825	0.189	0.793	0.293	0.151
5	10.625	0.250	−0.581	0.000	0.231
6	10.325	0.479	−2.641	0.000	2.372
7	10.625	0.457	−0.581	0.000	2.453
8	10.475	0.386	−1.611	0.000	3.563
9	10.400	0.503	−2.126	0.000	5.189
10	10.075	0.171	−4.357	0.000	9.046
11	10.200	0.668	−3.499	0.000	12.045
12	10.275	0.427	−2.984	0.000	14.529
13	10.450	0.252	−1.782	0.000	15.811
14	10.250	0.173	−3.156	0.000	18.466
15	10.175	0.222	−3.671	0.000	21.637
16	11.700	0.216	6.801	6.301	14.336
17	11.325	0.250	4.226	10.027	9.610
18	10.875	0.171	1.136	10.663	7.974
19	10.850	0.100	0.964	11.127	6.510
20	11.200	0.294	3.368	13.995	2.642
21	11.525	0.096	5.599	19.094	0.000
22	11.175	0.096	3.196	21.790	0.000
23	11.125	0.263	2.853	24.142	0.000
24	11.050	0.311	2.338	25.980	0.000
25	10.775	0.310	0.449	25.929	0.000
26	11.400	0.216	4.741	30.170	0.000
27	10.925	0.263	1.479	31.149	0.000
28	11.275	0.126	3.883	34.532	0.000
29	11.250	0.370	3.711	37.743	0.000
30	10.425	0.126	−1.954	35.289	1.454
31	10.150	0.238	−3.842	30.947	4.796
32	10.325	0.189	−2.641	27.806	6.937
33	10.575	0.275	−0.924	26.382	7.361
34	9.800	0.163	−6.245	19.637	13.106
Overall mean	10.710				
$\overline{S}$	0.268				
C_4	0.921				
n	4.000				
k	0.500				

There are S_{H_i} and S_{L_i} values greater than 4, hence the process is out of control.

(b) EWMA chart

Container	Average	Standard Deviation	W_i	LCL	UCL
1	10.550	0.311	10.670	10.644	10.808
2	10.525	0.287	10.634	10.628	10.808
3	10.625	0.275	10.631	10.620	10.808
4	10.825	0.189	10.680	10.616	10.808
5	10.625	0.250	10.666	10.548	10.871
6	10.325	0.479	10.581	10.548	10.871
7	10.625	0.457	10.592	10.548	10.871
8	10.475	0.386	10.563	10.548	10.871
9	10.400	0.503	10.522	10.548	10.871
10	10.075	0.171	10.410	10.548	10.871
11	10.200	0.668	10.358	10.548	10.871
12	10.275	0.427	10.337	10.548	10.871
13	10.450	0.252	10.365	10.548	10.871
14	10.250	0.173	10.336	10.548	10.871
15	10.175	0.221	10.296	10.548	10.871
16	11.700	0.216	10.647	10.548	10.871
17	11.325	0.250	10.817	10.548	10.871
18	10.875	0.171	10.831	10.548	10.871
19	10.850	0.100	10.836	10.548	10.871
20	11.200	0.294	10.927	10.548	10.871
21	11.525	0.096	11.076	10.548	10.871
22	11.175	0.096	11.101	10.548	10.871
23	11.125	0.263	11.107	10.548	10.871
24	11.050	0.311	11.093	10.548	10.871
25	10.775	0.310	11.013	10.548	10.871
26	11.400	0.216	11.110	10.548	10.871
27	10.925	0.263	11.064	10.548	10.871
28	11.275	0.126	11.117	10.548	10.871
29	11.250	0.370	11.150	10.548	10.871
30	10.425	0.126	10.969	10.548	10.871
31	10.150	0.238	10.764	10.548	10.871
32	10.325	0.189	10.654	10.548	10.871
33	10.575	0.275	10.634	10.548	10.871
34	9.800	0.163	10.426	10.548	10.871
Overall mean	10.710				
$\overline{S}$	0.268				
C_4	0.940				
n	4.000				
r	0.250				

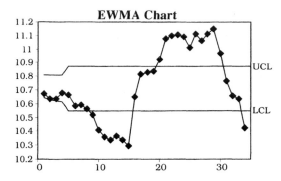

EWMA Chart

There are W_i values below the LCL and above the UCL, hence the process is out of statistical control.

(c) The results are the same for all of the parts. The process is out of statistical control.

19. (a) CUSUM Chart

Day	Mean Flow	Flow Standard Deviation	Z_i	S_{H_i}	S_{L_i}
1	0.065	0.023	10.050	9.550	0.000
2	0.059	0.006	7.050	16.100	0.000
3	0.053	0.008	4.001	19.601	0.000
4	0.052	0.007	3.340	22.440	0.000
5	0.054	0.007	4.763	26.703	0.000
6	0.053	0.007	3.848	30.051	0.000
7	0.053	0.008	4.001	33.552	0.000
8	0.052	0.006	3.645	36.696	0.000
9	0.046	0.008	0.747	36.944	0.000
10	0.045	0.008	−0.219	36.225	0.000
11	0.044	0.008	−0.269	35.456	0.000
12	0.045	0.006	−0.066	34.890	0.000
13	0.047	0.008	1.052	35.442	0.000
14	0.044	0.008	−0.422	34.520	0.000
15	0.041	0.007	−1.845	32.175	1.345
16	0.038	0.008	−3.370	28.305	4.215
17	0.038	0.008	−3.574	24.231	7.289
18	0.038	0.009	−3.675	20.056	10.464
19	0.038	0.008	−3.624	15.931	13.588
20	0.037	0.008	−4.234	11.197	17.323
21	0.036	0.008	−4.539	6.158	21.362
22	0.041	0.022	−2.150	3.508	23.012
23	0.042	0.007	−1.744	1.264	24.256
24	0.038	0.008	−3.624	0.000	27.380
25	0.039	0.008	−3.065	0.000	29.945
26	0.044	0.024	−0.320	0.000	29.766
27	0.042	0.007	−1.489	0.000	30.755
28	0.040	0.009	−2.404	0.000	32.660
29	0.041	0.018	−1.947	0.000	34.106
30	0.045	0.010	0.086	0.000	33.520
Overall mean	0.045				
$\overline{S}$	0.010				
C_4	0.989				
n	24.000				
k	0.500				

There are S_{H_i} and S_{L_i} values greater than 4, hence the process is out of statistical control.

(b) EWMA Chart

Day	Mean Flow	Flow Standard Deviation	W_i	LCL	UCL
1	0.065	0.023	0.050	0.042	0.048
2	0.059	0.006	0.052	0.041	0.049
3	0.053	0.008	0.052	0.040	0.050
4	0.052	0.007	0.052	0.040	0.050
5	0.054	0.007	0.053	0.040	0.050
6	0.053	0.007	0.053	0.034	0.050
7	0.053	0.008	0.053	0.040	0.050
8	0.052	0.006	0.053	0.040	0.050
9	0.046	0.008	0.052	0.040	0.050
10	0.045	0.008	0.049	0.040	0.050
11	0.044	0.008	0.048	0.040	0.050
12	0.045	0.006	0.047	0.040	0.050
13	0.047	0.008	0.047	0.040	0.050
14	0.044	0.008	0.046	0.040	0.050
15	0.041	0.007	0.045	0.040	0.050
16	0.038	0.008	0.043	0.040	0.050
17	0.038	0.008	0.042	0.040	0.050
18	0.038	0.009	0.041	0.040	0.050
19	0.038	0.008	0.040	0.040	0.050
20	0.037	0.008	0.039	0.040	0.050
21	0.036	0.008	0.038	0.040	0.050
22	0.041	0.022	0.039	0.040	0.050
23	0.042	0.007	0.040	0.040	0.050
24	0.038	0.008	0.039	0.040	0.050
25	0.039	0.008	0.039	0.040	0.050
26	0.044	0.024	0.040	0.040	0.050
27	0.042	0.007	0.041	0.040	0.050
28	0.040	0.009	0.041	0.040	0.050
29	0.041	0.018	0.041	0.040	0.050
30	0.045	0.010	0.042	0.040	0.050
Overall mean	0.045				
$\overline{S}$	0.010				
C_4	0.940				
n	5.000				
r	0.250				

There are W_i values below the LCL and above the UCL, hence the process is out of statistical control.

(c) The results are the same for all of the parts. The process is out of statistical control.

21. (a) CUSUM Chart

Sample	Average	Standard Deviation	Z_i	S_{H_i}	S_{L_i}
1	19.800	0.255	−2.986	0.000	2.486
2	19.640	0.518	−3.993	0.000	5.978
3	19.980	0.507	−1.853	0.000	7.331
4	20.660	0.230	2.427	1.927	4.404
5	19.740	0.467	−3.363	0.000	7.267
6	19.540	0.297	−4.622	0.000	11.389
7	20.020	0.319	−1.601	0.000	12.490
8	20.100	0.122	−1.098	0.000	13.088
9	20.280	0.164	0.035	0.000	12.552
10	20.700	0.283	2.678	2.178	9.374
11	20.620	0.164	2.175	3.853	6.699
12	20.540	0.305	1.672	5.025	4.528
13	20.380	0.148	0.665	5.190	3.363
14	20.580	0.217	1.923	6.613	0.940
15	20.540	0.207	1.672	7.784	0.000
16	18.500	4.535	−11.167	0.000	10.667
17	20.080	0.164	−1.223	0.000	11.390
18	20.240	0.152	−0.216	0.000	11.107
19	20.320	0.286	0.287	0.000	10.320
20	20.280	0.179	0.035	0.000	9.785
21	20.220	0.239	−0.342	0.000	9.627
22	20.020	0.408	−1.601	0.000	10.728
23	20.300	0.187	0.161	0.000	10.067
24	19.980	0.531	−1.853	0.000	11.420
25	20.340	0.207	0.413	0.000	10.507
26	20.260	0.288	−0.091	0.000	10.097
27	20.280	0.130	0.035	0.000	9.562
28	20.300	0.245	0.161	0.000	8.901
29	20.460	0.219	1.168	0.668	7.233
30	20.400	0.141	0.790	0.958	5.943
31	20.340	0.270	0.413	0.871	5.030
32	20.340	0.270	0.413	0.784	4.117
33	20.120	0.259	−0.972	0.000	4.589
34	20.320	0.259	0.287	0.000	3.802
35	20.600	0.200	2.049	1.549	1.253
36	20.060	0.114	−1.349	0.000	2.102
37	20.060	0.378	−1.349	0.000	2.951
38	20.420	0.228	0.916	0.416	1.535
39	20.400	0.187	0.790	0.707	0.244
40	19.940	0.550	−2.104	0.000	1.849
41	20.320	0.148	0.287	0.000	1.062
42	20.560	0.329	1.797	1.297	0.000
43	20.580	0.370	1.923	2.721	0.000
44	20.500	0.625	1.420	3.640	0.000
45	20.940	0.167	4.189	7.329	0.000
46	20.860	0.134	3.685	10.515	0.000
47	20.880	0.228	3.811	13.826	0.000
48	20.380	0.239	0.665	13.991	0.000
49	20.480	0.286	1.294	14.784	0.000
50	20.520	0.228	1.546	15.830	0.000
Overall mean	20.274				
$\overline{S}$	0.352				
C_4	0.990				
n	5.000				
k	0.500				

There are S_{H_i} and S_{L_i} values greater than 4, hence the process is out of statistical control.

(b) EWMA chart

Sample	Average	Standard Deviation	W_i	Lower Control Limit	Upper Control Limit
1	19.800	0.255	20.156	20.155	20.394
2	19.640	0.518	20.027	20.125	20.423
3	19.980	0.507	20.015	20.111	20.438
4	20.660	0.230	20.176	20.103	20.445
5	19.740	0.467	20.067	20.094	20.455
6	19.540	0.297	19.935	20.094	20.455
7	20.020	0.319	19.957	20.094	20.455
8	20.100	0.122	19.992	20.094	20.455
9	20.280	0.164	20.064	20.094	20.455
10	20.700	0.283	20.223	20.094	20.455
11	20.620	0.164	20.322	20.094	20.455
12	20.540	0.305	20.377	20.094	20.455
13	20.380	0.148	20.378	20.094	20.455
14	20.580	0.217	20.428	20.094	20.455
15	20.540	0.207	20.456	20.094	20.455
16	18.500	4.535	19.967	20.094	20.455
17	20.080	0.164	19.995	20.094	20.455
18	20.240	0.152	20.057	20.094	20.455
19	20.320	0.286	20.122	20.094	20.455
20	20.280	0.179	20.162	20.094	20.455
21	20.220	0.239	20.176	20.094	20.455
22	20.020	0.409	20.137	20.094	20.455
23	20.300	0.187	20.178	20.094	20.455
24	19.980	0.531	20.128	20.094	20.455
25	20.340	0.207	20.181	20.094	20.455
26	20.260	0.288	20.201	20.094	20.455
27	20.280	0.130	20.221	20.094	20.455
28	20.300	0.245	20.241	20.094	20.455
29	20.460	0.219	20.295	20.094	20.455
30	20.400	0.141	20.322	20.094	20.455
31	20.340	0.270	20.326	20.094	20.455
32	20.340	0.270	20.330	20.094	20.455
33	20.120	0.259	20.277	20.094	20.455
34	20.320	0.259	20.288	20.094	20.455
35	20.600	0.200	20.366	20.094	20.455
36	20.060	0.114	20.289	20.094	20.455
37	20.060	0.378	20.232	20.094	20.455
38	20.420	0.228	20.279	20.094	20.455
39	20.400	0.187	20.309	20.094	20.455
40	19.940	0.550	20.217	20.094	20.455
41	20.320	0.148	20.243	20.094	20.455
42	20.560	0.329	20.322	20.094	20.455
43	20.580	0.370	20.387	20.094	20.455
44	20.500	0.625	20.415	20.094	20.455
45	20.940	0.167	20.546	20.094	20.455
46	20.860	0.134	20.625	20.094	20.455
47	20.880	0.228	20.688	20.094	20.455
48	20.380	0.239	20.611	20.094	20.455
49	20.480	0.286	20.579	20.094	20.455
50	20.520	0.228	20.564	20.094	20.455
Overall mean	20.274				
$\overline{S}$	0.352				
C_4	0.990				
n	5.000				
r	0.250				

EWMA Chart

There are W_i values below the LCL and above the UCL, hence the process is out of statistical control.

(c) The results are the same for all of the parts. The process is out of statistical control.

23. (a) CUSUM Chart

Day	Mean Weight	Standard Deviation Weight	Z_i	S_{H_i}	S_{L_i}
1	1894.670	31.330	−1.520	0.000	1.020
2	1924.670	27.600	2.071	1.571	0.000
3	1894.000	34.980	−1.600	0.000	1.100
4	1902.670	25.380	−0.562	0.000	1.163
5	1912.670	34.860	0.635	0.135	0.028
6	1896.000	39.120	−1.361	0.000	0.889
7	1908.000	21.570	0.076	0.000	0.313
8	1912.670	22.490	0.635	0.135	0.000
9	1937.920	33.090	3.657	3.292	0.000
10	1917.330	27.890	1.193	3.985	0.000
11	1889.330	20.840	−2.159	1.325	1.659
12	1910.000	18.090	0.315	1.140	0.844
13	1909.000	18.090	0.195	0.836	0.149
14	1900.000	26.200	−0.882	0.000	0.531
15	1915.330	31.160	0.953	0.453	0.000
16	1911.330	32.620	0.474	0.427	0.000
17	1912.680	22.750	0.636	0.563	0.000
18	1901.330	17.670	−0.723	0.000	0.223
19	1892.000	31.820	−1.840	0.000	1.563
20	1888.670	38.060	−2.238	0.000	3.301
21	1918.670	31.140	1.353	0.853	1.448
22	1904.670	39.260	−0.323	0.030	1.271
23	1909.330	22.590	0.235	0.000	0.536
24	1904.000	24.480	−0.403	0.000	0.439
25	1912.000	32.270	0.554	0.054	0.000
26	1896.670	18.200	−1.281	0.000	0.781
27	1923.330	38.210	1.911	1.411	0.000
Overall mean	1907.368				
$\overline{S}$	28.213				
C_4	0.975				
n	12.000				
k	0.500				

There are no S_{H_i} or S_{L_i} values greater than 4, hence there is no evidence that the process is out of statistical control.

(b) EWMA chart

Day	Mean Weight	Standard Deviation Weight	W_i	LCL	UCL
1	1894.670	31.330	1904.194	1901.103	1913.633
2	1924.670	27.600	1909.313	1899.537	1915.199
3	1894.000	34.980	1905.485	1898.781	1915.956
4	1902.670	25.380	1904.781	1898.383	1916.353
5	1912.670	34.860	1906.753	1897.896	1916.840
6	1896.000	39.120	1904.065	1897.896	1916.840
7	1908.000	21.570	1905.049	1897.896	1916.840
8	1912.670	22.490	1906.954	1897.896	1916.840
9	1937.920	33.090	1914.695	1897.896	1916.840
10	1917.330	27.890	1915.354	1897.896	1916.840
11	1889.330	20.840	1908.848	1897.896	1916.840
12	1910.000	18.090	1909.136	1897.896	1916.840
13	1909.000	18.090	1909.102	1897.896	1916.840
14	1900.000	26.200	1906.827	1897.896	1916.840
15	1915.330	31.160	1908.952	1897.896	1916.840
16	1911.330	32.620	1909.547	1897.896	1916.840
17	1912.680	22.750	1910.330	1897.896	1916.840
18	1901.330	17.670	1908.080	1897.896	1916.840
19	1892.000	31.820	1904.060	1897.896	1916.840
20	1888.670	38.060	1900.213	1897.896	1916.840
21	1918.670	31.140	1904.827	1897.896	1916.840
22	1904.670	39.260	1904.788	1897.896	1916.840
23	1909.330	22.590	1905.923	1897.896	1916.840
24	1904.000	24.480	1905.442	1897.896	1916.840
25	1912.000	32.270	1907.082	1897.896	1916.840
26	1896.670	18.200	1904.479	1897.896	1916.840
27	1923.330	38.210	1909.192	1897.896	1916.840
Overall mean	1907.368				
$\overline{S}$	28.213				
C_4	0.975				
n	12.000				
r	0.250				

EWMA Chart

There are no W_i values out of LCL and UCL, hence there is no evidence that the process is out of statistical control.

(c) The results in general are the same for all of the parts.

25. $USL = 210$, $LSL = 190$, $USL - LSL = 20$, $6\sigma = UCL - LCL = 220 - 180 = 40$, $\sigma = 6.667$

(a) $C_p = \dfrac{USL - LSL}{6\sigma} = \dfrac{20}{40} = 0.5$, $C_p < 1$, so the process can be expected to produce many nonconforming units.

$Z_{LSL} = \dfrac{LSL - \overline{X}}{\sigma} = \dfrac{190 - 200}{6.667} = -\dfrac{10}{6.667} = -1.5$, $Z_{USL} = \dfrac{USL - \overline{X}}{\sigma} = \dfrac{210 - 200}{6.667} = \dfrac{10}{6.667} = 1.5$,

$|Z_{\min}| = |Z_{LSL}| = |Z_{USL}| = 1.5$, $C_{pk} = \left|\dfrac{Z_{\min}}{3}\right| = \dfrac{1.5}{3} = 0.5$. The specification limits are equidistant from the mean, so

$C_p = C_{pk}$.

(b) proportion too small $= 0.5 - 0.4332 = 0.0668$
proportion too large $= 0.5 - 0.4332 = 0.0668$
proportion too small + proportion too large $= 0.1336$

(c) $Z_{LSL} = \dfrac{LSL - \overline{X}}{\sigma} = \dfrac{190 - 200}{3} = -\dfrac{10}{3} = -3.33$, $Z_{USL} = \dfrac{USL - \overline{X}}{\sigma} = \dfrac{210 - 200}{3} = \dfrac{10}{3} = 3.33$
proportion too small $= 0.5 - 0.49957 = 0.00043$
proportion too large $= 0.5 - 0.49957 = 0.00043$
proportion too small + proportion too large $= 0.00086$

(d) $|Z_{\min}| = 3 * C_{pk} = 3 * 1.33 = 3.99$. For the same specification limits and the same sample mean we have

$\sigma = \dfrac{10}{|Z_{\min}|} = \dfrac{10}{3.99} = 2.5$ and $UCL - LCL = 6\sigma = 15$, hence $LCL = 200 - 7.5 = 192.5$, $UCL = 200 + 7.5 = 207.5$. For

the same standard deviation and the same sample mean we have $LSL = \overline{X} - \sigma \times Z_{\min} = 200 - 3 \times 3.99 = 188$,
$USL = \overline{X} + \sigma \times Z_{\min} = 200 + 3 \times 3.99 = 212$

27. $LSL = 0.4$, $USL = 0.55$, $USL - LSL = 0.15$

(a) $C_p = \dfrac{USL - LSL}{6\sigma} = \dfrac{0.15}{6 \times 0.05} = \dfrac{0.15}{0.3} = 0.5$; $C_p < 1$, so the process can be expected to produce many nonconforming

units. $Z_{LSL} = \dfrac{LSL - \overline{X}}{\sigma} = \dfrac{0.4 - 0.5}{0.05} = -2$, $Z_{USL} = \dfrac{USL - \overline{X}}{\sigma} = \dfrac{0.55 - 0.5}{0.05} = 1$, $|Z_{\min}| = 1$, $C_{pk} = \left|\dfrac{Z_{\min}}{3}\right| = \dfrac{1}{3}$

(b) proportion too small $= 0.5 - 0.4772 = 0.0228$
proportion too large $= 0.5 - 0.3413 = 0.1587$
proportion too small + proportion too large $= 0.1815$

(c) $|Z_{\min}| = 3 \times C_{pk} = 3 \times 1.33 = 3.99$. For the same specification limits and the same sample mean the following should

hold $\sigma = \dfrac{0.05}{|Z_{\min}|} = \dfrac{0.05}{3.99} = 0.0125$ and $UCL - LCL = 6\sigma = 0.075$, so $LCL = 0.5 - 0.0375 = 0.4625$,
$UCL = 0.5 + 0.0375 = 0.5375$

29. The R chart evaluates the process stability and tests the out-of-control points. The $\overline{X}$ chart shows the existence of the central tendency. For correct process monitoring, both characteristics should be studied. Only when the control chart, which measures the variability within a group (R or s chart) indicates that inherent process variability is stable, is it possible to study the central tendency ($\overline{X}$ or $\overline{\overline{X}}$ chart).

31. The $\overline{X}$ chart indicates the shifts between the group averages, the CUSUM and EWMA charts indicate small shifts within the group averages.

33. This method is appropriate whenever sample data is used to make a decision about the acceptability of all units of production within an interval. Unfortunately, this method maximizes variations within a sample and is ineffective in detecting the shifts in process average.

35. If the cause of the out-of-control points has been found and eliminated, it is possible to remove the out-of-control points from the control limits calculations.

37. Calculation of the $\bar{\bar{X}}$ includes more items than one of the $\bar{X}$. Due to the central limit theorem, $\bar{\bar{X}}$ has a probability distribution closer to the normal distribution.

39. Specified tolerance limits are the boundaries beyond which the process should not function or perform main operations. These are the limits of process existence. Natural tolerance limits show the boundaries of the most typical process values.

41. (a)

Control Chart	
Sample/Subgroup Size	4.000
$\bar{R}$	3.314
R Chart	
D_3 Factor	0.000
D_4 Factor	2.282
Lower Control Limit	0.000
Center	3.314
Upper Control Limit	7.563

$\bar{X}$ Chart	
Average of Subgroup Averages	56.235
A_2 Factor	0.729
Lower Control Limit	53.819
Center	56.235
Upper Control Limit	58.651

(b) There are no points outside of the control limits and there is no evidence of a pattern in the R chart. The process is stable.

(c) There are points outside of the control limits on the $\bar{X}$ chart, hence the process is out of statistical control.

(d)

S Chart	
$\bar{S}$	1.471
B_3 factor	0.000
B_4 factor	2.266
Lower Control Limit	0.000
Center Line	1.471
Upper Control Limit	3.335

$\bar{X}$ Chart	
Average $\bar{X}$	56.235
A_3 factor	1.628
Lower Control Limit	53.839
Center Line	56.235
Upper Control Limit	58.632

(e) There are no points outside of the control limits on the s chart, hence the process is in a state of statistical control.

(f) There are points outside of the control limits on the $\overline{\overline{X}}$ chart, hence the process is out of statistical control.

(g) The results are the same for all of the parts.

(h) CUSUM chart

Sample	Average	Standard Deviation	Z_i	S_{H_i}	S_{L_i}
1	56.750	2.062	0.644	0.144	0.000
2	57.500	0.577	1.583	1.226	0.000
3	59.750	2.062	4.399	5.126	0.000
4	60.250	1.258	5.025	9.651	0.000
5	58.500	1.000	2.834	11.985	0.000
6	59.250	2.500	3.773	15.258	0.000
7	58.250	0.957	2.521	17.280	0.000
8	59.000	1.414	3.460	20.240	0.000
9	53.250	0.500	−3.738	16.003	3.238
10	55.000	1.633	−1.547	13.956	4.284
11	50.500	0.577	−7.180	6.276	10.964
12	52.750	3.096	−4.363	1.412	14.828
13	56.500	0.577	0.331	1.243	13.997
14	57.250	1.258	1.270	2.013	12.227
15	57.000	1.155	0.957	2.470	10.771
16	54.750	1.258	−1.860	0.110	12.130
17	56.000	0.816	−0.295	0.000	11.925
18	55.000	1.414	−1.547	0.000	12.972
19	56.750	0.957	0.644	0.144	11.829
20	55.250	1.708	−1.234	0.000	12.562
21	55.750	2.062	−0.608	0.000	12.670
22	55.500	1.732	−0.921	0.000	13.091
23	56.750	1.258	0.644	0.144	11.948
24	57.000	1.414	0.957	0.601	10.491
25	55.500	0.577	−0.921	0.000	10.912
26	58.000	1.414	2.209	1.709	8.203
27	54.500	2.380	−2.173	0.000	9.876
28	56.000	0.816	−0.295	0.000	9.671
29	57.500	2.082	1.583	1.083	7.589
30	57.000	1.633	0.957	1.539	6.132
31	53.250	2.500	−3.738	0.000	9.369
32	54.000	2.160	−2.799	0.000	11.668
33	57.750	1.500	1.896	1.396	9.272
34	53.250	1.500	−3.738	0.000	12.510
35	57.250	1.708	1.270	0.770	10.740
Overall mean	56.236				
$\overline{S}$	1.472				
C_4	0.921				
n	4.000				
k	0.500				

(i) EWMA chart

EWMA Chart

There is a shift in the process mean.

(j) The results are the same for all of the parts. The process is stable and out of statistical control. The EWMA chart indicates a shift in the process mean with the magnitude of one standard deviation.

(k) $LSL = 53$, $USL = 57$, $USL - LCL = 4$,

$$C_p = \frac{USL - LSL}{6\sigma} = \frac{4}{6 \times 1.47} = 0.45, \; C_p < 1, \text{ so the}$$

process can be expected to produce many nonconforming units.

$$Z_{LSL} = \frac{LSL - \overline{X}}{\sigma} = \frac{53 - 56.236}{1.47} = -2.2,$$

$$Z_{USL} = \frac{USL - \overline{X}}{\sigma} = \frac{57 - 56.236}{1.47} = 0.52, \; |Z_{min}| = 0.52,$$

$$C_{pk} = \left| \frac{Z_{min}}{3} \right| = \frac{0.52}{3} = 0.173$$

43. (a)

Control Chart	
Sample/Subgroup Size	3.000
$\overline{R}$	9.960
R Chart	
D_3 Factor	0.000
D_4 Factor	2.575
Lower Control Limit	0.000
Center	9.960
Upper Control Limit	25.647

$\overline{X}$ Chart	
Average of Subgroup Averages	35.680
A_2 Factor	1.0230
Lower Control Limit	25.491
Center	35.680
Upper Control Limit	45.869

R Chart

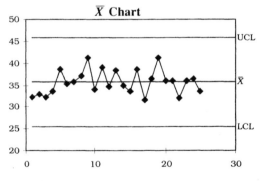

$\overline{X}$ Chart

(b) There are no points outside of the control limits and there is no evidence of a pattern in the R chart. The process is stable.

(c) There are no points outside of the control limits on the $\overline{X}$ chart, hence the process is in a state of statistical control.

(d)

S Chart	
$\overline{S}$	5.223
B_3 factor	0.000
B_4 factor	2.568
Lower Control Limit	0.000
Center Line	5.223
Upper Control Limit	13.413

$\overline{X}$ Chart	
Average $\overline{X}$	35.680
A_3 factor	1.953
Lower Control Limit	25.479
Center Line	35.680
Upper Control Limit	45.881

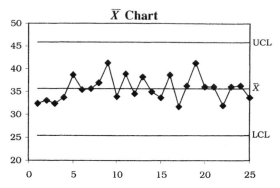

(e) There are no points outside of the control limits and there is no evidence of a pattern in the *s* chart. The process is stable.

(f) There are no points outside of the control limits on the $\overline{X}$ chart, hence the process is in a state of statistical control.

(g) The results are the same for all of the parts.

(h) CUSUM chart

Sample	Average	Standard Deviation	Z_i	S_{H_i}	S_{L_i}
1	32.333	2.517	−1.065	0.000	0.565
2	33.000	2.646	−0.858	0.000	0.358
3	32.333	2.082	−1.065	0.000	0.565
4	33.667	2.082	−0.651	0.000	0.151
5	38.667	9.074	0.901	0.401	0.000
6	35.333	3.055	−0.134	0.000	0.000
7	35.667	3.215	−0.030	0.000	0.000
8	37.000	5.568	0.384	0.000	0.000
9	41.333	12.662	1.730	1.230	0.000
10	34.000	1.732	−0.548	0.000	0.048
11	39.000	10.440	1.005	0.505	0.000
12	34.667	4.509	−0.341	0.000	0.000
13	38.333	4.933	0.798	0.298	0.000
14	35.000	8.888	−0.237	0.000	0.000
15	33.667	4.163	−0.651	0.000	0.151
16	38.667	6.658	0.901	0.401	0.000
17	31.667	5.686	−1.272	0.000	0.772
18	36.333	2.082	0.177	0.000	0.000
19	41.333	7.572	1.730	1.230	0.000
20	36.000	4.000	0.073	0.000	0.000
21	36.000	5.568	0.073	0.000	0.000
22	32.000	4.583	−1.169	0.000	0.669
23	36.000	4.359	0.073	0.000	0.000
24	36.333	9.292	0.177	0.000	0.000
25	33.667	3.215	−0.651	0.000	0.151
Overall mean	35.764				
$\overline{S}$	5.307				
C_4	0.952				
n	3.000				
k	0.500				

(i) EWMA chart

(j) The process is stable and in a state of statistical control. The EWMA chart does not indicate a shift in the process mean with the magnitude of one standard deviation.

45. (a)

Moving Range Chart	
$\overline{MR}$	1.018
D_3 factor	0.000
D_4 factor	3.267
Lower Control Limit	0.000
Center Line	1.018
Upper Control Limit	3.325

Individual Value Chart	
$\overline{X}$	1.496
E_2 factor	2.659
Lower Control Limit	−1.210
Center Line	1.496
Upper Control Limit	4.202

(b) There are no points outside of the control limits on the *MR* chart, hence the process is in a state of statistical control.

(c) There are no points outside of the control limits on the *X* chart, hence the process is in a state of statistical control.

(d)

Individual Value Chart	
$\overline{X}$	1.496
S	0.908
C_4 factor	0.990
Lower Control Limit	−1.257
Center Line	1.496
Upper Control Limit	4.249

(e) There are no points outside of the control limits on the *X* chart, hence the process is in a state of statistical control.

(f) The results are the same for all of the parts.

47. (a)

Moving Range Chart	
$\overline{MR}$	0.005
D_3 factor	0.000
D_4 factor	3.267
Lower Control Limit	0.000
Center Line	0.005
Upper Control Limit	0.017

Individual Value Chart	
$\overline{X}$	2.000
E_2 factor	2.659
Lower Control Limit	1.987
Center Line	2.000
Upper Control Limit	2.015

(b) There are points outside of the control limits on the *MR* chart, hence the process is out of statistical control.

(c) There are points outside of the control limits on the *X* chart, hence the process is out of statistical control. There is a negative trend in this process.

(d)

Individual Value Chart	
$\overline{X}$	2.000
S	0.045
C_4 factor	0.990
Lower Control Limit	1.866
Center Line	2.001
Upper Control Limit	2.136

(e) There are no points outside of the control limits. The process is in a state of statistical control.

(f) The *MR* method controls the neighbor points variability and can be small or large for the trend processes. The SD method controls common variability, and its results are more accurate.

(g) There is a trend in this data that may indicate problems with either the data production or measurement.

(h) Based on the *MR* chart, we conclude that the process is not stable, and therefore, the calculation of the capability index is not correct.

(i) The process is not stable, therefore, the calculation of the proportions of the nonconforming items is not correct.

49. Thickness for Tablet 54 is 0.115.

(a) Hardness

Moving Range Chart	
$\overline{MR}$	0.319
D_3 factor	0.000
D_4 factor	3.267
Lower Control Limit	0.000
Center Line	0.319
Upper Control Limit	1.041

Individual Value Chart	
$\overline{X}$	3.808
E_2 factor	2.659
Lower Control Limit	2.961
Center Line	3.808
Upper Control Limit	4.656

(b) There are points outside of the control limits on the *MR* chart, hence the process is not stable.

(c) Based on the *MR* chart, the process is not stable, hence the calculation of the capability index is not correct.

There are points outside of control limits, hence the process is not stable. The process is in a state of statistical control.

(d) Thickness

Moving Range Chart	
$\overline{MR}$	0.001
D_3 factor	0.000
D_4 factor	3.267
Lower Control Limit	0.000
Center Line	0.001
Upper Control Limit	0.004

Individual Value Chart	
$\overline{X}$	0.112
E_2 factor	2.659
Lower Control Limit	0.109
Center Line	0.112
Upper Control Limit	0.115

There are points outside of the control limits, hence the process is not stable.

There are points outside of the control limits, hence this process is out of statistical control.

$\overline{X}$ Chart (Standard Deviation Method)

There are points outside of the control limits, hence this process is out of statistical control.

(e) There are points outside of the control limits on the *MR* chart, hence the process is not stable.

(f) Based on the *MR* chart, the process is not stable, hence the calculation of the capability index is not correct.

51. Answers will vary.

53. Answers will vary.

chapter 8

Estimation Procedures

1. $\bar{X} \pm Z \dfrac{\sigma}{\sqrt{n}} = 85 \pm 1.96 \dfrac{8}{\sqrt{64}} = 85 \pm 1.96;\ 83.04 < \mu < 86.96$

3. $\bar{X} \pm t_{n-1} \dfrac{S}{\sqrt{n}} = 75 \pm 2.03 \dfrac{24}{\sqrt{36}} = 75 \pm 8.12;\ 66.88 < \mu < 83.12$

5. (a) $\bar{X} \pm Z \dfrac{\sigma}{\sqrt{n}} = 1.99 \pm 1.96 \dfrac{0.05}{\sqrt{100}} = 1.99 \pm 0.0098;\ 1.9802 < \mu < 1.9998$

 (b) No. As σ is known and $n = 100$, based on the central limit theorem, we may assume that the sampling distribution of $\bar{X}$ is approximately normal.

 (c) An individual value of 2.02 is 0.60 of the standard deviation above the sample mean of 1.99. The confidence interval represents bounds on the estimate of a sample of 100, not an individual value.

 (d) $\bar{X} \pm Z \dfrac{\sigma}{\sqrt{n}} = 1.97 \pm 1.96 \dfrac{0.05}{\sqrt{100}} = 1.97 \pm 0.0098;\ 1.9602 < \mu < 1.9798$

 A shift of 0.02 units in the sample average shifts the confidence interval by the same distance without affecting the width of the resulting interval.

7. $\bar{X} - 1069.563;\ S = 227.4276;\ n = 35$

 (a) $\bar{X} \pm t_{n-1} \dfrac{S}{\sqrt{n}} = 1069.563 \pm 2.03 \dfrac{227.4276}{\sqrt{35}} = 1069.563 \pm 78.124;\ 991.439 < \mu < 1147.687$

 (b) All individual observations must be represented by independent, identically distributed normal random values, i.e., they must be a random Gaussian sample. The assumption is probably correct, because the sample kurtosis and sample skewness are equal to 0.72283 and 0.29377, respectively, for sample size of 35. The same conclusion may be derived from a normal probability plot.

9. $\bar{X} = 64.484;\ S = 2.41106;\ n = 50$

 (a) $\bar{X} \pm t_{n-1} \dfrac{S}{\sqrt{n}} = 64.484 \pm 2.0096 \dfrac{2.41106}{\sqrt{50}} = 64.484 \pm 0.685;\ 63.80 < \mu < 65.17$

 (b) All individual observations must be represented by independent, identically distributed normal random values, i.e., they must be a random Gaussian sample. The assumption is probably correct, because the sample kurtosis and sample skewness are equal to –0.8846 and 0.180138, respectively, for a sample size of 50. The same conclusion may be derived from a normal probability plot.

11. $\bar{X} = 9.08;\ S = 0.81584;\ n = 36$

 (a) $\bar{X} \pm t_{n-1} \dfrac{S}{\sqrt{n}} = 9.08 \pm 2.03 \dfrac{0.81584}{\sqrt{36}} = 9.08 \pm 0.276;\ 8.80 < \mu < 9.36$

 (b) All individual observations must be represented by independent, identically distributed random values, i.e., they must be a random Gaussian sample. A closer approximation would be obtained if this were a sample from a normal distribution. The assumption is probably correct, because the sample kurtosis and sample skewness are equal to 0.571098 and –0.57151, respectively, for a sample size of 36. The same conclusion may be derived from a normal probability plot.

13. (a) **Confidence Interval for Variance**

Sample Standard Deviation	2.1
Sample Size	30
Confidence Level	95%
df	29
Sum of Squares	127.89
Lower Chi-Square Value	16.04705
Upper Chi-Square Value	45.72228
Interval Lower Limit for Variance	2.797105
Interval Upper Limit for Variance	7.969689
Interval Lower Limit for Standard Deviation	1.672455
Interval Upper Limit for Standard Deviation	2.823064

$2.797 < \sigma^2 < 7.97$; $1.672 < \sigma < 2.823$

(b) All individual observations must be independent, identically distributed random values, i.e., they must be a random Gaussian sample.

15. **Confidence Interval for Variance**

Sample Standard Deviation	21.4
Sample Size	18
Confidence Level	95%
df	17
Sum of Squares	7785.32
Lower Chi-Square Value	7.564179
Upper Chi-Square Value	30.19098
Interval Lower Limit for Variance	257.8691
Interval Upper Limit for Variance	1029.235
Interval Lower Limit for Standard Deviation	16.0583
Interval Upper Limit for Standard Deviation	32.0817

$257.879 < \sigma^2 < 1029.235$; $16.058 < \sigma < 32.082$

17. (a) **Confidence Interval for Variance**

Sample Standard Deviation	0.405763
Sample Size	30
Confidence Level	95%
df	29
Sum of Squares	4.774667
Lower Chi-Square Value	16.04705
Upper Chi-Square Value	45.72228
Interval Lower Limit for Variance	0.104428
Interval Upper Limit for Variance	0.297542
Interval Lower Limit for Standard Deviation	0.323153
Interval Upper Limit for Standard Deviation	0.545474

$0.1044 < \sigma^2 < 0.2975$; $0.323 < \sigma < 0.545$

(b) All individual observations must be represented by independent identically distributed normal random values, i.e., they must be a random Gaussian sample. There are some doubts about the validity of this assumption because both sample kurtosis and sample skewness are not close to zero (they are equal to –0.44915 and –0.62772, respectively, for a sample size of 30). From the normal probability plot, we conclude that the initial sample can be normal as well. A more precise answer to this question can be provided by testing the corresponding hypothesis (see chapter 9).

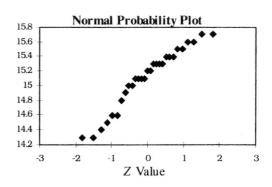

(c) No. The standard deviation is greater than 0.323 with a probability greater than 0.95.

19. (a) $\overline{X} \pm t_{n-1} S \sqrt{1 + \dfrac{1}{n}} = 195.3 \pm 2.11 \cdot 21.4 \sqrt{1 + \dfrac{1}{18}} = 195.3 \pm 46.39$; $148.81 < X_f < 241.69$

(b) Part (a) is an interval estimation for an individual value rather than for a mean, therefore, it is wider than the confidential interval in 8.6 (a). Both of the intervals are centered at 195.3.

21. (a) $\overline{X} \pm t_{n-1} S \sqrt{1 + \dfrac{1}{n}} = 6.7328 \pm 2.06 \cdot 0.0658 \sqrt{1 + \dfrac{1}{25}} = 6.7328 \pm 0.4518$; $6.281 < X_f < 7.185$

(b) This is an interval estimation for an individual value rather than for a mean, therefore, it is wider than the confidential interval in 8.8 (a). Both of the intervals are centered at 6.7328.

23. (a) $\overline{X} \pm t_{n-1} S \sqrt{1 + \dfrac{1}{n}} = 273.085 \pm 2.023 \cdot 25.21135 \sqrt{1 + \dfrac{1}{40}} = 273.085 \pm 51.636$; $221.449 < X_f < 324.721$

(b) This is an interval estimation for an individual value, not for a mean, therefore, it is wider than the confidential interval in 8.8 (a). Both of the intervals are centered at 273.085.

25. $\overline{X} = 195.3$; $S = 21.4$; $n = 18$

(a) $p = 0.90$, $n = 18$, $K_2 = 2.376$

$\overline{X} \pm K_2 = 195.3 \pm 2.376 \times 21.4 = 195.3 \pm 50.846$

Tolerance estimate is $(144.454;\ 246.146)$.

(b) $p = 0.1$, $n = 18$, $K_1 = 1.974$

$\overline{X} - K_1 S = 195.3 - 1.974 \times 21.4 = 195.3 - 42.24$

$= 153.06$

(c) The result of 8.6 (a) provides an interval estimate for a mean, the result of 8.19 (a) gives the prediction interval for the single future observation (it is, therefore, wider than the former), whereas this result gives an interval estimate for a given portion (90%) of the observations; therefore, it is the largest.

27. $\overline{X} = 6.7328$; $S = 0.0658$; $n = 25$

(a) $p = 0.95$, $K_2 = 2.984$

$\overline{X} \pm K_2 S = 6.7328 \pm 2.984 \times 0.0658 = 6.7328 \pm 0.1963$

Tolerance estimate is $(6.5365;\ 6.9291)$

(b) It is not correct to compare this tolerance interval with the previous two because they have different confidence levels.

29. $\overline{X} = 273.085$; $S = 25.21135$; $n = 40$

(a) $p = 0.9$, $K_2 = 2.253$

$\overline{X} \pm K_2 S = 273.085 \pm 2.253 \times 25.21 = 273.085 \pm 56.344$

Tolerance estimate is $(216.741;\ 329.429)$.

(b) $p = 0.05$, $K_1 = 2.125$

   $\overline{X} + K_1 S = 273.085 + 2.125 \times 25.21 = 273.085 + 53.571 = 326.656$

(c) It is not correct to compare this tolerance interval with the previous two because they have different confidence levels.

31.

Confidence Interval Estimate for the Mean	
Sample Size	63
Number of Successes	40
Confidence Level	95%
Sample Proportion	0.634920635
Z Value	−1.95996108
Standard Error of the Proportion	0.060657302
Interval Half Width	0.118885951
Interval Lower Limit	0.516034684
Interval Upper Limit	0.753806586

$0.516 < \pi < 0.754$

33.

Confidence Interval Estimate for the Mean	
Sample Size	1126
Number of Successes	114
Confidence Level	99%
Sample Proportion	0.101243339
Z Value	−2.57583451
Standard Error of the Proportion	0.008989491
Interval Half Width	0.023155441
Interval Lower Limit	0.078087898
Interval Upper Limit	0.12439878

$0.078 < \pi < 0.124$

35. (a)

Confidence Interval Estimate for the Mean	
Sample Size	1425
Number of Successes	722
Confidence Level	95%
Sample Proportion	0.506666667
Z Value	−1.95996108
Standard Error of the Proportion	0.013244146
Interval Half Width	0.025958011
Interval Lower Limit	0.480708656
Interval Upper Limit	0.532624678

(b)

Confidence Interval Estimate for the Mean	
Sample Size	1425
Number of Successes	115
Confidence Level	90%
Sample Proportion	0.080701754
Z Value	−1.644853
Standard Error of the Proportion	0.007215431
Interval Half Width	0.011868323
Interval Lower Limit	0.068833431
Interval Upper Limit	0.092570078

(c)

Confidence Interval Estimate for the Mean	
Sample Size	1425
Number of Successes	588
Confidence Level	99%
Sample Proportion	0.412631579
Z Value	−2.57583451
Standard Error of the Proportion	0.013041547
Interval Half Width	0.033592866
Interval Lower Limit	0.379038713
Interval Upper Limit	0.446224445

37. The t distribution is used in the interval estimate procedure when information about the variance is not available.

39. The estimated objects are different, so the estimators are different as well. Both of the point estimates are the same (sample average), but the interval for the mean estimate is narrower.

41. It depends on the problem context and the type pf results derived. If we are interested in lower or upper values, we need to construct one-sided tolerance and confidence intervals. For a model without any preference for the positive or negative differences of the observed values and their mean, it is appropriate to construct two-sided confidence and tolerance intervals.

43.

Mean	438.3333
Standard Deviation	261.5013
Sample Variance	68382.91
Kurtosis	5.753448
Skewness	2.060448
Count	36
Confidence Level(95.0%)	88.47941

(a)

Confidence Interval Estimate for the Mean	
Sample Standard Deviation	261.5013
Sample Mean	438.3333
Sample Size	36
Confidence Level	95%
Standard Error of the Mean	43.58355
Degrees of Freedom	35
t Value	2.030110409
Interval Half Width	88.4794185
Interval Lower Limit	349.85
Interval Upper Limit	526.81

(b)

Confidence Interval For Variance	
Sample Standard Deviation	261.5013
Sample Size	36
Confidence Level	95%
df	35
Sum of Squares	2393403
Lower Chi-Square Value	20.56938
Upper Chi-Square Value	53.20331
Interval Lower Limit for Variance	44985.97
Interval Upper Limit for Variance	116357.5
Interval Lower Limit for Standard Deviation	212.099
Interval Upper Limit for Standard Deviation	341.1122

(c) All individual observations must be represented by independent, identically distributed normal random values, i.e., they must be a random Gaussian sample. The assumption is probably correct, because the sample kurtosis is equal to 5.753448 for a sample size of 36. The same conclusion may be derived from a normal probability plot.

Normal Probability Plot

(d) $\overline{X} \pm t_{n-1} S \sqrt{1 + \dfrac{1}{n}} = 438.333 \pm 2.03 \times 261.5 \sqrt{1 + \dfrac{1}{36}} = 438.333 \pm 538.17,\ (0;\ 976.5)$

(e) $\overline{X} \pm K_2 S = 438.333 \pm 3.276 \times 261.5 = 438.333 \pm 856.674,\ K_2 = 3.276,\ (0;\ 1295.007)$

(f) The result of part (a) provides an interval estimate for a mean, the result of part (d) gives the prediction interval for the single future observation whereas the result of part (e) gives an interval estimate for a certain portion (99%) of the observations.

45. Height

Mean	157.0833
Standard Deviation	46.3199
Sample Variance	2145.533
Kurtosis	−0.91332
Skewness	−0.27951
Count	21
Confidence Level (95.0%)	21.08456

(a)

Confidence Interval Estimate for the Mean	
Sample Standard Deviation	46.3199
Sample Mean	157.0833
Sample Size	21
Confidence Level	95%
Standard Error of the Mean	10.10783085
Degrees of Freedom	20
t Value	2.085962478
Interval Half Width	21.0845559
Interval Lower Limit	136.00
Interval Upper Limit	178.17

(b)

Confidence Interval For Variance	
Sample Standard Deviation	46.3199
Sample Size	21
Confidence Level	95%
df	20
Sum of Squares	42910.66
Lower Chi-Square Value	9.590772
Upper Chi-Square Value	34.16958
Interval Lower Limit for Variance	1255.815
Interval Upper Limit for Variance	4474.161
Interval Lower Limit for Standard Deviation	35.43748
Interval Upper Limit for Standard Deviation	66.88917

(c) All individual observations must be independent, identically distributed normal random values, i.e., they must represent a random Gaussian sample. The same conclusion may be derived from a normal probability plot.

Normal Probability Plot

(d) $\overline{X} \pm t_{n-1}S\sqrt{1+\dfrac{1}{n}} = 157.08 \pm 2.086 \times 46.32\sqrt{1+\dfrac{1}{21}} = 157.08 \pm 98.898,\ (58.182;\ 255.978)$

(e) $\overline{X} \pm K_2 S = 157.08 \pm 3.621 \times 46.32 = 157.08 \pm 167.72,\ (0;\ 324.8)$

(f) The result of part (a) provides an interval estimate for a mean, the result of part (d) gives the prediction interval for the single future observation, whereas the result of part (e) gives an interval estimate for a certain portion (99%) of the observations.

dbh

Mean	29.28571
Standard Deviation	14.79237
Sample Variance	218.8143
Kurtosis	−1.22175
Skewness	0.172381
Count	21
Confidence Level (95.0%)	6.733404

(a)

Confidence Interval Estimate for the Mean	
Sample Standard Deviation	14.79237
Sample Mean	29.28577
Sample Size	21
Confidence Level	95%
Standard Error of the Mean	3.227959773
Degrees of Freedom	20
t Value	2.085962478
Interval Half Width	6.733402968
Interval Lower Limit	22.55
Interval Upper Limit	36.02

(b)

Confidence Interval For Variance	
Sample Standard Deviation	14.79273
Sample Size	21
Confidence Level	95%
df	20
Sum of Squares	4376.497
Lower Chi-Square Value	9.590772
Upper Chi-Square Value	34.16958
Interval Lower Limit for Variance	128.0817
Interval Upper Limit for Variance	456.3237
Interval Lower Limit for Standard Deviation	11.31732
Interval Upper Limit for Standard Deviation	21.36174

(c) All individual observations must be independent, identically distributed normal random values, i.e., they must represent a random Gaussian sample. The same conclusion may be derived from a normal probability plot.

Normal Probability Plot

(d) $\overline{X} \pm t_{n-1}S\sqrt{1+\dfrac{1}{n}} = 29.286 \pm 2.086 \times 14.79\sqrt{1+\dfrac{1}{21}} = 29.286 \pm 31.578, (0; 60.864)$

(e) $\overline{X} \pm K_2 S = 29.286 \pm 3.621 \times 14.79 = 29.286 \pm 53.554, (0; 82.84)$

(f) The result of part (a) provides an interval estimate for a mean, the result of part (d) gives the prediction interval for the single future observation, whereas the result of part (e) gives an interval estimate for a certain portion (99%) of the observations.

Bark

Mean	2.219048
Standard Deviation	0.916307
Sample Variance	0.839619
Kurtosis	0.121937
Skewness	0.829526
Count	21
Confidence Level (95.0%)	0.417098

(a) **Confidence Interval Estimate for the Mean**

Sample Standard Deviation	0.916307
Sample Mean	2.219048
Sample Size	21
Confidence Level	95%
Standard Error of the Mean	0.19995458
Degrees of Freedom	20
t Value	2.085962478
Interval Half Width	0.417097752
Interval Lower Limit	1.80
Interval Upper Limit	2.64

(b) **Confidence Interval For Variance**

Sample Standard Deviation	0.9163
Sample Size	21
Confidence Level	95%
df	20
Sum of Squares	16.79211
Lower Chi-Square Value	9.590772
Upper Chi-Square Value	34.16958
Interval Lower Limit for Variance	0.491435
Interval Upper Limit for Variance	1.750861
Interval Lower Limit for Standard Deviation	0.701024
Interval Upper Limit for Standard Deviation	1.323201

(c) All individual observations must be independent, identically distributed normal random values, i.e., they must represent a random Gaussian sample. The same conclusion may be derived from a normal probability plot.

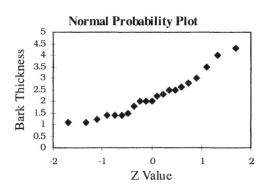

Normal Probability Plot

(d) $\overline{X} \pm t_{n-1} S \sqrt{1 + \dfrac{1}{n}} = 2.22 \pm 2.086 \times 0.92 \sqrt{1 + \dfrac{1}{21}} = 2.22 \pm 1.96$, (0.26; 4.18)

(e) $\overline{X} \pm K_2 S = 2.22 \pm 3.621 \times 0.92 = 2.22 \pm 3.33$, (0; 5.55)

(f) The result of part (a) provides an interval estimate for a mean, the result of part (d) gives the prediction interval for the single future observation, whereas the result of part (e) gives an interval estimate for a certain portion (99%) of the observations.

chapter 9

Introduction to Hypothesis Testing

1. (a) $H_0: \mu = 70$ pounds; the cloth has an average breaking strength of 70 pounds.

$H_1: \mu \ne 70$ pounds; the cloth has an average breaking strength that differs from 70 pounds.

(b)

Z Test of Hypothesis for the Mean	
Null Hypothesis	$\mu = 70$
Level of Significance	0.05
Population Standard Deviation	3.5
Sample Size	49
Sample Mean	69.1
Standard Error of the Mean	0.5
Z Test Statistic	−1.8

Two-Tail Test	
Lower Critical Value	−1.95996108
Upper Critical Value	1.959961082
p-value	0.071860531
Do not reject the null hypothesis	

Decision rule: Reject H_0 if $Z < -1.96$ or $Z > 1.96$. Test statistic: $Z = \dfrac{\bar{X} - \mu}{\sigma/\sqrt{n}} = \dfrac{69.1 - 70}{3.5/\sqrt{49}} = -1.8$. Decision: Because $-1.96 < Z < 1.96$, do not reject H_0. There is insufficient evidence to conclude that the cloth has an average breaking strength that differs from 70 pounds for the 0.05 significance level.

(c) p-value = 0.072. This is the probability of obtaining a test statistic $|Z|$ equal to or greater than the result obtained from the sample data given that the null hypothesis is true.

(d)

Z Test of Hypothesis for the Mean	
Null Hypothesis	$\mu = 70$
Level of Significance	0.05
Population Standard Deviation	1.75
Sample Size	49
Sample Mean	69.1
Standard Error of the Mean	0.25
Z Test Statistic	−3.6

Two-Tail Test	
Lower Critical Value	−1.95996108
Upper Critical Value	1.959961082
p-value	0.000318291
Reject the null hypothesis	

Decision rule: Reject H_0 if $Z < -1.96$ or $Z > 1.96$. Test statistic: $Z = \dfrac{\bar{X} - \mu}{\sigma/\sqrt{n}} = \dfrac{69.1 - 70}{1.75/\sqrt{49}} = -3.6$. Decision: Because $Z < -1.96$, reject H_0. There is sufficient evidence to conclude that the cloth has an average breaking strength that differs from 70 pounds for the 0.05 significance level.

(e)

Z Test of Hypothesis for the Mean	
Null Hypothesis	$\mu = 70$
Level of Significance	0.05
Population Standard Deviation	3.5
Sample Size	49
Sample Mean	69
Standard Error of the Mean	0.5
Z Test Statistic	−2

Two-Tail Test	
Lower Critical Value	−1.95996108
Upper Critical Value	1.959961082
p-value	0.045500124
Reject the null hypothesis	

Decision rule: Reject H_0 if $Z < -1.96$ or $Z > 1.96$. Test statistic: $Z = \dfrac{\overline{X} - \mu}{\sigma/\sqrt{n}} = \dfrac{69 - 70}{3.5/\sqrt{49}} = -2$. Decision: Because $Z < -1.96$, reject H_0. There is sufficient evidence to conclude that the cloth has an average breaking strength that is different from the 70 pound breaking strength.

3. (a) $H_0: \mu = 375$ hours; the light bulbs in a large shipment have an average life of 375 hours.

   $H_1: \mu \neq 375$ hours; the light bulbs in a large shipment have an average life that differs from 375 hours.

(b)

Z Test of Hypothesis for the Mean	
Null Hypothesis	$\mu = 375$
Level of Significance	0.05
Population Standard Deviation	100
Sample Size	50
Sample Mean	350
Standard Error of the Mean	14.14213562
Z Test Statistic	-1.76776695

Two-Tail Test	
Lower Critical Value	-1.95996108
Upper Critical Value	1.959961082
p-value	0.077099777
Do not reject the null hypothesis	

Decision rule: Reject H_0 if $Z < -1.96$ or $Z > 1.96$. Test statistic: $Z = \dfrac{\overline{X} - \mu}{\sigma/\sqrt{n}} = \dfrac{350 - 375}{100/\sqrt{50}} = -1.77$. Decision: Because $-1.96 < Z < 1.96$, do not reject H_0. There is insufficient evidence that the average light bulb life is different from 375 hours for the 0.05 significance level.

(c) Based on the result of Chapter 8, problem 4, the null hypothesis is rejected, because 375 hours does not belong to the central confidence interval. The conclusions for each problem will be different due to the different sample sizes.

5. (a) $H_0: \mu = 9.0$; the average energy efficiency rating of window-mounted large-capacity air-conditioning units is 9.0.

   $H_1: \mu \neq 9.0$; the average energy efficiency rating of window-mounted large-capacity air-conditioning units differs from 9.0.

   Decision rule: Reject H_0 if $|t| > 2.03$.

   Test statistic: $t = \dfrac{\overline{X} - \mu}{S/\sqrt{n}} = \dfrac{9.211 - 9}{0.3838/\sqrt{36}} = 3.30$

   Decision: Because $|t| > 2.03$, reject H_0.

   There is sufficient evidence to conclude that the average energy rating of window-mounted large-capacity air-conditioning units is not equal to 9.0 for the 0.05 significance level.

(b) The following assumptions are made: (1) The computed numerical data are independently drawn and represent a random sample from a population that is normally distributed. (2) The sample population is not very small or very skewed. Note that the t test is robust, so if the sample size is large and the central limit theorem applies, the t test does not loose much power even if the distribution departs from normal.

(c) p-value = 0.002. This is the probability of obtaining a test statistic $|t|$ equal to or greater than the result obtained from the sample data given that the null hypothesis is true.

(d)

t Test of Hypothesis for the Mean	
Null Hypothesis	$\mu = 9$
Level of Significance	0.05
Sample Size	36
Sample Mean	9.155555556
Sample Standard Deviation	0.410187723
Standard Error of the Mean	0.068364621
Degrees of Freedom	35
t Test Statistic	2.275380955

Two-Tail Test	
Lower Critical Value	-2.03011041
Upper Critical Value	2.030110409
p-value	0.029115712
Reject the null hypothesis	

Decision rule: Reject H_0 if $|t| > 2.03$. Test statistic: $t = \dfrac{\overline{X} - \mu}{S/\sqrt{n}} = \dfrac{9.155 - 9}{0.41/\sqrt{36}} = 2.275$. Decision: Because $|t| > 2.03$,

reject H_0. There is sufficient evidence to conclude that the average energy rating of window-mounted large-capacity air-conditioning units is not equal to 9.0 and EER for the 0.05 significance level.

7. (a) $H_0: \mu = 15$ ounces; the average weight of the raisin boxes is 15 ounces.

$H_1: \mu \neq 15$ ounces; the average weight of the raisin boxes differs from 15 ounces.

t Test of Hypothesis for the Mean	
Null Hypothesis	$\mu = 15$
Level of Significance	0.05
Sample Size	30
Sample Mean	15.11333333
Sample Standard Deviation	0.405763081
Standard Error of the Mean	0.074081864
Degrees of Freedom	29
t Test Statistic	1.529839112

Two-Tail Test	
Lower Critical Value	−2.04523076
Upper Critical Value	2.045230758
p-value	0.136892688
Do not reject the null hypothesis	

Decision rule: Reject H_0 if $|t| > 2.05$.

Test statistic: $t = \dfrac{\overline{X} - \mu}{S/\sqrt{n}} = \dfrac{15.1133 - 15}{0.4058/\sqrt{30}} = 1.53$.

Decision: Because $|t| < 2.05$, do not reject H_0.

There is insufficient evidence to conclude that the average weight of the raisin boxes is different from 15 ounces for the 0.05 significance level.

(b) The following assumptions are made: (1) The computed numerical data must be independently drawn and represent a random sample from a population that is normally distributed. (2) The sample population is not very small or very skewed. Note that the *t* test is robust, so if the sample size is large and the central limit theorem applies, the *t* test does not loose much power even if the distribution departs from normal.

(c)

t Test of Hypothesis for the Mean	
Null Hypothesis	$\mu = 15$
Level of Significance	0.05
Sample Size	30
Sample Mean	15.18
Sample Standard Deviation	0.490882386
Standard Error of the Mean	0.089622452
Degrees of Freedom	29
t Test Statistic	2.008425299

Two-Tail Test	
Lower Critical Value	−2.04523076
Upper Critical Value	2.045230758
p-value	0.05399146
Do not reject the null hypothesis	

Decision rule: Reject H_0 if $|t| > 2.045$. Test statistic: $t = \dfrac{\overline{X} - \mu}{S/\sqrt{n}} = \dfrac{15.18 - 15}{0.4909/\sqrt{30}} = 2.008$. Decision: Because

$|t| < 2.045$, do not reject H_0. There is insufficient evidence to conclude that the mean weight per box is different from 15 ounces for the 0.05 significance level.

9.   (a) $H_0: \mu = 350$ psi; the mean bursting pressure of the PVC irrigation pipe is 350 psi.

   $H_1: \mu < 350$ psi; the mean bursting pressure of the PVC irrigation pipe is less than 350 psi.

t Test of Hypothesis for the Mean	
Null Hypothesis	$\mu = 350$
Level of Significance	0.05
Sample Size	10
Sample Mean	407.3
Sample Standard Deviation	28.86385668
Standard Error of the Mean	9.127552915
Degrees of Freedom	9
t Test Statistic	6.277695734

Lower-Tail Test	
Lower Critical Value	–1.83311386
p-value	0.999927613
Do not reject the null hypothesis	

Decision rule: Reject H_0 if $t < -1.83$.

Test statistic: $t = \dfrac{\overline{X} - \mu}{S/\sqrt{n}} = \dfrac{407.3 - 350}{28.864/\sqrt{10}} = 6.28$.

Decision: Because $t > -1.83$, do not reject H_0.

There is insufficient evidence to conclude that the average bursting pressure is less than 350 psi for the 0.05 significance level.

   (b)   The following assumptions are made: (1) The numerical data must be independently drawn and represent a random sample from a population that is normally distributed. (2) The sample population is not very small or very skewed. Note that the *t* test is robust, so if the sample size is large and the central limit theorem applies, the *t* test does not loose much power even if the distribution departs from normal.

11.   (a) $H_0: \mu_1 = \mu_2$; the mean talking time of the nickel-cadmium batteries is the same as the mean talking time of the nickel-metal hydride batteries.

   $H_1: \mu_1 \neq \mu_2$; the mean talking time of the nickel-cadmium batteries is different than the mean talking time of the nickel-metal hydride batteries.

t-Test: Two-Sample Assuming Equal Variances	Cadmium	Metal Hydride
Mean	70.748	79.728
Variance	195.7884	226.0296
Observations	25	25
Pooled Variance	210.909	
Hypothesized Mean Difference	0	
df	48	
t Stat	–2.18617	
$p(T \leq t)$ one-tail	0.016856	
t Critical one-tail	1.677224	
$p(T \leq t)$ two-tail	0.033712	
t Critical two-tail	2.010634	

Decision rule: Reject H_0 if $|t| > 2.01$.

Test statistic: $t = \dfrac{(\overline{X}_1 - \overline{X}_2) - (\mu_1 - \mu_2)}{\sqrt{S_p^2(1/n_1 + 1/n_2)}} = \dfrac{70.748 - 79.728}{\sqrt{210.909(1/25 + 1/25)}} = -2.18$.

Decision: Because $t < -2.01$, reject H_0.

There is a significant difference between the two means because the two-tail *p*-value is less than 0.05.

   (b)   In part (a) it is assumed that numerical data are sampled from normally distributed populations having equal variances. The pooled *t* test is not sensitive to moderate departures from normality if the sample size is large.

(c) $p(T \le t) = 0.034$. This is the probability of obtaining a test statistic $|t|$ equal to or greater than the result obtained from the sample data given that the null hypothesis is true.

(d) $H_0: \mu_1 = \mu_2$, $H_1: \mu_1 \ne \mu_2$

t-Test: Two-Sample Assuming Unequal Variances

	Cadmium	Metal Hydride
Mean	70.748	79.728
Variance	195.7884	226.0296
Observations	25	25
Hypothesized Mean Difference	0	
df	48	
t Stat	−2.18617	
$p(T \le t)$ one-tail	0.016856	
t Critical one-tail	1.677224	
$p(T \le t)$ two-tail	0.033712	
t Critical two-tail	2.010634	

Decision rule: Reject H_0 if $|t| > 2.010634$. Test statistic: $t = \dfrac{(\overline{X}_1 - \overline{X}_2) - (\mu_1 - \mu_2)}{\sqrt{S_p^2(1/n_1 + 1/n_2)}} = -2.18617$. Decision: Because

$|t| < -2.010634$, reject H_0. There is a significant difference between the two means because the two-tail p-value is less than 0.05.

(e) In the separate variance t test, it is assumed that the data are sampled from two normally distributed populations.

(f) $p(T \le t)$ two-tail $= 0.034$. This is the probability of obtaining a test statistic $|t|$ equal to or greater than the result obtained from the sample data, given that the null hypothesis is true.

(g) We must reject the null hypothesis and conclude that the population means are unequal. This is true whether we assume that the populations have equal variances.

13. (a) $H_0: \mu_1 = \mu_2$; the mean airflow value observed for Carnes 3-Way diffusers is the same as the mean airflow value observed for Krueger 4-Way diffusers.

$H_1: \mu_1 \ne \mu_2$; the mean airflow value observed for Carnes 3-Way diffusers is different than the mean airflow value observed for Krueger 4-Way diffusers.

t-Test: Two-Sample Assuming Equal Variances

	Carnes	Kruger
Mean	247.5	244.3
Variance	1557.398	732.6633
Observations	50	50
Pooled Variance	1145.031	
Hypothesized Mean Difference	0	
df	98	
t Stat	0.472837	
$p(T \le t)$ one-tail	0.31869	
t Critical one-tail	1.660551	
$p(T \le t)$ two-tail	0.637381	
t Critical two-tail	1.984467	

Decision rule: Reject H_0 if $|t| > 1.98$.

Test statistic: $t = \dfrac{(\overline{X}_1 - \overline{X}_2) - (\mu_1 - \mu_2)}{\sqrt{S_p^2(1/n_1 + 1/n_2)}} = \dfrac{247.5 - 244.3}{\sqrt{1145.031(1/50 + 1/50)}} = 0.473$.

Decision: Because $|t| < 1.98$, do not reject H_0.

There is no significant difference between the two means because the two-tail p-value is greater than 0.05.

(b) It is assumed that the data are sampled from normally distributed populations having equal variances.

(c) $p(T \leq t)$ two-tail = 0.637. This is the probability of obtaining a test statistic $|t|$ equal to or greater than the result obtained from the sample data given that the null hypothesis is true.

15. (a) $H_0 : \mu_1 = \mu_2$; the average processing time in Plant A is the same as the average processing time in Plant B.

$H_1 : \mu_1 \neq \mu_2$; the average processing time in Plant A is different than the average processing time in Plant B.

t-Test: Two-Sample Assuming Equal Variances		
	Plant A	**Plant B**
Mean	9.382	11.3535
Variance	15.98123	26.27748
Observations	20	20
Pooled Variance	21.12935	
Hypothesized Mean Difference	0	
df	38	
t Stat	−1.35629	
$p(T \leq t)$ one-tail	0.091505	
t Critical one-tail	1.685953	
$p(T \leq t)$ two-tail	0.18301	
t Critical two-tail	2.024394	

Decision rule: Reject H_0 if $|t| > 2.02$.

Test statistic: $t = \dfrac{(\overline{X}_1 - \overline{X}_2) - (\mu_1 - \mu_2)}{\sqrt{S_p^2(1/n_1 + 1/n_2)}} = \dfrac{9.382 - 11.3535}{\sqrt{21.2935(1/20 + 1/20)}} = -1.36$.

Decision: Since $|t| < 2.02$, do not reject H_0.

There is no significant difference between the two means because the two-tail p-value is greater than 0.05.

(b) It is assumed that the processing time in each plant is normally distributed and that the variances in the two plants are equal.

(c) There are some doubts about the validity of the assumptions made in part (b) because the data from both plants are slightly skewed. This is shown below in the box-and-whisker plot. The skewness is probably not enough to seriously affect the results.

(c)

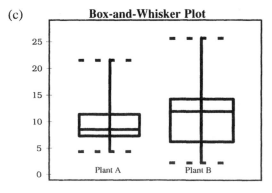

Box-and-Whisker Plot

(d) $p(T \leq t)$ two-tail = 0.183. This is the probability of obtaining a test statistic $|t|$ equal to or greater than the result obtained from the sample data, given that the null hypothesis is true.

17. (a) $f_l = 0.429$; $f_u = 2.20$.   (b) $f_l = 0.362$; $f_u = 2.57$.   (c) $f_l = 0.297$; $f_u = 3.09$.

(d) $f_l = 0.258$; $f_u = 3.50$.

19. $H_0: \sigma_1^2 = \sigma_2^2$; the two pumping plants have the same population variance.

$H_1: \sigma_1^2 \neq \sigma_2^2$; the two pumping plants have different population variances.

F-Test Two-Sample for Variances		
	Polonio Pass	**Devil's Den**
Mean	4076.5	4275.25
Variance	277676.6	334540.7
Observations	20	20
df	19	19
F	0.830023	
$P(F \leq f)$ one-tail	0.344415	
F Lower Critical one-tail	0.461201	

Decision rule: Reject H_0 if $F < 0.461$.

Test statistic: $F = \dfrac{s_1^2}{s_2^2} = \dfrac{277676.6}{334540.7} = 0.830$.

Decision: Since $F > 0.830$, reject H_0.

There is no significant difference between the two variances because the *p*-value is greater than 0.05.

21. (a) $H_0: \sigma_1^2 = \sigma_2^2$; the two battery types have the same population variance in talking time.

$H_1: \sigma_1^2 \neq \sigma_2^2$; the two battery types have different population variances in talking time.

F-Test Two-Sample for Variances		
	Cadmium	**Metal Hydride**
Mean	70.748	79.728
Variance	195.7884	226.0296
Observations	25	25
df	24	24
F	0.866207	
$P(F \leq f)$ one-tail	0.363909	
F Lower Critical one-tail	0.504093	

Decision rule: Reject H_0 if $F < 0.504$.

Test statistic: $F = \dfrac{s_1^2}{s_2^2} = \dfrac{195.7884}{226.0296} = 0.866$.

Decision: Since $F > 0.504$, do not reject H_0.

There is no significant difference between the two variances because the *p*-value is greater than 0.05.

(b) Do not reject the null hypothesis, $\sigma_1^2 = \sigma_2^2$; it is, therefore, necessary to use a pooled-variance *t* test to calculate the difference in the two means.

23. (a) $H_0: \sigma_1^2 = \sigma_2^2$; the two lines have the same population variance.

$H_1: \sigma_1^2 > \sigma_2^2$; the variance in line A is greater than the variance in line B.

F Test for Differences in Two Means	
Level of Significance	0.05

Population 1 Sample	
Sample Size	11
Sample Standard Deviation	0.012

Population 2 Sample	
Sample Size	16
Sample Standard Deviation	0.005
F-Test Statistic	5.76
Population 1 Sample Degrees of Freedom	10
Population 2 Sample Degrees of Freedom	15

Upper-Tail Test	
Upper Critical Value	2.543715
p-value	0.001333
Reject the null hypothesis	

Decision rule: Reject H_0 if $F > 2.54$.

Test statistic: $F = \dfrac{s_1^2}{s_2^2} = \dfrac{0.012^2}{0.005^2} = 5.76$.

Decision: Since $F > 2.54$, reject H_0.

The variance in Line A is greater than the variance in Line B because the *p*-value for the upper-tail test is less than 0.05.

25. (a) $H_0: \mu_1 = \mu_2$; the average thickness measurements obtained by the nondestructive and the destructive method are the same.

$H_1: \mu_1 \neq \mu_2$; the average thickness measurements obtained by the nondestructive and the destructive method are different.

t-Test: Paired Two Sample for Means		
	Nondestructive Method	Destructive Method
Mean	229.1818	249.3636
Variance	29277.16	38313.85
Observations	11	11
Pearson Correlation	0.991909	
Hypothesized Mean Difference	0	
df	10	
t Stat	−1.97488	
$p(T \leq t)$ one-tail	0.03826	
t Critical one-tail	1.812462	
$p(T \leq t)$ two-tail	0.076521	
t Critical two-tail	2.228139	

Decision rule: Reject H_0 if $|t| > 2.23$.

Test statistic: $t = \dfrac{\overline{D} - \mu_{\overline{D}}}{S_{\overline{D}}/\sqrt{n}} = \dfrac{-20.1818 - 0}{33.89242/\sqrt{11}} = -1.97$.

Decision: Because $|t| < 2.23$, do not reject H_0.

There is no significant difference in the average measurement of thickness between the two methods because the *p*-value is greater than 0.05.

(b) It is assumed that the thickness in each method is normally distributed and that the variances in the two methods are equal.

(c) $p(T \leq t)$ two-tail $= 0.077$. This is the probability of obtaining a test statistic $|t|$ equal to or greater than the result obtained from the sample data given that the null hypothesis is true.

(d) $H_0: \mu_1 = \mu_2$, $H_1: \mu_1 \neq \mu_2$

t-Test: Two-Sample Assuming Unequal Variances	Nondestructive Method	Destructive Method
Mean	229.1818	249.3636
Variance	29277.16	38313.85
Observations	11	11
Hypothesized Mean Difference	0	
df	20	
t Stat	−0.25746	
$p(T \leq t)$ one-tail	0.399727	
t Critical one-tail	1.724718	
$p(T \leq t)$ two-tail	0.799453	
t Critical two-tail	2.085962	

There is no significant difference in the average thickness between the two methods because the *p*-value is greater than 0.05.

(e) For the significance level 0.05 (a) and (d) provides the same results.

(f) It is most appropriate to use the paired test because the data is obtained from repeated measurements of the same sample.

27. (a) $H_0: \mu_1 = \mu_2$; the average time for the two sorting methods is the same.

$H_1: \mu_1 \neq \mu_2$; the average time for the two sorting methods is different.

t-Test: Paired Two Sample for Means	Insert Sort	Selection Sort
Mean	5.05525	8.89175
Variance	0.031359	0.068681
Observations	40	40
Pearson Correlation	0.243727	
Hypothesized Mean Difference	0	
df	39	
t Stat	−87.2055	
$p(T \leq t)$ one-tail	1.27×10^{-46}	
t Critical one-tail	1.684875	
$p(T \leq t)$ two-tail	2.55×10^{-46}	
t Critical two-tail	2.022689	

Decision rule: Reject H_0 if $|t| > 2.02$.

Test statistic: $t = \dfrac{\overline{D} - \mu_{\overline{D}}}{S_{\overline{D}}/\sqrt{n}} = \dfrac{-3.8365 - 0}{0.27824/\sqrt{40}} = -87.2055$.

Decision: Because $|t| > 2.02$, reject H_0.

There is significant difference between the 2 average times because of the very small *p*-value.

(b) Two series of observations are obtained from the same set of items or individuals. The sample of the pair wise differences between two observations drawn for the same items must be a set of independent, identically normal distributed random values.

(c) $p(T \leq t)$ two-tail $= 2.55 \times 10^{-46}$. This is the probability of obtaining a test statistic $|t|$ equal to or greater than the result obtained from the sample data given that the null hypothesis is true.

29. (a) $H_0: \mu_1 = \mu_2$; the average gasoline mileage is the same for regular and high-octane gas.

$H_1: \mu_1 \neq \mu_2$; the average gasoline mileage is different for regular and high-octane gas.

t-Test: Paired Two Sample for Means		
	Regular	**High-octane**
Mean	27	27.5
Variance	66.66667	82.05556
Observations	10	10
Pearson Correlation	0.925401	
Hypothesized Mean Difference	0	
df	9	
t Stat	−0.45964	
$p(T \leq t)$ one-tail	0.328338	
t Critical one-tail	1.833114	
$p(T \leq t)$ two-tail	0.656677	
t Critical two-tail	2.262159	

Decision rule: Reject H_0 if $|t| > 2.26$.

Test statistic: $t = \dfrac{\overline{D} - \mu_{\overline{D}}}{S_{\overline{D}}/\sqrt{n}} = \dfrac{0.5 - 0}{3.44/\sqrt{10}} = -0.460$.

Decision: Because $|t| < 2.26$, do not reject H_0.

There is not significant difference between two average gasoline mileage values because the *p*-value is greater than 0.05.

(b) It is assumed that the distribution of the difference in the average gas mileage between regular and high-octane gas is approximately normal.

(c) $p(T \leq t)$ two-tail = 0.657. This is the probability of obtaining a test statistic $|t|$ equal to or greater than the result obtained from the sample data given that the null hypothesis is true.

31. (a) $H_0: \pi_1 = \pi_2$; the proportions of smokers that develop osteoporosis and non-smokers that develop osteoporosis are equal.

$H_1: \pi_1 \neq \pi_2$; the proportions of smokers that develop osteoporosis and non-smokers that develop osteoporosis differ.

Observed Frequencies: Smoking			
Osteoporosis	**Yes**	**No**	**Total**
Yes	22	16	38
No	10	28	38
Total	32	44	76

Expected Frequencies:Smoking			
Osteoporosis	**Yes**	**No**	**Total**
Yes	16	22	38
No	16	22	38
Total	32	44	76

Level of Significance	**0.05**
Number of Rows	2
Number of Columns	2
Degrees of Freedom	1
Critical Value	3.84146
Chi-Square Test Statistic	7.7728
p-value	0.0053
Reject the null hypothesis	

Decision rule: Reject H_0 if $\chi^2 > 3.841$. Test statistic: $\chi^2 = 7.773$. Decision: Because $\chi^2 < 3.841$, reject H_0. There is a significant relationship between lifestyle and osteoporosis for the 0.05 significance level.

(b) p-value $= 0.005$. This is the probability of obtaining a test statistic chi-square equal to or greater than the result obtained from the sample data given that the null hypothesis is true.

33. (a) $H_0: \pi_1 = \pi_2 = \pi_3$; the proportions of each type of reference found are equal in both types of program.
H_1: At least one proportion differs.

Observed Frequencies: References				
Optimization	Register	Immediate	Indirect	Total
Yes	88	29	47	164
No	186	45	88	319
Total	274	74	135	483

Expected Frequencies: References				
Optimization	Register	Immediate	Indirect	Total
Yes	93.0352	25.12629	45.83851	164
No	180.9648	48.87371	89.16149	319
Total	274	74	135	483

Level of Significance	0.05
Number of Rows	2
Number of Columns	3
Degrees of Freedom	2
Critical Value	5.991476
Chi-Square Test Statistic	1.361408
p-value	0.50626
Do not reject the null hypothesis	

Decision rule: Reject H_0 if $\chi^2 > 5.991$. Test statistic: $\chi^2 = 1.361$. Decision: Because $\chi^2 < 5.991$, do not reject H_0. There is no relationship between the type of the program and the type of references for the 0.05 significance level.

(b) p-value $= 0.506$. This is the probability of obtaining a test statistic chi-square equal to or greater than the result obtained from the sample data given that the null hypothesis is true.

35. (a) $H_0: \pi_A = \pi_B = \pi_C = \pi_D$; the proportions of patients on each of the four drug regimens suffering severe adverse effects are all equal.
H_1: At least one proportion is different.

Observed Frequencies: Drug Regimen					
Result	A	B	C	D	Total
Severe	714	785	754	820	3073
Not Severe	9630	9543	9042	9557	37772
Total	10344	10328	9796	10377	40845

Expected Frequencies: Drug Regimen					
Result	A	B	C	D	Total
Severe	778.2375	777.0338	737.0084	780.7203	3073
Not Severe	9565.762	9550.966	9058.992	9596.28	37772
Total	10344	10328	9796	10377	40845

Level of Significance	0.05
Number of Rows	2
Number of Columns	4
Degrees of Freedom	3
Critical Value	7.814725
Chi-Square Test Statistic	8.382645
p-value	0.038731
Reject the null hypothesis	

Decision rule: Reject H_0 if $\chi^2 > 7.815$. Test statistic: $\chi^2 = 8.383$. Decision: Because $\chi^2 > 7.815$, reject H_0. There is a significant difference among the 4 drug regimens with respect to the proportion of patients suffering severe adverse effects for the 0.05 significance level.

(b) There are 64.2 fewer severe reactions observed than expected with drug regimen A. Other regimens were less effective at reducing observed severe reactions compared to expected values. From the p-values shown in the above table for $\alpha = 0.05$ it can be concluded that the A and B drug regimens are not statsitically different. However, because regimen B is more expensive, regimen A is preferred.

37. (a) $\chi_L^2 = 10.520$, $\chi_U^2 = 46.928$ (b) $\chi_L^2 = 6.908$, $\chi_U^2 = 28.845$ (c) $\chi_L^2 = 5.892$, $\chi_U^2 = 22.362$

39. (a) $H_0: \sigma = 0.035$ inches; the standard deviation is equal to 0.035 inches.

$H_0: \sigma < 0.035$ inches; the standard deviation is less than 0.035 inches.

Chi-Square Test of Hypothesis for the Variance	
Null Hypothesis	$\sigma^2 = 0.001225$
Level of Significance	0.05
Sample Size	25
Sample Standard Deviation	0.025
df	24
Chi-Square Test Statistic	12.2449

Upper-Tail Test	
Lower Critical Value	13.84842
p-value	0.022994
Reject the null hypothesis	

Decision rule: Reject H_0 if $\chi^2 < 13.848$. Test statistic: $\chi^2 = 12.245$. Decision: Because $\chi^2 < 13.848$, reject H_0. The standard deviation of the population is less than 0.035 inch for the 0.05 significant level.

(b) It is assumed that the observed numerical data are sampled from a normally distributed population.

(c) p-value = 0.022994.

This is the probability of obtaining a test statistic of magnitude lower than the result obtained from the sample data given that the null hypothesis is true.

41. $H_0: \sigma = 0.100$; the standard deviation is equal to 0.100.

$H_1: \sigma > 0.100$; the standard deviation is greater than 0.100.

Chi-Square Test of Hypothesis for the Variance	
Null Hypothesis	$\sigma^2 = 0.01$
Level of Significance	0.05
Sample Size	31
Sample Standard Deviation	0.068303
df	30
Chi-Square Test Statistic	13.99603

Upper-Tail Test	
Upper Critical Value	43.77295
p-value	0.994297
Do not reject the null hypothesis	

Decision rule: Reject H_0 if $\chi^2 > 43.773$. Test statistic: $\chi^2 = 13.996$. Decision: Because $\chi^2 < 43.773$, do not reject H_0. The sample standard deviation is not greater than 0.100 percent For 0.05 significance level.

43. $H_0: \sigma = 100$; the standard deviation is equal to 100.

$H_1: \sigma \neq 100$; the standard deviation is not equal to 100.

Chi-Square Test of Hypothesis for the Variance	
Null Hypothesis	$\sigma^2 = 10000$
Level of Significance	0.05
Sample Size	12
Sample Standard Deviation	235.8256
df	11
Chi-Square Test Statistic	61.17507

Two-Tail Test	
Lower Critical Value	3.815742
Upper Critical Value	21.92002
p-value	1
Do not reject the null hypothesis	

Decision rule: Reject H_0 if $\chi^2 < 3.816$ or $\chi^2 > 21.920$. Test statistic: $\chi^2 = 61.175$. Decision: Because $\chi^2 > 21.920$, reject H_0. Standard deviation is significantly different from 100 for the 0.05 significance level.

45. $H_0: M_1 = M_2$; the population medians are equal.

$H_1: M_1 \neq M_2$; the population medians are different.

Ballast Efficiency Factor

Wilcoxon Rank Sum Test	
Level of Significance	0.05

Population 1 Sample	
Sample Size	4
Sum of Ranks	10

Population 2 Sample	
Sample Size	6
Sum of Ranks	45
Warning: Large-scale approximation formula not designed for small sample sizes.	
Total Sample Size n	10
T_1 Test Statistic	10
T_1 Mean	22
Standard Error of T_1	4.690416
Z Test Statistic	−2.55841

Two-Tail Test	
Lower Critical Value	−1.95996
p-value	1.959961
Upper Critical Value	0.010515
Reject the null hypothesis	

Decision rule: Reject H_0 if $|Z| > 1.96$. Test statistic: $Z = -2.558$. Decision: Because $|Z| > 1.96$, reject H_0. These two methods have different population medians for 0.05 significance level.

Light Output

Wilcoxon Rank Sum Test	
Level of Significance	0.05

Population 1 Sample	
Sample Size	4
Sum of Ranks	34

Population 2 Sample	
Sample Size	6
Sum of Ranks	21
Warning: Large-scale approximation	
formula not designed for small sample sizes.	
Total Sample Size n	10
T_1 Test Statistic	34
T_1 Mean	22
Standard Error of T_1	4.690416
Z Test Statistic	2.558409

Two-Tail Test	
Lower Critical Value	−1.95996
Upper Critical Value	1.959961
p-value	0.010515
Reject the null hypothesis	

Decision rule: Reject H_0 if $|Z| > 1.96$. Test statistic: $Z = 2.558409$. Decision: Because $|Z| > 1.96$, reject H_0. These two methods have different population medians for 0.05 significance level.

Total Harmonic Distortion

Wilcoxon Rank Sum Test	
Level of Significance	0.05

Population 1 Sample	
Sample Size	4
Sum of Ranks	17

Population 2 Sample	
Sample Size	6
Sum of Ranks	38
Warning: Large-scale approximation	
formula not designed for small sample sizes.	
Total Sample Size n	10
T_1 Test Statistic	17
T_1 Mean	22
Standard Error of T_1	4.690416
Z Test Statistic	−1.066

Two-Tail Test	
Lower Critical Value	−1.95996
Upper Critical Value	1.959961
p-value	0.286422
Do not reject the null hypothesis	

Decision rule: Reject H_0 if $|Z| > 1.96$. Test statistic: $Z = -1.066$. Decision: Because $|Z| < 1.96$, do not reject H_0. These two methods have the same population median for the 0.05 significance level.

Power Factor

Wilcoxon Rank Sum Test	
Level of Significance	0.05

Population 1 Sample	
Sample Size	4
Sum of Ranks	31.5

Population 2 Sample	
Sample Size	6
Sum of Ranks	23.5
Warning: Large-scale approximation	
formula not designed for small sample sizes.	
Total Sample Size n	10
T_1 Test Statistic	31.5
T_1 Mean	22
Standard Error of T_1	4.690416
Z Test Statistic	2.025407

Two-Tail Test	
Lower Critical Value	−1.95996
Upper Critical Value	1.959961
p-value	0.042825
Reject the null hypothesis	

Decision rule: Reject H_0 if $|Z| > 1.96$. Test statistic: $Z = 2.025407$. Decision: Because $|Z| > 1.96$, reject H_0. These two methods have different population medians for 0.05 significance level.

Lamp Temperature

Wilcoxon Rank Sum Test	
Level of Significance	0.05

Population 1 Sample	
Sample Size	4
Sum of Ranks	32

Population 2 Sample	
Sample Size	6
Sum of Ranks	23
Total Sample Size n	10
T_1 Test Statistic	32
T_1 Mean	22
Standard Error of T_1	4.690416
Z Test Statistic	2.132007

Two-Tail Test	
Lower Critical Value	−1.95996
Upper Critical Value	1.959961
p-value	0.033006
Reject the null hypothesis	

Decision rule: Reject H_0 if $|Z| > 1.96$. Test statistic: $Z = 2.132007$. Decision: Because $|Z| > 1.96$, reject H_0. These two methods have different population medians for 0.05 significance level.

Ballast Temperature

Wilcoxon Rank Sum Test	
Level of Significance	0.05

Population 1 Sample	
Sample Size	4
Sum of Ranks	34

Population 2 Sample	
Sample Size	6
Sum of Ranks	21
Warning: Large-scale approximation	
formula not designed for small sample sizes.	
Total Sample Size n	10
T_1 Test Statistic	34
T_1 Mean	22
Standard Error of T_1	4.690416
Z Test Statistic	2.558409

Two-Tail Test	
Lower Critical Value	−1.95996
Upper Critical Value	1.959961
p-value	0.010515
Reject the null hypothesis	

Decision rule: Reject H_0 if $|Z| > 1.96$. Test statistic: $Z = 2.558409$. Decision: Because $|Z| > 1.96$, reject H_0. These two methods have different population medians for the 0.05 significance level.

47. (a) $H_0: M_1 = M_2$; the population medians are equal.

$H_1: M_1 \neq M_2$; the population medians are different.

Wilcoxon Rank Sum Test	
Level of Significance	0.05

Population 1 Sample	
Sample Size	30
Sum of Ranks	790

Population 2 Sample	
Sample Size	45
Sum of Ranks	2060
Total Sample Size n	75
T_1 Test Statistic	790
T_1 Mean	1140
Standard Error of T_1	92.46621
Z Test Statistic	−3.78517

Two-Tail Test	
Lower Critical Value	−1.95996
Upper Critical Value	1.959961
p-value	0.000154
Reject the null hypothesis	

Decision rule: Reject H_0 if $|Z| > 1.96$. Test statistic: $Z = -3.785$. Decision: Because $|Z| > 1.96$, reject H_0. These two variables have different population medians for the 0.05 significance level.

(b) p-value = 0.0002. This is the probability of obtaining a test statistic of magnitude equal to or greater than the result obtained from the sample data given that the null hypothesis is true.

(c) These two batteries have both different means and different medians for 0.05 significance level.

49. (a) $H_0: M_1 = M_2$; the population medians are equal.

$H_1: M_1 \neq M_2$; the population medians are different.

Wilcoxon Rank Sum Test	
Level of Significance	0.05

Population 1 Sample	
Sample Size	20
Sum of Ranks	345.5

Population 2 Sample	
Sample Size	20
Sum of Ranks	474.5
Total Sample Size n	40
T_1 Test Statistic	345.5
T_1 Mean	410
Standard Error of T_1	36.96846
Z Test Statistic	−1.74473

Two-Tail Test	
Lower Critical Value	−1.95996
Upper Critical Value	1.959961
p-value	0.081032
Do not reject the null hypothesis	

Decision rule: Reject H_0 if $|Z| > 1.96$. Test statistic: $Z = -1.745$. Decision: Because $|Z| < 1.96$, do not reject H_0. These two variables have the same population medians for 0.05 significance level.

(b) p-value $= 0.081$. This is the probability of obtaining a test statistic of magnitude equal to or greater than the result obtained from the sample data given that the null hypothesis is true.

(c) These two variables have both equal means and equal medians for 0.05 significance level.

51. A Type I error occurs when the null hypothesis is rejected when in fact it is true and should not be rejected. The probability of occurrence of Type I error is the level of significance. A Type II error occurs when the null hypothesis is not rejected when in fact it is false and should be rejected.

53. For the one-side alternatives it is necessary to use a one-tailed test procedure. For the $H_1: \theta \neq \theta_0$ alternatives one should perform a two-tailed test.

55. If the $(1 - \alpha)\%$ confidence interval does not contain the parameter value tested in the null hypothesis, this null hypothesis should be rejected for the confidence level α. For a one-tailed test it is necessary to construct a one-tailed confidence intervals.

57. The pooled-variance t test is selected when two samples are randomly and independently drawn from populations such that the populations are normally distributed and have equal variances.

59. The Wilcoxon rank sum test can be used with ordinal data when sample sizes are small and it cannot be assumed that the data in each group are taken from normally distributed populations.

61. For related populations the results obtained from one group are not independent of those obtained from all other groups.

63. The paired t test is used when two sets of data are selected for the same set of items or individuals and when the sample of difference scores is randomly and independently drawn from a population that is normally distributed.

65. By performing a chi-square test for various sample pairs of contingency tables and by taking into account their p-values, one can select groups with significantly different proportions of success.

67. $H_0 : \sigma_1 = \sigma_2$; the variances are equal.

$H_1 : \sigma_1 \neq \sigma_2$; the variances are not equal.

F-Test Two-Sample for Variances		
	Variable 1	**Variable 2**
Mean	909.65	1018.35
Variance	8893.464	9389.874
Observations	40	40
df	39	39
F	0.947133	
$P(F \leq f)$ one-tail	0.433093	
F Critical one-tail	0.586694	

There is no significant difference between the two variances.

$H_0 : \mu_1 = \mu_2$; the two means are equal.

$H_1 : \mu_1 \neq \mu_2$; the two means are not equal.

t-Test: Two-Sample Assuming Equal Variances		
	Variable 1	**Variable 2**
Mean	909.65	1018.35
Variance	8893.464	9389.874
Observations	40	40
Pooled Variance	9141.669	
Hypothesized Mean Difference	0	
df	78	
t Stat	–5.08431	
$p(T \leq t)$ one-tail	1.24×10^{-6}	
t Critical one-tail	1.664625	
$p(T \leq t)$ two-tail	2.47×10^{-6}	
t Critical two-tail	1.990848	

There is a significant difference between the two means.

69. *pH*

$H_0 : \sigma_1 = \sigma_2$; the variances are equal.

$H_1 : \sigma_1 \neq \sigma_2$; the variances are not equal.

F-Test Two-Sample for Variances		
	Variable 1	**Variable 2**
Mean	5.203333	5.3
Variance	0.096479	0.100291
Observations	12	12
df	11	11
F	0.961989	
$P(F \leq f)$ one-tail	0.474955	
F Critical one-tail	0.35487	

There is no significant difference between the two variances.

$H_0 : \mu_1 = \mu_2$; the two means are equal.

$H_1 : \mu_1 \neq \mu_2$; the two means are not equal.

t-Test: Two-Sample Assuming Equal Variances		
	Variable 1	**Variable 2**
Mean	5.203333	5.3
Variance	0.096479	0.100291
Observations	12	12
Pooled Variance	0.098385	
Hypothesized Mean Difference	0	
df	22	
t Stat	−0.7549	
$p(T \le t)$ one-tail	0.229158	
t Critical one-tail	1.717144	
$p(T \le t)$ two-tail	0.458316	
t Critical two-tail	2.073875	

There is no significant difference between the two means.

Conductivity

$H_0:\sigma_1 = \sigma_2$; the variances are equal.

$H_1:\sigma_1 \ne \sigma_2$; the variances are not equal.

F-Test Two-Sample for Variances		
	Variable 1	**Variable 2**
Mean	0.80125	0.596167
Variance	0.078195	0.017882
Observations	12	12
df	11	11
F	4.372871	
$P(F \le f)$ one-tail	0.010805	
F Critical one-tail	2.817927	

There is a significant difference between the two variances.

$H_0:\mu_1 = \mu_2$; the two means are equal.

$H_1:\mu_1 \ne \mu_2$; the two means are not equal.

t-Test: Two-Sample Assuming Unequal Variances		
	Variable 1	**Variable 2**
Mean	0.80125	0.596167
Variance	0.078195	0.017882
Observations	12	12
Pooled Volume	0	
Hypothesized Mean Difference	16	
t Stat	2.291988	
t stat	0.017902	
$p(T \le t)$ one-tail	1.745884	
t Critical one-tail	0.035805	
$p(T \le t)$ two-tail	2.119905	

There is a significant difference between the two means.

Total Aerobic Microbial Population

$H_0: \sigma_1 = \sigma_2$; the variances are equal.

$H_1: \sigma_1 \neq \sigma_2$; the variances are not equal.

F-Test Two-Sample for Variances	Variable 1	Variable 2
Mean	5.666667	3.333333
Variance	157.1515	57.33333
Observations	12	12
df	11	11
F	2.741015	
$P(F \leq f)$ one-tail	0.054512	
F Critical one-tail	2.817927	

There are some doubts about the significance of the difference between the two variances, because the *p*-value is approximately 0.05. Therefore, consider both procedures for testing the hypothesis about the mean equality.

$H_0: \mu_1 = \mu_2$; the two means are equal.

$H_1: \mu_1 \neq \mu_2$; the two means are not equal.

t-Test: Two-Sample Assuming Equal Variances	Variable 1	Variable 2
Mean	5.666667	3.333333
Variance	157.1515	57.33333
Observations	12	12
Pooled Variance	107.2424	
Hypothesized Mean Difference	0	
df	22	
t Stat	0.551911	
$p(T \leq t)$ one-tail	0.293286	
t Critical one-tail	1.717144	
$p(T \leq t)$ two-tail	0.586573	
t Critical two-tail	2.073875	

t-Test: Two-Sample Assuming Unequal Variances	Variable 1	Variable 2
Mean	5.666667	3.333333
Variance	157.1515	57.33333
Observations	12	12
Hypothesized Mean Difference	0	
df	18	
t Stat	0.551911	
$p(T \leq t)$ one-tail	0.293898	
t Critical one-tail	1.734063	
$p(T \leq t)$ two-tail	0.587797	
t Critical two-tail	2.100924	

The result is the same for both assumptions; there is no significant difference between the two means.

Total Organic Carbon (TOC)

$H_0: \sigma_1 = \sigma_2$; the variances are equal.

$H_1: \sigma_1 \neq \sigma_2$; the variances are not equal.

F-Test Two-Sample for Variances		
	Variable 1	**Variable 2**
Mean	174.6667	173.5
Variance	7752.97	10796.27
Observations	12	12
df	11	11
F	0.718115	
$P(F \leq f)$ one-tail	0.296119	
F Critical one-tail	0.35487	

There is no significant difference between the two variances.

$H_0: \mu_1 = \mu_2$; the two means are equal.

$H_1: \mu_1 \neq \mu_2$; the two means are not equal.

t-Test: Two-Sample Assuming Equal Variances		
	Variable 1	**Variable 2**
Mean	174.6667	173.5
Variance	7752.97	10796.27
Observations	12	12
Pooled Variance	9274.621	
Hypothesized Mean Difference	0	
df	22	
t Stat	0.029674	
$p(T \leq t)$ one-tail	0.488297	
t Critical one-tail	1.717144	
$p(T \leq t)$ two-tail	0.976595	
t Critical two-tail	2.073875	

There is no significant difference between the two means.

71. (a) $H_0: \pi_1 = \pi_2$; the two proportions are equal.

$H_1: \pi_1 \neq \pi_2$; the two proportions are not equal.

Observed Frequencies: Hearing Loss Caused by Hib			
Country	**Yes**	**No**	**Total**
Canada	57	44	101
US	83	60	143
Total	140	104	244

Expected Frequencies: Hearing Loss Caused by Hib			
Country	**Yes**	**No**	**Total**
Canada	57.95081967	43.0491803	101
US	82.04918033	60.9508197	143
Total	140	104	244

Level of Significance	0.05
Number of Rows	2
Number of Columns	2
Degrees of Freedom	1
Critical Value	3.841455
Chi-Square Test Statistic	0.062452
p-value	0.802661
Do not reject the null hypothesis	

There is no significant difference between the two population proportions.

(b)

Observed Frequencies: Treated with Dexamethasone			
Result	Yes	No	Total
Severe	8	27	35
Not severe	252	206	458
Total	260	233	493

Expected Frequencies: Treated with Dexamethasone			
Result	Yes	No	Total
Severe	18.45841785	16.5415822	35
Not severe	241.5415822	216.458418	458
Total	260	233	493

Level of Significance	0.01
Number of Rows	2
Number of Columns	2
Degrees of Freedom	1
Critical Value	6.634891
Chi-Square Test Statistic	13.49803
p-value	0.000239
Reject the null hypothesis	

There is a significant difference between the two population proportions.

(c)

Observed Frequencies: Treated with Dexametazone			
Problem	Yes	No	Total
Neurological deficit	25	38	63
Hearing loss	365	329	694
Total	390	367	757

Expected Frequencies: Treated with Dexametazone			
Problem	Yes	No	Total
Neurological deficit	32.45706737	30.5429326	63
Hearing loss	357.5429326	336.457067	694
Total	390	367	757

Level of Significance	0.01
Number of Rows	2
Number of Columns	2
Degrees of Freedom	1
Critical Value	6.634891
Chi-Square Test Statistic	3.854724
p-value	0.049606
Do not reject the null hypothesis	

There is no significant difference between the two population proportions.

73. To check the assumptions let us construct the multiple Box-and-Whisker plot. The normal distribution assumption appears valid based on the plot.

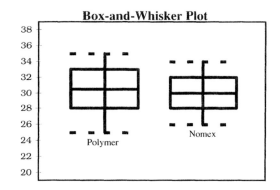

$H_0: \sigma_1 = \sigma_2$; the variances are equal.

$H_1: \sigma_1 \neq \sigma_2$; the variances are not equal.

F-Test Two-Sample for Variances		
	Variable 1	**Variable 2**
Mean	30.44828	29.89655
Variance	7.327586	5.238916
Observations	29	29
df	28	28
F	1.398684	
$P(F \leq f)$ one-tail	0.190023	
F Critical one-tail	1.882078	

There is no significant difference between the two variances for the 0.05 significance level.

$H_0: \mu_1 = \mu_2$; the two means are equal.

$H_1: \mu_1 \neq \mu_2$; the two means are not equal.

t-Test: Two-Sample Assuming Equal Variances		
	Variable 1	**Variable 2**
Mean	30.44828	29.89655
Variance	7.327586	5.238916
Observations	29	29
Pooled Variance	6.283251	
Hypothesized Mean Difference	0	
df	56	
t Stat	0.838135	
$p(T \leq t)$ one-tail	0.202759	
t Critical one-tail	1.672522	
$p(T \leq t)$ two-tail	0.405518	
t Critical two-tail	2.003239	

There is no significant difference between the two means for the 0.05 significance level.

chapter 10

The Design of Experiments: One Factor and Randomized Block Experiments

1. (a) $H_0: \mu_1 = \mu_2 = \mu_3$, H_1: Not all of the means are equal

Anova: Single Factor

		Summary		
Groups	**Count**	**Sum**	**Average**	**Variance**
Vegetable	5.000	2199.000	439.800	4435.200
Canola	5.000	2834.000	566.800	2443.700
Safflower	5.000	2139.000	427.800	2149.200

			ANOVA			
Source of Variation	**SS**	**df**	**MS**	**F**	**p-value**	**F_{crit}**
Between Groups	59323.330	2.000	29661.670	9.856	0.030	3.885
Within Groups	36112.400	12.000	3009.367			
Total	95435.730	14.000				

Decision rule: Reject H_0 if $F > 3.885$. Test statistic: $F = 9.856$. Decision: Because $F > 3.885$, reject H_0. There is a significant difference between the average number of popped kernels for these three oils.

(b)

Tukey Kramer Multiple Comparisons	
Group 1	
Sample Mean	439.800
Sample Size	5.000
Group 2	
Sample Mean	566.800
Sample Size	5.000
Group 3	
Sample Mean	427.800
Sample Size	5.000
MSW	3009.367
Q Statistic	3.060

Group 1 to Group 2 Comparison	
Absolute Difference	127.000
Standard Error of Difference	24.533
Critical Range	75.071
Means are different	

Group 1 to Group 3 Comparison	
Absolute Difference	12.000
Standard Error of Difference	24.533
Critical Range	75.071
Means are not different	

Group 2 to Group 3 Comparison	
Absolute Difference	139.000
Standard Error of Difference	24.533
Critical Range	75.071
Means are different	

Groups	**Group-to-group Means Comparison**		
	1–2	1–3	2–3
Means	different	not different	different

There is a significant difference between the means μ_1 and μ_2, and the means μ_2 and μ_3. Due to the absence of a significant difference between μ_1 and μ_3, one can conclude that μ_2 is significantly different from all others.

(c) Canola oil should be used to maximize the number of popped kernels. The average number of popped kernels is the greatest for Canola oil. Canola oil significantly differs from the average number of popped kernels from the other oils. (Canola oil is the best for the popcorn making if we do not take into account other parameters of these oils.)

3. (a) $H_0: \mu_1 = \mu_2 = \mu_3$, H_1: Not all of the means are equal.
Anova: Single Factor

Summary				
Groups	**Count**	**Sum**	**Average**	**Variance**
Run 1	10.000	6.620	0.662	0.024
Run 2	10.000	7.520	0.752	0.045
Run 3	10.000	6.860	0.686	0.028

ANOVA						
Source of Variation	**SS**	**df**	**MS**	**F**	**p-value**	F_{crit}
Between Groups	0.043	2.000	0.022	0.674	0.518	3.354
Within Groups	0.870	27.000	0.032			
Total	0.914	29.000				

Decision rule: Reject H_0 if $F > 3.354$. Test statistic: $F = 0.674$. Decision: Because $F < 3.354$, do not reject H_0. There is no significant difference between the average amounts of sulfides for the three runs for the 0.05 level.

(b) Although no significant difference between the averages were found, a Tukey Kramer Multiple Comparisons should still be completed.

Tukey Kramer Multiple Comparisons	
Group 1	
Sample Mean	0.662
Sample Size	10.000
Group 2	
Sample Mean	0.752
Sample Size	10.000
Group 3	
Sample Mean	0.686
Sample Size	10.000
MSW	0.0322
Q Statistic	2.900

Group 1 to Group 2 Comparison	
Absolute Difference	0.090
Standard Error of Difference	0.057
Critical Range	0.165
Means are different	

Group 1 to Group 3 Comparison	
Absolute Difference	0.024
Standard Error of Difference	0.057
Critical Range	0.165
Means are not different	

Group 1 to Group 4 Comparison	
Absolute Difference	22.008
Standard Error of Difference	1.371
Critical Range	5.224
Means are not different	

Group 2 to Group 3 Comparison	
Absolute Difference	0.066
Standard Error of Difference	0.057
Critical Range	0.165
Means are not different	

Group-to-Group Means Comparison		
Groups	1–2	1–3	2–3
Means	Not different	Not different	Not different

There are no significant differences between any of the pairs of means.

(c) (1) The assumptions of randomness and independence appear to be valid. These assumptions are necessary for the sampling procedure.

(2) The assumption of normality of errors appears to be valid.

(3) The assumption of homogeneity of variance appears to be valid for the first and second samples. The third sample does not appear to hold to the assumption. Bartlet's test may be used to test this hypothesis.

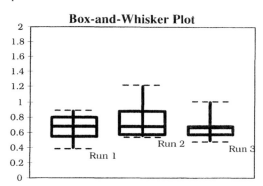

Box-and-Whisker Plot

5. (a) $H_0: \mu_A = \mu_B = \mu_C$, H_1: Not all of the means are equal.

Anova: Single Factor

Summary				
Groups	Count	Sum	Average	Variance
A	5.000	450.100	90.020	0.877
B	5.000	455.300	91.060	1.093
C	5.000	467.500	93.500	2.325

ANOVA						
Source of Variation	SS	df	MS	F	p-value	F_{crit}
Between Groups	31.909	2.000	15.955	11.144	0.002	3.885
Within Groups	17.180	12.000	1.432			
Total	49.089	14.000				

Decision rule: Reject H_0 if $F > 3.885$. Test statistic: $F = 11.144$. Decision: Because $F > 3.885$, reject H_0. There is significant difference between the average reflectance for the different machines for the 0.05 level.

(b)

Tukey Kramer Multiple Comparisons	
Group 1	
Sample Mean	90.020
Sample Size	5.000
Group 2	
Sample Mean	91.060
Sample Size	5.000
Group 3	
Sample Mean	93.500
Sample Size	5.000
MSW	1.432
Q Statistic	3.770

Group 1 to Group 2 Comparison	
Absolute Difference	1.040
Standard Error of Difference	0.535
Critical Range	2.017
Means are not different	

Group 1 to Group 3 Comparison	
Absolute Difference	3.480
Standard Error of Difference	0.535
Critical Range	2.017
Means are different	

Group 2 to Group 3 Comparison	
Absolute Difference	2.440
Standard Error of Difference	0.535
Critical Range	2.017
Means are different	

Groups	Group-to-group Means Comparison		
	1–2	1–3	2–3
Means	Not different	Different	Different

There is a significant difference between the third mean and all others.

(c) Machine C should be recommended because its average reflectance is significantly greater than the averages of the other two.

7. (a) $H_0: \mu_1 = \mu_2 = \mu_3 = \mu_4 = \mu_5 = \mu_6$, H_1: Not all of the means are equal.
    Anova: Single Factor

Groups	Summary			
	Count	**Sum**	**Average**	**Variance**
Column 1	8.000	4117.000	514.625	17228.840
Column 2	8.000	3893.000	486.625	20580.840
Column 3	8.000	3923.000	490.375	3708.554
Column 4	8.000	4058.000	507.250	11095.070
Column 5	8.000	3676.000	459.500	15778.000
Column 6	8.000	3596.000	449.500	18549.710

ANOVA						
Source of Variation	**SS**	**df**	**MS**	**F**	***p*-value**	F_{crit}
Between Groups	26511.850	5.000	5302.371	0.366	0.869	2.438
Within Groups	608587.100	42.000	14490.170			
Total	635099.000	47.000				

Decision rule: Reject H_0 if $F > 2.438$. Test statistic: $F = 0.366$. Decision: Because $F < 2.438$, do not reject H_0. There is no significant difference between the average tensile strengths for the different time period.

(b) Although no significant difference between the averages was found, a Tukey Kramer Multiple Comparisons should be done to complete the analysis.

Critical range $= 4.23 \sqrt{\dfrac{14490.17}{2}\left(\dfrac{1}{8} + \dfrac{1}{8}\right)} = 180$.

Let us denote $d_{ij} = \left| \overline{X}_{.i} - \overline{X}_{.j} \right|$

	i–j				
Groups	1–2	1–3	1–4	1–5	1–6
d_{ij}	224.000	194.000	59.000	441.000	521.000
Decision	Different	Different	Not different	Different	Different

	i–j				
Groups	2–3	2–4	2–5	2–6	3–4
d_{ij}	30.000	165.000	217.000	297.000	135.000
Decision	Not different	Not different	Different	Different	Not different

	i–j				
Groups	3–5	3–6	4–5	4–6	5–6
d_{ij}	247.000	337.000	382.000	462.000	80.000
Decision	Different	Different	Different	Different	Not different

(c)

(d) There are no clear patterns in this data. From the box-and-whisker plot it can be concluded that the average stresses measured over time periods 5 and 6 are significantly lower than those measured over time periods 1, 2, 3 and 4. However, because there are no significant differences between the average stresses measured over time periods 5 and 6, we cannot determine which of these two average stresses is the lowest. Further, the average stress measured over time period 1 is significantly higher than those measured over time periods 2, 3, 5, and 6. Although the average stress measured over time period 1 is also higher than that measured over time period 4, this result is not significant.

9. (a) $H_0: \mu_1 = \mu_2 = \mu_3$, H_1: At least one of the means is different.

Anova: Two-Factor Without Replication

Summary	Count	Sum	Average	Variance
Two days	40.000	119.640	2.991	0.246
Seven days	40.000	141.765	3.544	0.254
28 days	40.000	182.380	4.560	0.232

ANOVA						
Source of Variation	SS	df	MS	F	*p*-value	F_{crit}
Rows	21.170	39.000	0.543	5.752	2.92×10^{-11}	1.553
Columns	50.628	2.000	25.314	268.256	1.09×10^{-35}	3.114
Error	7.361	78.000	0.094			
Total	79.159	119.000				

Decision rule: Reject H_0 if $F > 3.114$. Test statistic: $F = 268.256$. Decision: Because $F > 3.114$, reject H_0. There is evidence of a difference among the average compressive strengths after 2, 7 and 28 days.

(b) critical range $= 3.38 \sqrt{\dfrac{0.094366}{40}} = 0.16417$. Let us denote $d_{ij} = \left| \overline{X}_{.i} - \overline{X}_{.j} \right|$

	i–j		
Groups	1–2	1–3	2–3
d_{ij}	0.553	1.569	1.015
Decision	Different	Different	Different

There are significant differences for all pairs of means for the 0.05 level.

(c) Estimated relative efficiency: $RE = \dfrac{(r-1)MSBL + r(c-1)MSE}{(rc-1)MSE} = \dfrac{39 \cdot 0.54822 + 40 \cdot 2 \cdot 0.094366}{119 \cdot 0.094366} = 2.576$

(d)

Box-and-Whisker Plot

(e) Compressive strength increases as the number of days after pouring increases, within a range of 2 to 28 days.

11. (a) $H_0: \mu_1 = \mu_2 = \mu_3 = \mu_4$, H_1: At least one of the means is different.

Anova: Two-Factor Without Replication

Summary	Count	Sum	Average	Variance
1	4.000	90.900	22.725	0.069
2	4.000	217.600	54.400	4.620
3	4.000	39.300	9.825	1.249
4	4.000	85.900	21.475	2.729
5	4.000	52.700	13.175	0.769
6	4.000	177.900	44.475	64.369
7	4.000	63.100	15.775	12.429
8	4.000	75.000	18.750	15.843
Fear	8.000	222.600	27.825	328.656
Happiness	8.000	203.300	25.413	258.313
Depression	8.000	191.000	23.875	224.196
Calmness	8.000	185.500	23.188	221.216

ANOVA						
Source of Variation	SS	df	MS	F	*p*-value	F_{crit}
Rows	7021.865	7.000	1003.124	102.858	8.3×10^{-15}	2.488
Columns	101.433	3.000	33.811	3.467	0.034	3.072
Error	204.803	21.000	9.753			
Total	7328.100	31.000				

Decision rule: Reject H_0 if $F > 3.072$. Test statistic: $F = 3.467$. Decision: Because $F > 3.072$, reject H_0. There is a significant difference among the average measured skin potentials for the emotions for the 0.05 level.

(b) critical range $= 3.95 \sqrt{\dfrac{9.7525}{8}} = 4.361$. Let us denote $d_{ij} = \left| \overline{X}_{.i} - \overline{X}_{.j} \right|$

	i–j					
Groups	1–2	1–3	1–4	2–3	2–4	3–4
d_{ij}	2.413	3.950	4.638	1.538	2.225	0.688
Decision	Not different	Not different	Different	Not different	Not different	Not different

There is a significant difference between μ_1 and μ_4 for the 0.05 level.

(c) Estimated relative efficiency: $RE = \dfrac{(r-1)MSBL + r(c-1)MSE}{(rc-1)MSE} = \dfrac{7 \cdot 1003.121 + 8 \cdot 3 \cdot 9.7525}{31 \cdot 9.7525} = 24$

(d) There is a significant difference among the average measured skin potentials for the emotions for the 0.05 level. Paired comparisons show that this effect exists for the fear and the calmness groups at a significant level.

13. (a) $H_0: M_1 = M_2 = M_3$, H_1: At least one of the medians is different.

Kruskal Wallis Rank Test	
Level of Significance	0.050
Group 1	
Sum of Ranks	119.000
Sample Size	8.000
Group 2	
Sum of Ranks	112.000
Sample Size	8.000
Group 3	
Sum of Ranks	69.000
Sample Size	8.000
Sum of Squared Ranks/Sample Size	3933.250
Sum of Sample Sizes	24.000
Number of groups	3.000
H Test Statistic	3.665
Critical Value	5.991
p-Value	0.160
Do not reject the null hypothesis	

Decision rule: reject H_0 if $H > 5.991$. Test statistic: $H = 3.665$. Decision: Because $H < 5.991$, do not reject H_0. There is no significant temperature effect on the median life of the three types of electronic components.

(b) Temperature does not have a significant effect on the failure time because of the large p-value of 0.16.

15. (a) $H_0: M_1 = M_2 = M_3 = M_4$, H_1: At least one of the medians is different

Kruskal Wallis Rank Test	
Level of Significance	0.050
Group 1	
Sum of Ranks	55.000
Sample Size	10.000
Group 2	
Sum of Ranks	174.000
Sample Size	10.000
Group 3	
Sum of Ranks	277.000
Sample Size	10.000
Group 4	
Sum of Ranks	314.000
Sample Size	10.000
Sum of Squared Ranks/Sample Size	20862.600
Sum of Sample Sizes	40.000
Number of groups	4.000
H Test Statistic	29.653
Critical Value	7.815
p-Value	1.63×10^{-6}
Reject the null hypothesis	

Decision rule: reject H_0 if $H > 7.815$. Test statistic: $H = 29.653$. Decision: Because $H > 7.815$, reject H_0. There is evidence of a difference in the median distance traveled by the golf balls of different design.

(b) There are no differences in the results of 10.2 and 10.15 because the initial assumptions of the ANOVA appear to be valid (see the Box-and-Whisker Plot). There is no significant difference between the means and the medians.

Box-and-Whisker Plot

17. (a) $H_0: M_1 = M_2 = M_3 = M_4 = M_5 = M_6$, H_1: At least one of the medians is different.

j	1	2	3	4	5	6
T_j	224.000	199.500	189.000	221.500	179.500	162.500
n_j	8.000	8.000	8.000	8.000	8.000	8.000

$$H = \left[\frac{12}{n(n+1)} \sum_{j=1}^{6} \frac{T_j^2}{n_j} \right] - 3(n+1) = \left[\frac{12}{48 \cdot 49} \cdot \frac{1}{8}(224^2 + 199.5^2 + 189^2 + 221.5^2 + 179.5^2 + 162.5^2) \right] - 3 \cdot 49 = 1.8431.$$

Decision rule: Reject H_0 if $H > 11.071$. Decision: Because $H < 11.071$, do not reject H_0. There is no significant difference in the median tensile strengths for the six time periods.

(b) There are no differences in the results of 10.7 and 10.17 because the initial assumptions of the ANOVA appear to be valid. There is no significant difference between the means and the medians.

19. Only two assumptions can be tested graphically—the normality and homogeneity of variance. It is possible to see skewness, kurtosis, mean squared displacement using the multiple Box-and-Whisker Plot.

21. The main assumptions of the ANOVA are:
   (a) Randomness and Independence.
   (b) Normality.
   (c) Homogeneity of variance.

23. The Kruskal-Wallis should be selected when the measurements are ordinal over all of the sample groups, and the common population distributions are continuous. Under these assumptions, the hypothesis about equal medians with common alternative can be tested. Thus, the Kruskal-Wallis procedure makes less stringent assumptions than the F test. As a result, for completely randomized designs, the Kruskal-Wallis test is more powerful than the F test, when the more stringent assumptions of the F test cannot be met.

25. In the randomized block design models, there are repeated measurements or matched samples (blocks) for the various levels of the study factor (treatments). The purpose of blocking is to remove as much block or subject variability as possible, so that the focus is on differences among the c treatment conditions. Thus, the reason for selecting a randomized block F test (instead of a completely randomized test) is to provide a more efficient analysis by reducing the experimental error and thereby obtaining more precise results. Obviously, a randomized block F test makes more stringent assumptions than does a completely randomized test: in addition to the assumptions of the one-way analysis of variance listed in Problem 21, it should also be assumed that there is no interacting effects between the treatments and the blocks.

27. (a) $H_0: \mu_1 = \mu_2 = \mu_3 = \mu_4$, H_1: At least one of the means is different.

Anova: Single Factor

		Summary		
Groups	**Count**	**Sum**	**Average**	**Variance**
0.0 cc	10.000	6519.000	651.900	3390.989
0.5 cc	10.000	5897.000	589.700	4256.678
1.0 cc	10.000	5629.000	562.900	3727.878
2.0 cc	10.000	5705.000	570.500	2490.722

			ANOVA			
Source of Variation	**SS**	**df**	**MS**	**F**	**p-value**	**F_{crit}**
Between Groups	48901.100	3.000	16300.370	4.702	0.007	2.866
Within Groups	124796.400	36.000	3466.567			
Total	173697.500	39.000				

Decision rule: Reject H_0 if $F > 2.866$. Test statistic: $F = 4.702$. Decision: Because $F > 2.866$, reject H_0 for the 0.05 level.

(b)

Tukey Kramer Multiple Comparisons	
Group 1	
Sample Mean	651.900
Sample Size	10.000
Group 2	
Sample Mean	589.700
Sample Size	10.000
Group 3	
Sample Mean	562.900
Sample Size	10.000
Group 4	
Sample Mean	570.500
Sample Size	10.000
MSW	3466.567
Q Statistic	3.810

Group 1 to Group 2 Comparison	
Absolute Difference	62.200
Standard Error of Difference	18.619
Critical Range	70.937
Means are not different	

Group 1 to Group 3 Comparison	
Absolute Difference	89.000
Standard Error of Difference	18.619
Critical Range	70.937
Means are different	

Group 1 to Group 4 Comparison	
Absolute Difference	81.400
Standard Error of Difference	18.619
Critical Range	70.937
Means are different	

Group 2 to Group 3 Comparison	
Absolute Difference	26.800
Standard Error of Difference	18.619
Critical Range	70.937
Means are not different	

Group 2 to Group 4 Comparison	
Absolute Difference	19.200
Standard Error of Difference	18.619
Critical Range	70.937
Means are not different	

Group 3 to Group 4 Comparison	
Absolute Difference	7.600
Standard Error of Difference	18.619
Critical Range	70.937
Means are not different	

critical range = 70.93732. Let us denote $d_{ij} = \left| \overline{X}_{.i} - \overline{X}_{.j} \right|$

			i–j			
Groups	1–2	1–3	1–4	2–3	2–4	3–4
d_{ij}	62.200	89.000	81.400	26.800	19.200	7.600
Decision	Not different	Different	Different	Not different	Not different	Not different

There is a significant difference between the means μ_1 and μ_3, and the means μ_1 and μ_4 for the 0.05 level.

(c)

Box-and-Whisker Plot

(d) The drug reading for the 0.0 cc formulation is significantly larger than those for the 1.0 cc and the 2.0 cc formulations. The drug reading for the 0.0 cc formulation is also larger than that for the 0.5 cc formulation; this result, however, is not significant.

29. *Conductivity*

(a) $H_0: \mu_1 = \mu_2 = \mu_3 = \mu_4 = \mu_5$, H_1: At least one of the means is different.
Anova: Single Factor

	Summary			
Groups	**Count**	**Sum**	**Average**	**Variance**
6	9.000	13237.000	1470.778	103990.400
7	9.000	15392.000	1710.222	11880.440
8	9.000	11902.000	1322.444	6697.528
9	9.000	16100.000	1788.889	28479.860
10	9.000	9551.000	1061.222	15093.440
11	9.000	11410.000	1267.778	4619.444

			ANOVA			
Source of Variation	**SS**	**df**	**MS**	**F**	**p-value**	F_{crit}
Between Groups	3443266.000	5.000	688653.200	24.197	4.51×10^{-12}	2.409
Within Groups	1366089.000	48.000	28460.190			
Total	4809355.000	53.000				

Decision rule: Reject H_0 if $F > 2.409$. Test statistic: $F = 24.197$. Decision: Because $F > 2.409$, reject H_0.

(b) There is evidence of a difference in the conductivity of the wells.

Hardness

(a) $H_0: \mu_1 = \mu_2 = \mu_3 = \mu_4 = \mu_5$, H_1: At least one of the means is different.
Anova: Single Factor

	Summary			
Groups	**Count**	**Sum**	**Average**	**Variance**
7	9.000	8553.000	950.333	10698.250
8	9.000	6742.000	749.111	1224.361
9	9.000	9785.000	1087.222	21044.440
10	9.000	2289.000	254.333	94.000
11	9.000	2730.000	303.333	471.750

ANOVA					
Source of Variation	**SS**	**df**	**MS**	**F**	**p-value**	**F_{crit}**
Within Groups	5095229.000	4.000	1273807.000	189.935	1.92×10^{-25}	2.606
Within Groups	268262.400	40.000	6706.561			
Total	5363491.000	44.000				

Decision rule: Reject H_0 if $F > 2.606$. Test statistic: $F = 189.935$. Decision: Because $F > 2.606$, reject H_0.

(b) There is evidence of a difference in the hardness of the wells.

Chloride

(a) $H_0: \mu_1 = \mu_2 = \mu_3 = \mu_4 = \mu_5$, H_1: At least one of the means is different.

Anova: Single Factor

Summary				
Groups	**Count**	**Sum**	**Average**	**Variance**
6	9.000	3160.000	351.111	2221.611
7	9.000	1459.000	162.111	646.611
8	9.000	896.000	99.556	13.278
9	9.000	1448.000	160.889	1018.361
10	9.000	1989.000	221.000	207.500
11	9.000	1209.000	134.333	196.250

ANOVA					
Source of Variation	**SS**	**df**	**MS**	**F**	**p-value**	**F_{crit}**
Within Groups	358216.600	5.000	71643.320	99.883	3.57×10^{-24}	2.409
Within Groups	34428.890	48.000	717.269			
Total	392645.500	53.000				

Decision rule: Reject H_0 if $F > 2.409$. Test statistic: $F = 99.883$. Decision: Because $F > 2.409$, reject H_0.

(b) There is evidence of a difference in the level of chloride of the wells.

chapter 11

The Design of Experiments: Factorial Designs

1. | **Two-way ANOVA: Breaking Strength versus Operator; Machine**

```
Analysis of Variance for Breaking Strength
Source        DF      SS        MS       F        P
Operator       3    301.11    100.37    26.57    0.000
Machine        2    329.39    164.69    43.60    0.000
Interaction    6     86.39     14.40     3.81    0.008
Error         24     90.67      3.78
Total         35    807.56
```

(a) $H_0: \mu_A = \mu_B = \mu_C = \mu_D$, H_1: At least one of the means is different.

Decision rule: Reject H_0 if $F > 3.01$. Test statistic: $F = 26.57$. Decision: Because $F > 3.01$, reject H_0. There is evidence of a difference in the breaking strengths of wool serge material due to the operator.

(b) $H_0: \mu_I = \mu_{II} = \mu_{III}$, H_1: At least one of the means is different.

Decision rule: Reject H_0 if $F > 3.40$. Test statistic: $F = 43.60$. Decision: Because $F > 3.40$, reject H_0. There is evidence of a difference in the breaking strengths of wool serge material due to the machine.

(c) H_0: There is no interaction between the operator and the machine.

H_1: There is interaction between the operator and the machine.

Decision rule: Reject H_0 if $F > 2.51$. Test statistic: $F = 3.81$. Decision: Because $F > 2.51$, reject H_0. There is a significant interaction between operator and machine for the 0.05 level.

(d) (1)
```
                            Individual 95% CI
Operator      Mean    ---------+---------+---------+---------+--
A            112.00                                    (----*----)
B            110.56                              (----*-----)
C            104.33    (----*-----)
D            109.56                        (----*-----)
                      ---------+---------+---------+---------+--
                       105.00    107.50    110.00    112.50
```

(2)
```
                            Individual 95% CI
Machine       Mean    --+---------+---------+---------+---------
I            113.08                                  (---*----)
II           105.75    (----*----)
III          108.50                   (----*----)
                      --+---------+---------+---------+---------
                      105.00    107.50    110.00    112.50
```

(e) (1) critical range $= Q_U \sqrt{\dfrac{MSE}{rn'}} = 3.90 \sqrt{\dfrac{3.78}{4 \cdot 3}} = 2.189$. Let us denote $d_{ij} = \left| \overline{X}_{i.} - \overline{X}_{j.} \right|$

Group-to-Group Means Comparison					
Groups	A–B	A–C	A–D	B–C	B–D	C–D
d_{ij}	1.44	7.67	2.44	5.67	1	5.23
Means	Not different	Different	Different	Different	Not different	Different

There are significant differences between average breaking strengths produced by operator C and average breaking strengths produced by each of the others for the 0.05 level. The average breaking strengths produced by Operations A and D are also different at this significance level.

(2) critical range $= Q_U \sqrt{\dfrac{MSE}{rn'}} = 3.53 \sqrt{\dfrac{3.78}{4 \cdot 3}} = 1.98$. Let us denote $\Delta_{ij} = \left| \overline{X}_{.i} - \overline{X}_{.j} \right|$

Group-to-Group Means Comparison		
Groups	I—II	I—III	II—III
Δ_{ij}	7.33	4.58	5.75
Means	Different	Different	Different

There are significant differences in average breaking strengths for all pairs of machines for the 0.05 significance level.

(f) Operators create fabric of varying strengths depending on which machines individuals use. One suggestion is to use the 12 operator-machine combinations as the levels of a single factor and completely analyze the data by performing a one-way ANOVA.

(g) For the random effect model one can provide test statistic $F = \dfrac{MSFA}{MSAB} = \dfrac{100.37}{14.40} = 6.97$. Decision rule: reject H_0 if $F > 4.76$. Decision: Because $F = 6.97 > 4.76$, reject H_0. There is a significant difference in the breaking strengths of wool serge material due to the operator for both fixed-effects and random-effects models for the 0.05 significance level.

3.

```
Two-way ANOVA: Fabric Removed versus Fabric; Treatment


Analysis of Variance for Fabric r
Source          DF        SS         MS        F         P
Fabric          1        49.0       49.0       4.88      0.047
Treatment       1       756.3      756.3      75.31      0.000
Interaction     1        42.3       42.3       4.21      0.063
Error          12       120.5       10.0
Total          15       968.0
```

(a) $H_0 : \mu_C = \mu_P$, $H_1 : \mu_C = \mu_P$
Decision rule: Reject H_0 if $F > 4.75$. Test statistic: $F = 4.88$. Decision: Because $F > 4.75$, reject H_0. There is a significant difference in the average number of inches of a fabric burned after a flame test due to the type of fabric for the 0.05 significance level.

(b) $H_0 : \mu_X = \mu_Y$, $H_1 : \mu_X \neq \mu_Y$
Decision rule: Reject H_0 if $F > 4.75$. Test statistic: $F = 75.31$. Decision: Because $F > 75.31$, reject H_0. There is evidence of a difference in the average number of inches of a fabric burned after a flame test due to the treatment applied.

(c) H_0: There is no interaction between the fabric and the treatment.
H_1: There is interaction between the fabric and the treatment.
Decision rule: Reject H_0 if $F > 4.75$. Test statistic: $F = 4.21$. Decision: Because $F < 4.75$, do not reject H_0. There is no significant interaction between the fabric and the treatment for the 0.05 significance level.

(d) (1)

```
       Fabric       Mean    Individual 95% CI
                            ------+---------+---------+---------+------+-----
       C            35.3    (-----------*-----------)
       P            38.8                        (-----------*-----------)
                            ------+---------+---------+---------+------+-----
                            34.0      36.0      38.0      40.0
```

(2)

```
       Treatment    Mean    Individual 95% CI
                            -----+---------+---------+---------+------+------
       X            43.9                                  (----*----)
       Y            30.1    (----*----)
                            -----+---------+---------+---------+------+------
                            30.0      35.0      40.0      45.0
```

(e) There is a significant difference in the average number of inches of fabric burned after a flame test, due to both the type of fabric and the treatment applied, but there is no significant interaction between the fabric and the treatment effects for the 0.05 significance level.

5.

Two-way ANOVA: Particle Size versus Operator; Resin Railcar

```
Analysis of Variance for Particle
Source         DF      SS       MS       F       P
Operator        2     20.90    10.45    7.18    0.004
Resin railcar   7    283.87    40.55   27.85    0.000
Interaction    14     14.14     1.01    0.69    0.759
Error          24     34.94     1.46
Total          47    353.86
```

(a) $H_0: \mu_1 = \mu_2 = \mu_3$, H_1: At least one of the means is different.

Decision rule: Reject H_0 if $F > 3.74$. Test statistic: $F = \dfrac{MSFA}{MSAB} = \dfrac{10.5}{1.01} = 10.4$. Decision: Because $F > 3.74$, reject

H_0. There is evidence of a difference in the average particle size of the resin due to the operator.

(b) $H_0: \mu_1 = \mu_2 = ... = \mu_8$, H_1: At least one of the means is different.

Decision rule: Reject H_0 if $F > 2.76$. Test statistic: $F = \dfrac{MSFB}{MSAB} = \dfrac{40.6}{1.01} = 40.2$. Decision: Because $F > 2.76$, reject

H_0. There is evidence of a difference in the average particle size of the resin due to the resin railcar.

(c) H_0: There is no interaction between the operator and the resin railcar.

H_1: There is interaction between the operator and the resin railcar.

Decision rule: Reject H_0 if $F > 2.13$. Test statistic: $F = 0.69$. Decision: Because $F < 2.13$, do not reject H_0. There is no significant interaction between the operator and the resin railcar.

(d) (1)

```
       Operator     Mean    Individual 95% CI
                            ----------+---------+---------+---------+-
       1            32.94                        (--------*--------)
       2            32.68                    (--------*--------)
       3            31.43    (--------*--------)
                            ----------+---------+---------+---------+-
                            31.50      32.20      32.90      33.60
```

```
(2)                              Individual 95% CI
    Resin railcar    Mean    --------+---------+---------+---------+---
    1               35.65                                  (----*----)
    2               34.62                               (----*----)
    3               29.85      (----*----)
    4               29.47    (----*----)
    5               30.85         (----*----)
    6               30.20      (----*----)
    7               32.72              (-----*----)
    8               35.47                              (----*----)
                            --------+---------+---------+---------+---
                              30.00     32.00     34.00     36.00
```

(e) There is evidence of a difference in the average particle size of the resin both due to the operator and due to the resin railcar. However, there is no significant interaction between the operator and resin railcar.

(f) (1) $H_0: \mu_1 = \mu_2 = \mu_3$, H_1: At least one of the means is different

Decision rule: Reject H_0 if $F > 3.40$. Test statistic: $F = 7.18$. Decision: Because $F > 3.40$, reject H_0. There is a significant difference in the average particle size of the resin due to the operator for the 0.05 significance level.

(2) $H_0: \mu_1 = \mu_2 = ... = \mu_8$, H_1: At least one of the means is different

Decision rule: Reject H_0 if $F > 2.42$. Test statistic: $F = 27.85$. Decision: Because $F > 2.42$, reject H_0. There is evidence of a difference in the average particle size of the resin due to the resin railcar.

(3) H_0: There is no interaction between the operator and the resin railcar.

H_1: There is interaction between the operator and the resin railcar.

Decision rule: Reject H_0 if $F > 2.13$. Test statistic: $F = 0.69$. Decision: Because $F < 2.13$, do not reject H_0. There is no significant interaction between the operator and resin railcar.

CONCLUSION: Results of (a)–(c) and (f) are the same. *There is no difference in testing H_0 for random and fixed effects.*

7.

ANOVA: Distance versus Design; Weight and Size

```
Factor       Type  Levels  Values
Design       fixed    2     C    S
Weight       fixed    2     H    L
Size         fixed    2     L    S
```

Analysis of Variance for Distance

Source	DF	SS	MS	F	P
Design	1	7906.5	7906.5	11.45	0.002
Weight	1	116.3	116.3	0.17	0.685
Size	1	14663.3	14663.3	21.24	0.000
Design*Weight	1	657.0	657.0	0.95	0.339
Design*Size	1	24255.0	24255.0	35.14	0.000
Weight*Size	1	4027.5	4027.5	5.83	0.024
Design*Weight*Size	1	318.8	318.8	0.46	0.503
Error	24	16566.3	690.3		
Total	31	68510.7			

(a) $H_0: \mu_S = \mu_C$, $H_1: \mu_S \neq \mu_C$

Decision rule: Reject H_0 if $F > 4.26$. Test statistic: $F = 11.45$. Decision: Because $F > 4.26$, reject H_0. There is a significant effect on the distance due to design for the 0.05 significance level.

(b) $H_0: \mu_L = \mu_H$, $H_1: \mu_L \neq \mu_H$

Decision rule: Reject H_0 if $F > 4.26$. Test statistic: $F = 0.17$. Decision: Because $F < 4.26$, do not reject H_0. There is no significant effect on the distance due to weight.

(c) $H_0: \mu_s = \mu_l$, $H_1: \mu_s \neq \mu_l$

Decision rule: Reject H_0 if $F > 4.42$. Test statistic: $F = 21.24$. Decision: Because $F > 4.26$, reject H_0. There is evidence of an effect on the distance due to size.

(d) Based on small p-values, there are significant interactions between the design and the size and between the weight and the size.

(e) **Main Effects Plot—Data Means Distance**

(f) **Interaction Plot—Data Means for Distance**

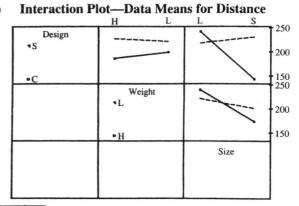

(g)

Treatment Combinations	Notation	Average Response
Simple, light, small	abc	242.5
Simple, light, large	abC	158.8
Simple, heavy, small	aBc	219.0
Simple, heavy, large	aBC	201.5
Complex, light, small	Abc	129.8
Complex, light, large	AbC	240.5
Complex, heavy, small	ABc	235.5
Complex, heavy, large	ABC	243.8

$$A = \frac{1}{4n'}[Abc + AbC + ABc + ABC - abc - abC - aBc - aBC] = 1.73$$

$$B = \frac{1}{4n'}[aBc + aBC + ABc + ABC - abc - abC - Abc - AbC] = 8.02$$

$$C = \frac{1}{4n'}[abC + aBC + AbC + ABC - abc - aBc - Abc - ABc] = 1.11$$

$$AB = \frac{1}{4n'}[abc + abC + ABc + ABC - Abc - aBc - AbC - aBC] = 5.61$$

$$AC = \frac{1}{4n'}[abc + aBc + AbC + ABC - abC - aBC - Abc - ABc] = 13.77$$

$$BC = \frac{1}{4n'}[abc + Abc + aBC + ABC - abC - aBc - ABc - AbC] = -2.27$$

$$ABC = \frac{1}{4n'}[abC + aBc + Abc + ABC - ABc - AbC - aBC - abc] = -10.55$$

(h)

**Normal Probability Plot for
Main Effects and Interactions**

(i) Effects *ABC* and *AC* are farthest from the line $x = 0$. These factor combinations must be included in the ANOVA model.

(j) In parts (a)–(d) the actual effects of significant factors were obscured by the use of insignificant factor combination terms in the ANOVA model.

(k) Based on average distances in part (g), complex design, heavy weight and large size (average distance is 243.8 inch) or simple design, light weight and small size (average distance is 242.5 inch) should be used.

9. (a)

Ring Osculation	Cage Design	Heat Treatment	Relative Life	Notation
L	L	L	17	*abc*
H	L	L	25	*Abc*
L	H	L	19	*aBc*
L	L	H	26	*abC*
H	H	L	21	*ABc*
H	L	H	85	*AbC*
L	H	H	16	*aBC*
H	H	H	128	*ABC*

$$A = \frac{1}{4n'}[Abc + AbC + ABc + ABC - abc - abC - aBc - aBC] = 45$$

$$B = \frac{1}{4n'}[aBc + aBC + ABc + ABC - abc - abC - Abc - AbC] = 8$$

$$C = \frac{1}{4n'}[abC + aBC + AbC + ABC - abc - aBc - Abc - ABc] = 43$$

$$AB = \frac{1}{4n'}[abc + abC + ABc + ABC - Abc - aBc - AbC - aBC] = 12$$

$$AC = \frac{1}{4n'}[abc + aBc + AbC + ABC - abC - aBC - Abc - ABc] = 40$$

$$BC = \frac{1}{4n'}[abc + Abc + aBC + ABC - abC - aBc - ABc - AbC] = 9$$

$$ABC = \frac{1}{4n'}[abC + aBc + Abc + ABC - ABc - AbC - aBC - abc] = 15$$

(b) **Main Effects Plot—Data Means for Relative Life**

(c) **Interaction Plot—Data Means for Relative Life**

(d)

Normal Probability Plot for Main Effects and Interactions

ML Estimates—95% CI

ML Estimates
Mean 24.5357
StDev 16.1087

Goodness of Fit
AD * 2.119

(e) From the graph it appears that all factors and their combinations have significant effects on the relative life of the bearings.

(f)

Analysis of Variance for Relative

Source	DF	SS	MS	F	P
Ring osc	1	4095	4095	3.99	0.116
Cage des	1	120	120	0.12	0.749
Heat tre	1	3741	3741	3.65	0.129
Error	4	4105	1026		
Total	7	12061			

There are no significant factors.

(g) Factors *A* (ring osculation) and *C* (heat treatment) are significant.

11. (a)

Relative Volatility	Bottom Composition	Top Composition	Feed Composition	Measured Efficiency	Notation
1.1	0.005	0.70	0.3	88	*abcd*
2.0	0.005	0.70	0.3	11	*Abcd*
1.1	0.200	0.70	0.3	31	*aCcd*
1.1	0.005	0.99	0.3	138	*abCd*
1.1	0.005	0.70	0.6	84	*abcD*
2.0	0.200	0.70	0.3	4	*ABcd*
2.0	0.005	0.99	0.3	18	*AbCd*
2.0	0.005	0.70	0.6	12	*AbcD*
1.1	0.200	0.99	0.3	80	*aBCd*
1.1	0.200	0.70	0.6	31	*aBcD*
1.1	0.005	0.99	0.6	138	*abCD*
2.0	0.200	0.99	0.3	11	*ABCd*
2.0	0.200	0.70	0.6	4	*ABcD*
2.0	0.005	0.99	0.6	19	*AbCD*
1.1	0.200	0.99	0.6	85	*aBCD*
2.0	0.200	0.99	0.6	11	*ABCD*

Factors	Main Effect
A	73.125
B	31.375
C	29.375
D	0.387
AB	23.875
AC	22.375
AD	0.158
BC	0.158
BD	0.880
CD	1.129
ABC	0.158
ABD	1.378
ACD	1.129
BCD	0.158
ABCD	0.158

(b)

Main Effects Plot—Data Means for Measured Efficiency

(c)

Interaction Plot—Data Means for Measured Efficiency

(d)
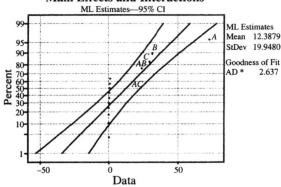
Normal Probability Plot for Main Effects and Interactions

(e) There are significant effects of A, B, C, AB and AC.

(f)

Analysis of Variance for Measured

Source	DF	SS	MS	F	P
Relative	1	21389.1	21389.1	54.67	0.000
Bottom c	1	3937.6	3937.6	10.06	0.009
Top comp	1	3451.6	3451.6	8.82	0.013
Feed com	1	0.6	0.6	0.00	0.970
Error	11	4303.7	391.2		
Total	15	33082.4			

The single factors A, B, and C have significant effects for the 0.05 significance level. Factor D is not significant at this level.

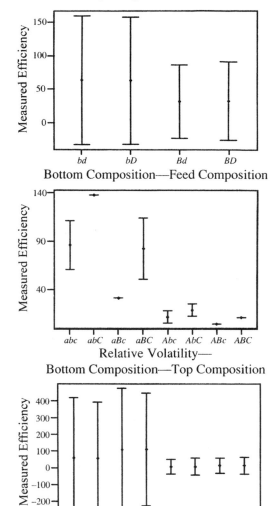

(g) The effects of *BC* and *ABC* are significant.

13. (a)

Balls	C. D.	G.	A.G.	A. life	A	B	C	D	AB + CD	AC + BD	AD + AD
S	S	S	N	0.31	a	b	c	d	+	+	+
M	M	S	N	2.17	A	B	c	d	+	–	–
M	S	M	N	1.37	A	b	C	d	–	+	–
M	S	S	L	1.38	A	b	c	D	–	–	+
S	M	M	N	0.92	a	B	C	d	–	–	+
S	M	S	L	0.73	a	B	c	D	–	+	–
S	S	M	L	0.95	a	b	C	D	+	–	–
M	M	M	L	2.57	A	B	C	D	+	+	+

Factors	Main Effect
A	1.145
B	0.595
C	0.305
D	0.215
AB + CD	0.400
AC + BD	–0.110
AD + BC	–0.010

(b)

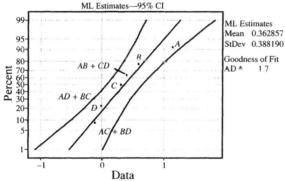

Normal Probability Plot for Main Effects and Interactions

ML Estimates—95% CI

ML Estimates
Mean 0.362857
StDev 0.388190

Goodness of Fit
AD *   1 7

(c) Factors *A* and *B* cause significant effects.

(d)   **Interaction Plot—Data Means for Average Life**

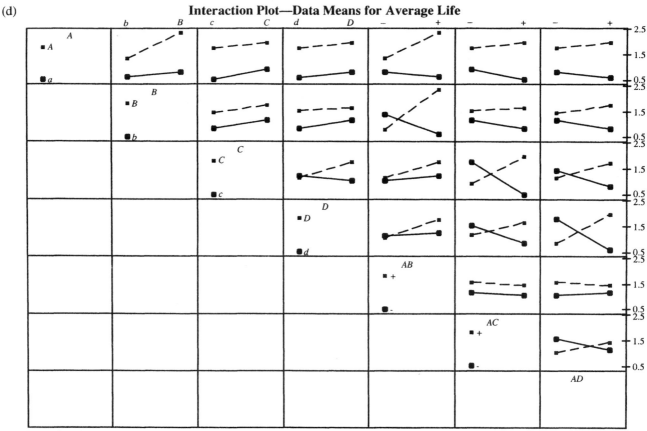

(e) Modified balls have an average life that is 1.14 higher than that of standard balls. A modified cage design resulted in and average life that is 0.60 higher than the standard cage design. There is no reason to suspect important interaction effects.

15. (a)

L.	P.	B.	R.	Score	A	B	C	D	AB + CD	AC + BD	AD + AD
75	0	0	N	89	a	b	c	d	+	+	+
100	5	0	N	87	A	B	c	d	+	−	−
100	0	2	N	71	A	b	C	d	−	+	−
100	0	0	Y	78	A	b	c	D	−	−	+
75	5	2	N	68	a	B	C	d	−	−	+
75	5	0	Y	76	a	B	c	D	−	+	−
75	0	2	Y	68	a	b	C	D	+	−	−
100	5	2	Y	67	A	B	C	D	+	+	+

Factors	Main effect
A	0.5
B	−2.0
C	−14.0
D	−6.5
AB + CD	4.5
AC + BD	0.5
AD + BC	0.0

(b)

**Normal Probability Plot for
Main Effects and Interactions**

(c) Single factors (C, D and B) are significant. The combination factor $AB + CD$ is also significant.

(d)

Interaction Plot—Data Means for Score

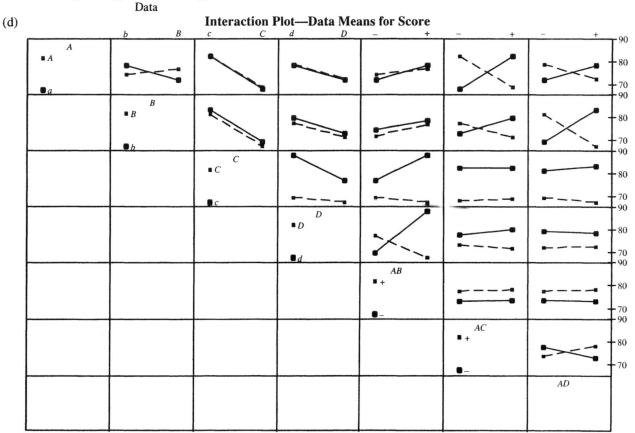

(e) Consumption of two cans of beer reduced the average score by 13.5. Playing the radio reduced the average score by 7. The interaction of lighting and practice time and/or beer consumption and radio playing seems important, but these two interactions cannot be separated by this fractional factorial design.

17. (a)

```
Fractional Factorial Fit: Yield of Oil versus CO2 Pressure; CO2 Temperature; ...

Estimated Effects and Coefficients for Yield (coded units)
Term                     Effect      Coef
Constant                            54.25
CO2 pres                   7.50       3.75
CO2 temp                  19.75       9.87
peanut m                   1.25       0.63
CO2 flow                  -0.00      -0.00
Peanut p                 -44.50     -22.25
CO2 pres*CO2 temp          5.25       2.63
CO2 pres*peanut m          1.25       0.62
CO2 pres*CO2 flow         -4.00      -2.00
CO2 pres*Peanut p         -7.00      -3.50
CO2 temp*peanut m          3.00       1.50
CO2 temp*CO2 flow         -1.75      -0.88
CO2 temp*Peanut p         -0.25      -0.13
peanut m*CO2 flow          2.25       1.12
peanut m*Peanut p          6.25       3.13
CO2 flow*Peanut p         -3.50      -1.75
```

(b) **Normal Probability Plot of the Effects**
(response is yield of, $\alpha = 0.10$)

A: CO_2 pressure
B: CO_2 temperature
C: Peanut moisture
D: CO_2 flow rate
E: Peanut particle size

(c) Factors *B* and *E* appear significant.

(d) **Interaction Plot—Data Means for Yield of Oil**

(e) Factors *B* and *E* are significant. The highest responses occur when the carbon dioxide pressure is high and the peanut particle size is low.

19. (a)

Treatment	Signal-to-Noise Ratio
(1)	15.644
a	4.425
b	20.491
ab	15.317

(b) Treatment combination b, consisting of receiver R^2 and amplifier B provides the highest signal to noise ratio.

(c) Results are the same.

21. Note: With the data provided in file *photo* MINITAB crashes. It produces the following error message: ** *Error* ** *One or more response is zero or negative. "Larger is Better" signal to noise ratio can not be calculated; execution aborted.*

The simplest thing to do is to compute the signal-to-noise ratios without using the software with the appropriate formula.

See Table (larger is better) on Problem 4.

$$SN_L = -10\log_{10}\frac{\sum_{i=1}^{n}\left(\frac{1}{Y_i}\right)^2}{n}0$$

23. (a)

Design	Weight	Size	SN_L
S	L	S	47.7
C	L	S	44.0
S	H	S	46.3
S	L	L	46.0
C	H	S	42.1
C	L	L	47.6
S	H	L	47.1
C	H	L	47.7

(b)–(c) There is no significant difference in SN_L values for various factor combinations. Worst combinations are CHS and CLS.

(d) The Taguchi approach does not contradict ANOVA, but it is less sensitive.

25. The randomized block design model deals with only *one* factor and matched items. The two-factor factorial design model evaluates the effects of *two* factors simultaneously.

27. To determine the interaction between the levels of factors V_i and V_j, $V_i \ne V_j$, $V_i, V_J \in \{A, B, C\}$ it is necessary to calculate test statistic $F = \dfrac{MSV_iV_j}{MSE}$ and compare it with critical value $F_{cr} = F_U(\alpha, df_1 df_2)$, where $df_1 = (l_i - 1)(l_j - 1)$, $df_2 = ijk(n' - 1)$, l_i is the number of levels of factor V_i, and l_j is the number of levels of factor V_j. Decision rule: Reject H_0 if $F > F_{cr}$. To determine the interaction between all three factors it is necessary to consider test statistic $F = \dfrac{MSABC}{MSE}$ and compare it with $F_{cr} = F_U(\alpha, df_1 df_2)$, where $df_1 = (i - 1)(j - 1)(k - 1)$, $df_2 = ilk(n' - 1)$, and i, j, k are numbers of levels of factors A, B, C, respectively. Decision rule: Reject H_0 if $F > F_{cr}$.

29. One-way design considers independent observations for various levels of only one factor. Two-way design deals with independent observations for various levels of two factors. In these cases the number of observations is not less than the number of all factor level combinations. Fractional factorial design considers binary factors only, but it is possible to analyze one or two more additional factors than for a standard factorial design.

31. In a fractional design, some of the effects are confounded with each other; that is, one cannot estimate all of the effects separately. For example, if factor A is confounded with a three-way interaction BCD, then the estimated effect for A also includes any effect due to interaction BCD. Effects that are confounded are said to be aliased. The alias structure describes the confounding that occurs in a design.

33. Inner arrays, or controllable factors should be the focus in the process improvement study. Outer arrays, or noise factors are environmental and represent conditions under which the product is expected to perform.

35. The Taguchi approach provides an advantage in quality engineering in that it leads to products that are robust against environmental variation and that are less sensitive to unit-to-unit variation. Some of the disadvantages to the Taguchi approach are summarized as follows: (1) Often fractional designs used with the Taguchi approach are Resolution III designs that contain a complicated confounding structure in which main effects are comfounded with simple two-factor interactions. Such designs may provide misleading results in circumstances when there is a lack of extensive experience with the process or when these designs are used without sufficient awareness of the design assumptions and limitations. (2) Implication that the separation of location and dispersion effects can always be accomplished merely by using a log transformation does not always seem right. The argument could be made that situations may exist in which a different transformation (or no transformation) is needed to obtain this separation. (3) The signal-to-noise ratio is often criticized over its complexity and inefficiency. Also, there are some problems with local and asymptotic properties of the SN estimators.

37.

Two-way ANOVA: Displacement versus Intensity; Location

```
Analysis of Variance for Displace
Source        DF       SS        MS        F        P
Intensity      2   0.004744  0.002372     7.35    0.005
Location       2   0.259926  0.129963   402.60    0.000
Interaction    4   0.000242  0.000060     0.19    0.942
Error         18   0.005811  0.000323
Total         26   0.270722
```

(a) $H_0: \mu_{860} = \mu_{1041} = \mu_{1246}$, H_1: At least one of the means is different.
Decision rule: Reject H_0, if $F > 3.55$. Test statistic: $F = 7.35$. Decision: Because $F > 3.55$, reject H_0. The effect of the clamp actuation intensity is significant for the 0.05 significance level.

(b) $H_0: \mu_1 = \mu_2 = \mu_3$, H_1: At least of the means is different.
Decision rule: Reject H_0, if $F > 3.55$. Test statistic: $F = 412.60$. Decision: Because $F > 3.55$, reject H_0. The location is a significant factor.

(c) H_0: There is no interaction between the clamp actuation intensity and location.
H_1: There is an interaction between the clamp actuation intensity and location.
Decision rule: Reject H_0 if $F > 2.93$. Test statistic: $F = 0.19$. Decision: Because $F < 2.93$, do not reject H_0. There is no significant interaction between the clamp actuation intensity and location.

(d)

```
                           Individual 95% CI
Intensity      Mean    --------+---------+---------+---------+---
  890        0.1965    (-------*-------)
 1041        0.2104          (-------*--------)
 1246        0.2289                       (--------*-------)
                       --------+---------+---------+---------+---
                          0.1950    0.2100    0.2250    0.2400
```

```
                           Individual 95% CI
location        Mean    ---------+---------+---------+---------+--
1             0.1453    (-*-)
2             0.3506                                    (-*--)
3             0.1398    (-*-)
                        ---------+---------+---------+---------+--
                          0.1800    0.2400    0.3000    0.3600
```

(e) The clamp actuation intensity, and the location of the fixture are both significant factors at a 0.05 significance level. There is no significant interaction between the clamp actuation intensity and location. Placing the clamp at a location of 1 or 3 with an intensity of 890 gives the lowest displacements.

39.

Penetration Rate

```
Analysis of Variance for penetration.
Source                  DF        SS        MS       F       P
Rake ang                 1     94.58     94.58    5.23   0.052
Thrust                   1    280.73    280.73   15.52   0.004
Speed                    1    121.00    121.00    6.69   0.032
Rake ang*Thrust          1     55.95     55.95    3.09   0.117
Rake ang*Speed           1      0.78      0.78    0.04   0.840
Thrust*Speed             1      4.14      4.14    0.23   0.645
Rake ang*Thrust*Speed    1      6.76      6.76    0.37   0.558
Error                    8    144.74     18.09
Total                   15    708.68
```

(a) There is no significant effect due to rake angle for the 0.05 significance level.
(b) There is significant effect due to thrust for the 0.05 significance level.
(c) There is significant effect due to speed for the 0.05 significance level.
(d) There are no significant factor interactions.

(e) **Main Effects Plot—Data Means for Penetration**

(f) **Interaction Plot—Data Means for Penetration**

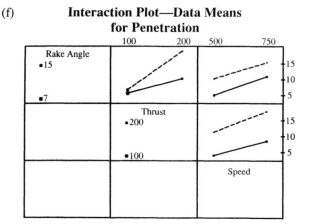

(g)

Estimated Effects and Coefficients for Penetration (coded units)					
Term	Effect	Coef	SE Coef	T	P
Constant		10.4075	1.063	9.79	0.000
Rake ang	4.8625	2.4313	1.063	2.29	0.052
Thrust	8.3775	4.1887	1.063	3.94	0.004
Speed	5.5000	2.7500	1.063	2.59	0.032
Rake ang*Thrust	3.7400	1.8700	1.063	1.76	0.117
Rake ang*Speed	−0.4425	−0.2212	1.063	−0.21	0.840
Thrust*Speed	1.0175	0.5088	1.063	0.48	0.645
Rake ang*Thrust*Speed	1.3000	0.6500	1.063	0.61	0.558

(h)

Normal Probability Plot of the Standardized Effects
(response is penetration, $\alpha = 0.05$)

(i)   There are significant effects due to all factors and interactions. Speed and thrust levels are most significant.

(j)   The ANOVA results indicate that none of the interaction factors are significant and that there is no significant effect due to the rake angle. Both the ANOVA results and the probability table agree that the thrust and speed are the most significant factors. Therefore, there are no significant differences in the results of parts (a)–(d) and part (i). It is important to note that the significance level used affects whether an effect is found to be significant.

(k)

```
Analysis of Means


     Summary Table
     Contents: number of nonmissing data cell mean
Rows: Rake ang      Columns:   Speed
            500         750       All
    7        4           4         8
             5.005     10.948    7.976
    15       4           4         8
            10.310     15.368   12.839
  All        8           8        16
             7.658     13.158   10.408
Rows: Rake ang      Columns:   Thrust
            100         200       All
    7        4           4         8
             5.658     10.295    7.976
    15       4           4         8
             6.780     18.898   12.839
  All        8           8        16
             6.219     14.596   10.408
Rows: Thrust        Columns:   Speed
            500         750       All
  100        4           4         8
             3.978      8.460    6.219
  200        4           4         8
            11.338     17.855   14.596
  All        8           8        16
             7.658     13.157   10.407
```

The highest penetration rate corresponds to rake angle of 15, a thrust of 200 and a speed of 750.

(l)

Rake Angle	Thrust	Speed	SN_L
7	100	500	3.4
7	100	750	16.3
7	200	500	17.3
7	200	750	18.5
15	100	500	14.7
15	100	750	18.0
15	200	500	23.5
15	200	750	27.0

(m) The highest SN_L corresponds to a rank angle of 15°, 200 pounds of thrust, and a speed of 750 rpm; the same as in part (k).

(n) The best choice would be a rake angle of 15°, a thrust of 200 pounds and a speed of 750 rpm.

(o) Conclusions for parts (n) and (k) are the same.

Torque

```
Analysis of Variance for Torque
Source                   DF        SS        MS       F        P
Rake ang                  1      18.1      18.1    0.10    0.757
Thrust                    1    6045.1    6045.1   34.29    0.000
Speed                     1     315.1     315.1    1.79    0.218
Rake ang*Thrust           1      10.6      10.6    0.06    0.813
Rake ang*Speed            1      68.1      68.1    0.39    0.552
Thrust*Speed              1     217.6     217.6    1.23    0.299
Rake ang*Thrust*Speed     1      52.6      52.6    0.30    0.600
Error                     8    1410.5     176.3
Total                    15    8137.4
```

(a) There is no significant effect due to rake angle.
(b) There is a significant effect due to thrust.
(c) There is no significant effect due to speed.
(d) There are no significant factor interactions.

(e)

Main Effects Plot—Data Means for Torque

(f)

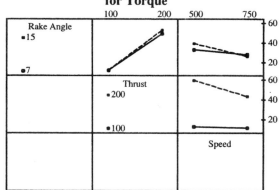

Interaction Plot—Data Means for Torque

(g) **Estimated Effects and Coefficients for Torque (coded units)**

```
Term                    Effect      Coef    SE Coef        T        P
Constant                          31.688      3.320     9.55    0.000
Rake ang                 2.125     1.062      3.320     0.32    0.757
Thrust                  38.875    19.438      3.320     5.86    0.000
Speed                   -8.875    -4.438      3.320    -1.34    0.218
Rake ang*Thrust          1.625     0.813      3.320     0.24    0.813
Rake ang*Speed          -4.125    -2.063      3.320    -0.62    0.552
Thrust*Speed            -7.375    -3.687      3.320    -1.11    0.299
Rake ang*Thrust*Speed   -3.625    -1.813      3.320    -0.55    0.600
```

(h)

(i) There is a significant effect of factor B (Thrust).

(j) Results of parts (a)–(d) and part (i) are the same.

(k) The only significant factor is the thrust level, which should be set at 100 pounds.

(l)

Rake Angle	Thrust	Speed	SN_S
7	100	500	−21.9
7	100	750	−23.1
7	200	500	−34.7
7	200	750	−33.8
15	100	500	−23.5
15	100	750	−21.3
15	200	500	−36.4
15	200	750	−32.3

(m) Significantly higher SN_S values correspond to 100 thrust and 750 or 500 speed levels.

(n) It will be reasonable to recommend 15 (rake angle), 100 (thrust), and 750 (speed) levels.

(o) Results of parts (k)–(n) does not contradict each other.

41. Answers will vary.   **43.** Answers will vary.

chapter 12

Simple Linear Regression and Correlation

1. (a) The Y-intercept, b_0, indicates that when $X = 0$, the expected valued of Y is 2.

(b) The slope b_1 indicates that for a one unit increase in X the expected change in Y is 5 units.

(c) $\hat{Y} = 2 + 5 = 2 + 5(3) = 17$

(d) (1) yes   (2) no   (3) no   (4) yes   (5) no

3.   **Regression Analysis for Film**   (a) Linear trend, Better result – logarithmic trend

Regression Analysis for Film

(b) Regression Analysis

Regression Statistics	
Multiple R	0.738
R^2	0.544
Adjusted R^2	0.509
Standard Error	171.794
Observations	15.000

ANOVA

	df	SS	MS	F	Significance F
Regression	1.000	458161.080	458161.080	15.524	0.002
Residual	13.000	383672.240	29513.249		
Total	14.000	841833.330			

	Coefficients	Standard Error	t Stat	p-value	Lower 95%	Upper 95%
Intercept	770.433	133.928	5.753	6.681×10^{-05}	481.099	1059.767
Distance	19.969	5.068	3.940	0.002	9.020	30.919

(c) The slope, b_1 represents the expected change in Y (19.969) per unit change in X.

(d) $\hat{Y}(20) = 770.43 + 19.969 \times 20 = 1169.81$

(e) (1) Regression Analysis

Regression Statistics	
Multiple R	0.853
R^2	0.728
Adjusted R^2	0.707
Standard Error	185.289
Observations	15.000

ANOVA

	df	SS	MS	F	Significance F
Regression	1.000	1192184.100	1192184.100	34.725	5.298×10^{-5}
Residual	13.000	446315.850	34331.989		
Total	14.000	1638500.000			

	Coefficients	Standard Error	t Stat	p-value	Lower 95%	Upper 95%
Intercept	531.835	144.4484	3.682	0.003	219.774	843.897
Distance	32.212	5.466	5.893	5.298×10^{-5}	20.403	44.022

(2) The slope (distance) by represents the expected change in Y (32.212) per unit change in X.

(3) $\hat{Y}(20) = 531.835 + 32.212 \times 20 = 1176.075$

5. (a) **Regression Analysis for Hardness**

(b) Regression Analysis

Regression Statistics	
Multiple R	0.679
R^2	0.461
Adjusted R^2	0.445
Standard Error	3.048
Observations	35.000

ANOVA

	df	SS	MS	F	Significance F
Regression	1.000	262.560	262.560	28.258	7.265×10^{-6}
Residual	33.000	306.624	9.292		
Total	34.000	569.184			

	Coefficients	Standard Error	t Stat	p-value	Lower 95%	Upper 95%
Intercept	15.055	2.953	5.098	1.381×10^{-5}	9.047	21.062
Tensile Strength	0.228	0.043	5.316	7.265×10^{-6}	0.141	0.316

(c) The slope, b_1 represents the expected change in Y (0.22847) per unit change in X.

(d) $\hat{Y}(70) = 15.1 + 0.228 \times 70 = 31.0$

7. (a)

Regression Analysis for Pumpkin

(b) Regression Analysis

Regression Statistics	
Multiple R	0.968
R^2	0.937
Adjusted R^2	0.934
Standard Error	3.260
Observations	23.000

ANOVA

	df	SS	MS	F	Significance F
Regression	1.000	3334.239	3334.239	313.650	4.203×10^{-14}
Residual	21.000	223.239	10.630		
Total	22.000	3557.478			

	Coefficients	Standard Error	t Stat	p-value	Lower 95%	Upper 95%
Intercept	33.293	1.372	24.272	7.566×10^{-17}	30.440	36.145
Circumference	0.011	0.001	17.710	4.203×10^{-14}	0.010	0.013

(c) The slope (circumference) represents the expected change in Y (0.0114) per unit change in X.

(d) $X = 60$ does not fall within the range of X, so it is incorrect to use the regression equation for this prediction.

(e) Because circumference is such a strong predictor of weight, the farmer might want to sell the pumpkins on the basis of circumference.

9. $SST = SSR + SSE$; $SSR = 120$, $SST \geq 0$, then $SST \geq 120$ and $SST \neq 110$.

11. (a) $SST = 238035858$, $SSR = 235668542$, $r^2 = \dfrac{235668542}{238035858} = 0.9900547$. 99% of the variation is explained by the independent variable in the regression model.

(b) $S_{XY} = \sqrt{\dfrac{SSE}{n-2}} = \sqrt{\dfrac{2367315}{17}} = 373.167$

(c) Based on the large r^2 value, one can conclude that the regression model is adequate for predicting the actual frequency of a generator.

13. (a) $SSR = 437.64447$, $SST = 449.76$, $r^2 = \dfrac{437.644}{449.76} = 0.973$. 97.3% of the variation is explained by the independent variable in the regression model.

(b) $S_{XY} = \sqrt{\dfrac{SSE}{n-2}} = \sqrt{\dfrac{12.115529}{23}} = 0.726$

(c) Based on the large r^2 value, one can conclude that the regression model is adequate for predicting the weight of the mail received.

15. A stratification pattern exists due to the decreasing variation in the data.

17. (a)–
(b)

The homoscedasticity and independence assumptions both appear to be valid. The assumption of normality appears to be valid. Gaussian simple linear regression is adequate.

19. (a)–
(b)

The homoscedasticity and independence assumptions both appear to be valid. The assumption of normality appears to be valid. The Gaussian simple linear regression is adequate.

21. (a)–
(b)

The homoscedasticity and independence assumptions both appear to be valid.

The assumption of normality appears to be valid. The Gaussian simple linear regression is adequate.

23. (a) $H_0: \beta_1 = 0$, $H_1: \beta_1 \neq 0$

Test statistic: $t = 41.138$, p-value is 1.8×10^{-18}. Decision: Because the p-value is less than 0.05, reject the null hypothesis. There is a significant linear relationship between X and Y.

(b) $b_1 \pm t_{n-2} S_{b_1} = 1.081 \pm t_{17} 0.026 = 1.081 \pm 2.110 \cdot 0.026 = 1.081 \pm 0.055$, $P(1.026 \leq \beta_1 \leq 1.137) \approx 0.95$. The confidence interval constructed above does not include zero, so the linear dependence of Y on X is significant.

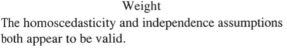

25. (a) $H_0: \beta_1 = 0$, $H_1: \beta_1 \neq 0$

Test statistic: $t = 28.824$, p-value is 1.48×10^{-19}. Decision: Because the p-value is less than 0.05, reject the null hypothesis. There is a significant linear relationship between X and Y.

(b) $b_1 \pm t_{n-2} S_{b_1} = 0.030 \pm t_{23} 0.001 = 0.030 \pm 2.069 \cdot 0.001 = 0.030 \pm 0.002$, $P(0.028 \leq \beta_1 \leq 0.032) \approx 0.95$. The confidence interval constructed above does not include zero, so the linear dependence of Y on X is significant.

27. (a) $h = \dfrac{1}{n} + \dfrac{(X_0 - \overline{X})^2}{\sum_{i=1}^{n} (X_i - \overline{X})^2} = \dfrac{1}{20} + \dfrac{(2-2)^2}{20} = 0.05$. 95% confidence interval of the population average response:

$\hat{Y} \pm t_{18} S_{XY} \sqrt{h} = 11 \pm 2.100 \cdot 1 \cdot \sqrt{0.05} = 11 \pm 0.470$, $P(10.53 \leq \mu_{XY} \leq 11.470) \approx 0.95$

(b) 95% prediction interval of the individual response: $\hat{Y} \pm t_{18} S_{XY} \sqrt{1+h} = 11 \pm 2.101 \cdot 1 \cdot \sqrt{1.05} = 11 \pm 2.153$, $P(8.847 \leq Y_i \leq 13.153) \approx 0.95$

(c) $h = \dfrac{1}{n} + \dfrac{(X_0 - \overline{X})^2}{\sum_{i=1}^{n} (X_i - \overline{X})^2} = \dfrac{1}{20} + \dfrac{(4-2)^2}{20} = 0.25$. 95% confidence interval of the population average response:

$\hat{Y} \pm t_{18} S_{XY} \sqrt{h} = 17 \pm 2.101 \cdot 1 \cdot \sqrt{0.25} = 17 \pm 1.050$, $P(15.950 \leq \mu_{XY} \leq 18.050) \approx 0.95$

(d) 95% prediction interval of the individual response: $\hat{Y} \pm t_{18} S_{XY} \sqrt{1+h} = 17 \pm 2.101 \cdot 1 \cdot \sqrt{1.25} = 17 \pm 2.349$, $P(14.651 \leq Y_i \leq 19.349) \approx 0.95$

(e) The intervals for parts (c) and (d) are wider than parts (a) and (b) because point X is farther away from the central point, $\overline{X}$.

29.

Confidence Interval Estimate		For Average Predicted $Y\left(\hat{Y}\right)$	
X Value	3000.000	Interval Half Width	180.770
Confidence Level	95%	Confidence Interval Lower Limit	2973.623
Sample Size	19.000	Confidence Interval Upper Limit	3335.163
Degrees of Freedom	17.000		
t Value	2.110	For Individual Response Y	
Sample Mean	3131.579	Interval Half Width	807.801
Sum of Squared Difference	201521052.630	Prediction Interval Lower Limit	2346.592
Standard Error of the Estimate	373.167	Prediction Interval Upper Limit	3962.195
h Statistic	0.053		
Average Predicted $Y\left(\hat{Y}\right)$	3154.393		

(a) 95% confidence interval of the population average response: $\hat{Y} \pm t_{17} S_{XY} \sqrt{h} = 3154 \pm 181$, $P(2974 \leq \mu_{XY} \leq 3335) \approx 0.95$

(b) 95% prediction interval of the individual response: $\hat{Y} \pm t_{17} S_{XY} \sqrt{1+h} = 3154 \pm 808$, $P(2347 \leq Y_i \leq 3962) \approx 0.95$

(c) The prediction interval is wider than the confidence interval, because variations in the predicted individual values are wider than in the predicted average values.

31.

Confidence Interval Estimate	
X Value	500.000
Confidence Level	95%
Sample Size	25.000
Degrees of Freedom	23.000
t Value	2.069
Sample Mean	438.640
Sum of Squared Difference	496055.760
Standard Error of the Estimate	0.726
h Statistic	0.048
Average Predicted Y $\left(\hat{Y} \right)$	15.043

For Average Predicted Y $\left(\hat{Y} \right)$	
Interval Half Width	0.328
Confidence Interval Lower Limit	14.715
Confidence Interval Upper Limit	15.370

For Individual Response Y	
Interval Half Width	1.537
Prediction Interval Lower Limit	13.506
Prediction Interval Upper Limit	16.579

(a) 95% confidence interval of the population average response: $\hat{Y} \pm t_{23} S_{XY} \sqrt{h} = 15.0 \pm 0.328$,

   $P(14.7 \le \mu_{XY} \le 15.4) \approx 0.95$

(b) 95% prediction interval of the individual response: $\hat{Y} \pm t_{23} S_{XY} \sqrt{1+h} = 15.0 \pm 1.54$, $P(13.5 \le Y_i \le 16.6) \approx 0.95$

(c) The prediction interval is wider than the confidence interval, because variations in the predicted individual values are wider than in the predicted average values.

33. $r = +\sqrt{r^2} = +\sqrt{0.81} = 0.9$

35. $r^2 = \dfrac{SSR}{SST} = 1$, $r < 0$, $r = -1$

37. (a) $r = 0.543$

(b) $H_0: \rho = 0$, $H_1: \rho \ne 0$

Decision rule: Reject H_0 if $|t| > t_{14} = 2.1448$.

Test statistic: $t = \dfrac{r}{\sqrt{\left(1 - r^2\right)/(n - 2)}} = \dfrac{0.543}{\sqrt{0.705/14}} = 2.42$. Decision: Because $t > 2.14$, reject the null hypothesis.

There is a significant linear relationship between X and Y for the 0.05 significance level.

(c) Part (a) provides $r > 0$, and part (b) provides the significance of r. Therefore, there is a significant positive relationship between rainfall depth and runoff depth for the 0.05 significance level.

39. (a) $r = 0.992$

(b) $H_0: \rho = 0$, $H_1: \rho \ne 0$

Decision rule: Reject H_0 if $|t| > t_9 = 2.26$. Test statistic: $t = \dfrac{r}{\sqrt{\left(1 - r^2\right)/(n - 2)}} = \dfrac{0.992}{\sqrt{0.0161/9}} = 23.4$. Decision:

Because $|t| > 2.26$, reject H_0. There is a significant linear relationship between X and Y for the 0.05 significance level.

(c) Because there is a large significant correlation between the non-destructive and the destructive methods, it is not appropriate to consider the initial samples as independent. The paired test is more appropriate than the t test for this application.

41. (a) $r = 0.738$

(b) $H_0: \rho = 0$, $H_1: \rho \ne 0$

Decision rule: Reject H_0 if $|t| > t_{13} = 2.160$.

Test statistic: $t = \dfrac{r}{\sqrt{\left(1 - r^2\right)/(n - 2)}} = \dfrac{0.738}{\sqrt{0.456/13}} = 3.940$. Decision: Because $|t| > 2.160$, reject H_0.

There is a significant linear relationship between X and Y for the 0.05 significance level.

(c) Due to the linear dependence of $b_1 = \rho \sqrt{\dfrac{SSX}{SSY}}$, the two tests in problem 22 (a) and problem 41 (b) must give the same results for the same level.

43. (a) $r = 0.679$

(b) $H_0: \rho = 0$, $H_1: \rho \neq 0$

Decision rule: Reject H_0 if $|t| > t_{33} = 2.035$. Test statistic: $t = \dfrac{r}{\sqrt{(1-r^2)/(n-2)}} = \dfrac{0.679}{\sqrt{0.539/33}} = 5.32$. Decision:

Because $|t| > 2.03$, reject H_0. There is a significant linear relationship between X and Y for the 0.05 significance level.

(c) Due to the linear dependence $b_1 = \rho \sqrt{\dfrac{SSX}{SSY}}$ the two tests in problem 24 (a) and problem 43 (b) must give the same results for the same level .

45. (a) $r = 0.9681$

(b) $H_0: \rho = 0$, $H_1: \rho \neq 0$

Decision rule: Reject H_0 if $|t| > t_{21} = 2.0796$. Test statistic: $t = \dfrac{r}{\sqrt{(1-r^2)/(n-2)}} = \dfrac{0.968}{\sqrt{0.063/21}} = 17.7$. Decision:

Because $|t| > 2.080$, reject H_0. There is evidence of a linear relationship between X and Y for the 0.05 significance level.

(c) Due to the linear dependence of $b_1 = \rho \sqrt{\dfrac{SSX}{SSY}}$, the two tests 12.26 (a) and 12.45 (b) must give the same results for the same level.

47. The coefficient of determination measures the proportion of the variation that is explained by the independent variable in the regression model.

49. SSR $= 0$ for all $\hat{Y}_i = \overline{Y}$, $1 \leq i \leq n$.

51. Assumptions of regression analysis:

(1) Normality of error. It is possible to check the validity of this assumption by constructing the residual normal probability plot.

(2) Homoscedasticity. It is possible to check this assumption visually using the scatterplot.

(3) Independence of error. It is possible to check this assumption visually using the scatterplot and the residual plot.

53. (a)

(b)

(1) Different samples provide different scatter diagrams. For example, part (a) shows that the study index is positive.

(2) The value $X = 31$ does not belong to the range of independent values.

(3) Regression Analysis

Regression Statistics	
Multiple R	0.641
R^2	0.411
Adjusted R^2	0.381
Standard Error	2.141
Observations	22.000

ANOVA

	df	SS	MS	F	Significance F
Regression	1.000	63.836	63.836	13.928	0.001
Residual	20.000	91.664	4.583		
Total	21.000	155.500			

	Coefficients	Standard Error	t Stat	p-value	Lower 95%	Upper 95%
Intercept	18.618	4.609	4.039	0.001	9.003	28.233
Distance	−0.247	0.066	−3.732	0.001	−0.385	−0.109

(c) **Regression Analysis of the O-Ring Damage**

(d) The points are not concentrated around the regression line, so a simple linear model is not appropriate for this data set.

(e)

There is evidence of a residual tendency, so a simple linear regression model is not adequate to describe this data set.

55. (a)

Regression Analysis for Height

$y = 2.6732x + 78.796$
$R^2 = 0.7288$

(b) Regression Analysis

Regression Statistics	
Multiple R	0.854
R^2	0.729
Adjusted R^2	0.715
Standard Error	24.749
Observations	21.000

ANOVA

	df	SS	MS	F	Significance F
Regression	1.000	31273.267	31273.267	51.059	8.598×10^{-7}
Residual	19.000	11637.400	612.495		
Total	20.000	42910.667			

	Coefficients	Standard Error	t Stat	p-value	Lower 95%	Upper 95%
Intercept	78.796	12.215	6.451	3.493×10^{-6}	53.230	104.362
Diameter at Breast Height	2.673	0.374	7.146	8.598×10^{-7}	1.890	3.456

(c) $\hat{Y} = 78.796 + 2.673 \times X$

(d) The intercept, 78.80, represents the average value of Y for $X = 0$. The slope, 2.673, represents the expected change in Y per unit change in X.

(e) $\hat{Y}(30) = 78.80 + 2.67 \times 30 = 158.99$

(f) $X = 4.0$ does not fall within to the range of X, so it is not appropriate to use the regression equation for the prediction of X.

(g) $r^2 = 0.729$, 72.88% of variation is explained by the independent variable in the regression model.

(h) $r = +\sqrt{r^2} = \sqrt{0.729} = 0.854$

(i) $S_{XY} = \sqrt{\dfrac{\text{SSE}}{n-2}} = 24.749$

(j) There is not any evidence of a pattern in the residuals.

(k)

Normal Probability Plot

Diameter at Breast Height Residual Plot

	Coefficients	Standard Error	t Stat	p-value	Lower 95%	Upper 95%
Intercept	78.796	12.215	6.451	3.493×10^{-6}	53.230	104.362
Diameter at Breast Height	2.673	0.374	7.146	8.598×10^{-7}	1.890	3.456

The constructed simple linear regression is significant, because the *p*-values are less than 0.05.

(1)	**Confidence Interval Estimate**	
X Value		30.000
Confidence Level		95%
Sample Size		2.000
Degrees of Freedom		1.000
t Value		2.093
Sample Mean		29.286
Sum of Squared Difference		4376.290
Standard Error of the Estimate		24.749
h Statistic		0.0477
Average Predicted Y $(\hat{Y})$		158.993

For Average Predicted Y $(\hat{Y})$	
Interval Half Width	11.317
Confidence Interval Lower Limit	147.675
Confidence Interval Upper Limit	170.310

For Individual Response Y	
Interval Half Width	53.021
Prediction Interval Lower Limit	105.971
Prediction Interval Upper Limit	212.014

95% confidence interval of the population average response: $\hat{Y} \pm t_{16} S_{XY} \sqrt{h} = 158.99 \pm 11.32$,

$P(147.68 \le \mu_{XY} \le 170.31) \approx 0.95$

(m) (See part (l)) 95% prediction interval for the individual response: $\hat{Y} \pm t_{16} S_{XY} \sqrt{h+1} = 158.99 \pm 53.02$,

$P(105.97 \le Y_i \le 212.01) \approx 0.95$

(n) (See part (b)) $P(1.89 < \beta_1 < 3.46) \approx 0.95$

(o) The height of the redwood can be successfully approximated by the linear dependence of height on the diameter at breast height. However, the definition of "diameter at breast height" is vague and would depend on the person making the measurement. A better parameter for the approximation would be "diameter at five feet above the ground".

57. (a) **Regression Analysis of the Serum Cholesterol**

Calcium Intake

(b) Regression Analysis

Regression Statistics	
Multiple R	0.001
R^2	9.126×10^{-7}
Adjusted R^2	–0.091
Standard Error	0.393
Observations	13.000

ANOVA

	df	SS	MS	F	Significance F
Regression	1.000	1547×10^{-6}	1547×10^{-6}	1.004×10^{-5}	0.998
Residual	11.000	1.695	0.154		
Total	12.000	1.695			

	Coefficients	Standard Error	t Stat	p-value	Lower 95%	Upper 95%
Intercept	6.185	0.260	23.742	8.430×10^{-11}	5.611	6.758
Diameter at Breast Height	-1.61×10^{-6}	0.001	–0.003	0.998	–0.001	0.001

(c) $\hat{Y} = 6.1846 - 1.61 \times 10^{-6} \times X$

(d) The intercept, 6.1846, represents the average value of Y for $X = 0$. The slope, 1.61×10^6, represents the expected change in Y per unit change in X.

(e) $\hat{Y}(500) = 6.18 - 1.61 \times 10^{-6} \times 500 = 6.18$

(f) $X = 1500$ does not fall within the range of X, so it is appropriate to use a regression equation for the prediction of X.

(g) $r^2 = 9.13 \times 10^{-7}$, 0.00009% of the variation is explained by the independent variable in the regression model.

(h) $r = -\sqrt{r^2} = -9.55 \times 10^{-4}$

(i) $S_{XY} = \sqrt{\dfrac{\text{SSE}}{n-2}} = 0.393$

(j)

The normality of error and independence assumptions appear to be valid. The homoscedasticity assumption appears to be invalid.

(k)

	Coefficients	Standard Error	t Stat	p-value	Lower 95%	Upper 95%
Intercept	6.185	0.260	23.742	8.430×10^{-11}	5.611	6.758
Calcium Intake	-1.61×10^{-6}	0.001	-0.003	0.998	-0.001	0.001

The constructed simple linear regression is not significant because the slope p-values are greater than 0.05.

(l)

Confidence Interval Estimate	
X Value	500.000
Confidence Level	95%
Sample Size	13.000
Degrees of Freedom	11.000
t Value	2.201
Sample Mean	465.615
Sum of Squared Difference	596617.080
Standard Error of the Estimate	0.393
h Statistic	0.079
Average Predicted Y $\left(\hat{Y}\right)$	6.184

For Average Predicted Y $\left(\hat{Y}\right)$	
Interval Half Width	0.243
Confidence Interval Lower Limit	5.941
Confidence Interval Upper Limit	6.427

For Individual Response Y	
Interval Half Width	0.898
Prediction Interval Lower Limit	5.286
Prediction Interval Upper Limit	7.081

95% confidence interval of the population average response: $\hat{Y} \pm t_{11} S_{XY} \sqrt{h} = 6.1838 \pm 0.243$,

$P(5.94 \leq \mu_{XY} \leq 6.43) \approx 0.95$

(m)   (See part (l)) 95% prediction interval of serum cholesterol: $P(5.286 \leq Y_i \leq 7.081) \approx 0.95$

(n)   (See part (b)) 95% confidence interval estimate of the population slope: $P(-0.00112 < \beta_1 < 0.00112) \approx 0.95$. The simple linear regression model is not significant because the interval includes zero.

59. (a)

Correlations	
pH	-0.271
Conductivity	0.204
TAMP	-0.173
TOC	0.185

(b) $H_0: \rho = 0$, $H_1: \rho \neq 0$

Decision rule: Reject H_0 if $|t| > t_{10} = 2.2281$. Test statistic: $t = \dfrac{r}{\sqrt{(1 - r^2)/(n - 2)}}$.

Correlation	Test statistic	Decision
PH	−0.891	Do not reject H_0
Conductivity	0.661	Do not reject H_0
TAMP	−0.556	Do not reject H_0
TOC	0.595	Do not reject H_0

There are no significant correlations for 0.05 significance level.

chapter 13

Multiple Regression

1. (a) When the effect of X_2 is held constant, the response variable Y is expected to increase on average by 5 units for each additional unit of X_1. When the effect of X_1 is held constant, the response variable Y is expected to increase on average by 3 units for each additional unit of X_2.

   (b) The Y-intercept, 10, represents the portion of the measurement of Y that is not affected by the factors measured by X_1 and X_2.

   (c) The computed coefficient of multiple determination means that 60% of the variation can be explained by the variations in the X_1 and X_2.

3. Regression Analysis

Regression Statistics	
Multiple R	0.906
R^2	0.821
Adjusted R^2	0.816
Standard Error	1.944
Observations	89.000

ANOVA

	df	SS	MS	F	Significance F
Regression	2.000	1485.519	742.760	196.615	8.318×10^{-33}
Residual	86.000	324.885	3.778		
Total	88.000	1810.405			

	Coefficients	Standard Error	t Stat	p-value	Lower 95%	Upper 95%
Intercept	50.018	4.384	11.408	6.757×10^{-19}	41.302	58.734
Weight	−0.007	0.001	−7.895	8.611×10^{-12}	−0.009	−0.006
Length	−0.019	0.037	−0.508	0.613	−0.092	0.055

(a) $\hat{Y}_i = 50.01886 - 0.00741 \times X_{1i} - 0.018776 \times X_{2i}$, Gas mileage $= 50.01886 - 0.007421 \times$ Weight $- 0.018776 \times$ Length

(b) Slope −0.007421 represents the expected change in gas mileage per unit change in weight. Slope −0.018776 represents the expected change in gas mileage per unit change in length.

(c) $\hat{Y}_i = 50.019 - 0.00742 \times 3000 - 0.0188 \times 195 = 24.095$

(d) $R^2_{Y.12} = 0.821$, 82.1% of the variation can be explained by the variations in the X_1 and X_2.

5. Regression Analysis

Regression Statistics	
Multiple R	0.791
R^2	0.625
Adjusted R^2	0.518
Standard Error	0.032
Observations	10.000

ANOVA

	df	SS	MS	F	Significance F
Regression	2.000	0.012	0.006	5.844	0.032
Residual	7.000	0.007	0.001		
Total	9.000	0.020			

	Coefficients	Standard Error	*t* Stat	*p*–value	Lower 95%	Upper 95%
Intercept	1.590	0.362	4.395	0.003	0.735	2.446
Lamp Output	–0.024	0.010	–2.320	0.053	–0.048	0.001
Lamp Temperature	–0.002	0.003	–0.640	0.542	–0.011	0.006

(a) $\hat{Y}_i = 1.5900851 - 0.02368 \times X_{1i} - 0.002239 \times X_{2i}$,
   $BEF = 1.5900851 - 0.02368 \times \text{Lamp Output} - 0.002239 \times \text{Lamp Temperature}$

(b) Holding constant the lamp temperature, for each increase of light output by one foot candle, the average *BEF* is predicted to decrease by 0.0237 foot candle. Holding constant the light output, for each increase in lamp temperature of one degree Celsius, the average *BEF* is predicted to decrease by 0.002 footcandle.

(c) $\hat{Y}_i = 1.5900851 - 0.0237 \times 40 - 0.00224 \times 40 = 0.5533251$

(d) $R^2_{Y.12} = 0.625$, 62.5% of the variation can be explained by the variations in X_1 and X_2.

7.

The multiple linear regression model appears to be adequate.

9.

The linear dependence of Y on X_1 is not adequate.

There are some doubts about the validity of the multiple linear regression model.

11. (a) $\text{MSR} = \dfrac{\text{SSR}}{p} = \dfrac{60}{2} = 30$, $\text{MSR} = \dfrac{\text{SSR}}{n-p-1} = \dfrac{120}{18} = 6.67$

(b) $F = \dfrac{\text{MSR}}{\text{MSE}} = \dfrac{30}{6.(6)} = 4.5$

(c) $H_0: \beta_1 = \beta_2 = 0$, $H_1: \beta_1^2 + \beta_2^2 > 0$

Decision rule: Reject H_0 if $F > 3.555$. Test statistic: $F = 4.5$. Decision: Because $F > 3.555$, reject H_0. There is a significant linear relationship between Y and X_1, X_2 for the 0.05 significance level.

13. (a) $H_0: \beta_1 = \beta_2 = 0$, $H_1: \beta_1^2 + \beta_2^2 > 0$

Decision rule: Reject H_0 if $F > 3.103$. Test statistic: $F = 196.6$. Decision: Because $F > 3.103$, reject H_0. There is a significant linear relationship between MPG and the two explanatory variables for the 0.05 significance level.

(b) The p-value of 8.31×10^{-33} is the probability of obtaining an F statistic of 196.6 or larger when H_0 is true.

(c) The multiple regression model is significant, so there is a significant dependence between Y, X_1, and X_2. For a more precise investigation, it is necessary to construct interval estimators for β_1 and β_2.

15. (a) $H_0: \beta_1 = \beta_2 = 0$, $H_1: \beta_1^2 + \beta_2^2 > 0$

Decision rule: Reject H_0 if $F > 4.737$. Test statistic: $F = 5.844$. Decision: Because $F > 4.737$, reject H_0. There is a significant linear relationship between the height of the redwood trees and the two explanatory variables for the 0.05 significance level.

(b) The p-value of 0.032 is the probability of obtaining an F statistic of 5.844 or larger when H_0 is true.

(c) The multiple regression model is significant, so there is a significant dependence between Y, X_1, and X_2. For a more precise investigation, it is necessary to construct interval estimators for β_1 and β_2.

17. (a) $b_1 \pm t_{n-p-1}S_{b_1} = 0.791 \pm 2.179 \times 0.063 = 0.791 \pm 0.137$, $P(0.654 \le \beta_1 \le 0.928) \approx 0.95$. The confidence interval does not contain a zero, so there is a significant linear dependence of Y on X_1 for the $1 - 0.95 = 0.05$ significance level.

(b) $H_0': \beta_1 = 0$, $H_1': \beta_1 \ne 0$

Decision rule: Reject H_0' if $|t| > 2.179$. Test statistic: $t = \dfrac{b_1}{S_{b_1}} = \dfrac{0.79116}{0.063295} = 12.568$. Decision: Because $t > 2.1788$,

reject H_0'. There is a significant linear dependence of Y on X_1 in the model already containing X_2 for the 0.05 significance level.

$H_0'': \beta_2 = 0$, $H_1'': \beta_2 \ne 0$

Decision rule: Reject H_0'' if $|t| > 2.179$. Test statistic: $t = \dfrac{b_2}{S_{b_2}} = \dfrac{0.60484}{0.07174} = 8.431$. Decision: Because $t > 2.1788$,

reject H_0''. There is a significant linear dependence of Y on X_2 in the model already containing X_1 for the 0.05 significance level.

19. (a) $b_1 \pm t_{n-p-1}S_{b_1} = 0.265063 \pm 2.1009 \times 0.0570665 = 0.265063 \pm 0.119891$, $P(0.14517 \le \beta_1 \le 0.385) \approx 0.95$. The confidence interval does not contain zero, so there is a significant linear dependence of Y on X_1 for the $1 - 0.95 = 0.05$ significance level.

$b_2 \pm t_{n-p-1}S_{b_2} = 0.525899 \pm 2.1009 \times 2.8847485 = 0.525899 \pm 6.060568$, $P(-5.5347 \le \beta_2 \le 6.5865) \approx 0.95$. The confidence interval contains zero, so there is no significant linear dependence of Y on X_2 for the $1 - 0.95 = 0.05$ significance level.

(b) $H_0': \beta_1 = 0$, $H_1': \beta_1 \ne 0$

Decision rule: Reject H_0' if $|t| > 2.101$. Test statistic: $t = \dfrac{b_1}{S_{b_1}} = 4.645$. Decision: Because $|t| > 2.101$, reject H_0'.

There is a significant linear dependence of Y on X_1 in the model already containing X_2 for the 0.05 significance level.

$H_0'': \beta_2 = 0$, $H_1'': \beta_2 \ne 0$

Decision rule: Reject H_0'' if $|t| > 2.101$. Test statistic: $t = \dfrac{b_2}{S_{b_2}} = 0.182$. Decision: Because $|t| < 2.101$, do not reject

H_0''. There is no significant linear dependence of Y on X_2 in the model already containing X_1 for the 0.05 significance level. There is a significant linear dependence of Y only on the variable X_1 for the 0.05 significance level.

21. (a) $b_1 \pm t_{n-p-1}S_{b_1} = 0.000358 \pm 2.0262 \times 0.000128 = 0.000358 \pm 0.000260$, $P(0.00098 \le \beta_1 \le 0.0006173) \approx 0.95$. The confidence interval does not contain zero, so there is a significant linear dependence of Y on X_1 for the $1 - 0.95 = 0.05$ significance level.

$b_2 \pm t_{n-p-1}S_{b_2} = 0.013 \pm 2.026 \times 0.052 = 0.013 \pm 0.106$, $P(-0.093 \le \beta_2 \le 0.119) \approx 0.95$. The confidence interval contains zero, so there is no significant linear dependence of Y on X_2 for the $1 - 0.95 = 0.05$ significance level.

(b) $H_0': \beta_1 = 0$, $H_1': \beta_1 \neq 0$

Decision rule: Reject H_0' if $|t| > 2.026$. Test statistic: $t = \dfrac{b_1}{S_{b_1}} = 2.79$. Decision: Because $|t| > 2.026$, reject H_0' .

There is a significant linear dependence of Y on X_1 in the model already containing X_2 for the 0.05 significance level.

$H_0'': \beta_2 = 0$, $H_1'': \beta_2 \neq 0$

Decision rule: Reject H_0'' if $|t| > 2.026$. Test statistic: $t = \dfrac{b_2}{S_{b_2}} = 0.2495$. Decision: Because $|t| < 2.026$, do not reject

H_0'' . There is no significant linear dependence of Y on X_2 in the model already containing X_1 for the 0.05 significance level. There is a significant linear dependence of Y only on the variables X_1 for the 0.05 significance level.

23. Summary Output: All but Weight

Regression Statistics	
Multiple R	0.831
R^2	0.690
Adjusted R^2	0.687
Standard Error	2.538
Observations	89.000

ANOVA

	df	SS	MS	F	Significance F
Regression	1.000	1250.034	1250.034	194.074	7.16×10^{-24}
Residual	87.000	560.370	6.441		
Total	88.000	1810.404			

	Coefficients	Standard Error	t Stat	p-value	Lower 95%	Upper 95%
Intercept	75.961	3.790	20.0411	2.35×10^{-34}	68.428	83.495
Length	−0.284	0.020	−13.931	7.16×10^{-24}	−0.324	−0.243

Summary Output: All but Length

Regression Statistics	
Multiple R	0.906
R^2	0.820
Adjusted R^2	0.818
Standard Error	1.935
Observations	89.000

ANOVA

	df	SS	MS	F	Significance F
Regression	1.000	1484.545	1484.545	396.354	3.77×10^{-34}
Residual	87.000	325.859	3.746		
Total	88.000	1810.404			

	Coefficients	Standard Error	*t* Stat	*p*-value	Lower 95%	Upper 95%
Intercept	47.885	1.252	38.240	3.48×10^{-56}	45.396	50.374
Weight	−0.008	0.000	−19.909	3.77×10^{-34}	−0.009	−0.007

Regression Analysis

Coefficients of Partial Determination			
$SSR(X_1, X_2)$	1485.519		
SST	1810.404		
$SSR(X_2)$	1250.034	$SSR(X_1\|X_2)$	235.485
$SSR(X_1)$	1484.545	$SSR(X_2\|X_1)$	0.974
$R^2_{Y1.2}$	0.420		
$R^2_{Y2.1}$	0.003		

(a) H_0': Variable X_1 does not significantly improve the model once the variable X_2 has been included.

H_1': Variable X_1 significantly improves the model once the variable X_2 has been included.

Decision rule: Reject H_0' if $F > 3.952$. Test statistic: $F = \dfrac{SSR(X_1|X_2)}{MSE} = \dfrac{235.485}{3.778} = 62.33$. Decision: Because $F > 3.952$, reject H_0'. Variable X_1 significantly improves the model once the variable X_2 has been included.

H_0'': Variable X_2 does not significantly improve the model once the variable X_1 has been included.

H_1'': Variable X_2 significantly improves the model once the variable X_1 has been included.

Decision rule: Reject H_0'' if $F > 3.952$. Test statistic: $F = \dfrac{SSR(X_2|X_1)}{MSE} = \dfrac{0.974}{3.778} = 0.258$. Decision: Because $F < 3.952$, do not reject H_0''. Variable X_2 does not significantly improve the model once the variable X_1 has been included. Appropriate regression model is $\widehat{Y}_i = \beta_0 + \beta_1 X_{1i} + \varepsilon_i$.

(b) $R^2_{Y1.2} = \dfrac{SSR(X_1|X_2)}{SST - SSR(X_1 \text{ and } X_2) + SSR(X_1|X_2)} = 0.420$, 42.0% of the variation in Y can be explained by the variation of X_1.

$R^2_{Y2.1} = \dfrac{SSR(X_2|X_1)}{SST - SSR(X_1 \text{ and } X_2) + SSR(X_2|X_1)} = 0.003$, 0.3% of the variation in Y can be explained by the variation of X_2.

25. Summary Output: All but Light Output

Regression Statistics	
Multiple R	0.581
R^2	0.337
Adjusted R^2	0.254
Standard Error	0.040
Observations	10.000

ANOVA

	df	SS	MS	F	Significance F
Regression	1.000	0.007	0.007	4.072	0.0783
Residual	8.000	0.013	0.002		
Total	9.000	0.020			

	Coefficients	Standard Error	t Stat	p-value	Lower 95%	Upper 95%
Intercept	0.782	0.122	6.387	0.000	0.500	1.065
Lamp Temperature	−0.007	0.003	−2.018	0.078	−0.015	0.001

Summary Output: All but Lamp Temperature

Regression Statistics	
Multiple R	0.777
R^2	0.603
Adjusted R^2	0.554
Standard Error	0.031
Observations	10.000

ANOVA

	df	SS	MS	F	Significance F
Regression	1.000	0.012	0.012	12.175	0.008
Residual	8.000	0.008	0.001		
Total	9.000	0.020			

	Coefficients	Standard Error	t Stat	p-value	Lower 95%	Upper 95%
Intercept	1.672	0.326	5.135	0.001	0.921	2.423
Light Output	−0.028	0.008	−3.489	0.008	−0.046	−0.009

Regression Analysis

Coefficients of Partial Determination			
SSR(X_1, X_2)	0.012		
SST	0.020		
SSR(X_2)	0.007	SSR($X_1 \vert X_2$)	0.006
SSR(X_1)	0.012	SSR($X_2 \vert X_1$)	0.000
$R^2_{Y1.2}$	0.435		
$R^2_{Y2.1}$	0.055		

(a) H_0': Variable X_1 does not significantly improve the model once the variable X_2 has been included.

H_1': Variable X_1 significantly improves the model once the variable X_2 has been included.

Decision rule: Reject H_0' if $F > 5.59$. Test statistic: $F = \dfrac{\text{SSR}(X_1 \vert X_2)}{\text{MSE}} = \dfrac{0.006}{0.001} = 5.383$. Decision: Because $F < 5.59$, do not reject H_0'. Variable X_1 does not significantly improve the model once the variable X_2 has been included for the 0.05 significance level.

H_0'': Variable X_2 does not significantly improve the model once the variable X_1 has been included.

H_1'': Variable X_2 significantly improves the model once the variable X_1 has been included.

Decision rule: Reject H_0'' if $F > 5.59$. Test statistic: $F = \dfrac{\text{SSR}(X_2 \vert X_1)}{\text{MSE}} = \dfrac{0.000}{0.001} = 0.41$. Decision: Because $F < 5.59$, do not reject H_0''. Variable X_2 does not significantly improve the model once the variable X_1 has been included.

An appropriate regression model will not include linear terms on X_1 and X_2.

(b) $R^2_{Y1.2} = \dfrac{\text{SSR}(X_1 \vert X_2)}{\text{SST} - \text{SSR}(X_1 \text{ and } X_2) + \text{SSR}(X_1 \vert X_2)} = 0.435$, 43.5% of the variation in Y can be explained by the variation of X_1.

$$R^2_{Y2.1} = \frac{SSR(X_2 | X_1)}{SST - SSR(X_1 \text{ and } X_2) + SSR(X_2 | X_1)} = 0.055 \text{, } 5.5\% \text{ of the variation in } Y \text{ can be explained by the variation}$$

of X_2.

27. (a)

MPG Scatter Diagram

(b) Regression Analysis

Regression Statistics	
Multiple R	0.959
R^2	0.919
Adjusted R^2	0.912
Standard Error	1.663
Observations	28.000

ANOVA

	df	SS	MS	F	Significance F
Regression	2.000	782.825	391.412	141.460	2.338×10^{-14}
Residual	25.000	69.174	2.767		
Total	27.000	851.999			

	Coefficients	Standard Error	t Stat	p–value	Lower 95%	Upper 95%
Intercept	−7.556	1.424	−5.305	1.694×10^{-5}	−10.489	−4.623
Speed	1.272	0.076	16.792	3.992×10^{-15}	1.116	1.428
Speed^2	−0.015	0.001	−16.633	4.973×10^{-15}	−0.016	−0.013

$\hat{Y}_i = -7.556 + 1.272 \times X_i - 0.015 \times X_i^2$

(c) $\hat{Y}_i = -7.556 + 1.272 \times 55 - 0.015 \times 55^2 = 18.509$

(d) $H_0: \beta_1 = \beta_2 = 0$, $H_1: \beta_1^2 + \beta_2^2 > 0$

Decision rule: Reject H_0 if $F > 4.29$. Test statistic: $F = \dfrac{MSR}{MSE} = \dfrac{391.412}{2.767} = 141.460$. Decision: Because $F > 4.29$,

reject H_0. Curvilinear relationship between mileage and speed is significant.

(e) $R^2_{Y.12} = \dfrac{SSR}{SST} = \dfrac{782.825}{851.999} = 0.919$, 91.9% of the variation in Y can be explained by the constructed curvilinear
relationship.

(f) $R^2_{adj} = 1 - \left[(1 - R^2_{Y.12}) \dfrac{(n-1)}{(n-p-1)} \right] = 1 - \left[(1 - 0.919) \dfrac{27}{25} \right] = 0.912$

(g)

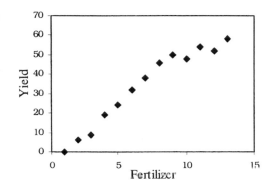

Normal Probability Plot

The constructed curvilinear regression seems to be adequate.

(h) H_0 : Including the curvilinear effect does not significantly improve the model ($\beta_2 = 0$).

H_1 : Including the curvilinear effect significantly improves the model ($\beta_2 \neq 0$).

Decision rule: Reject H_0 if $|t| > 2.060$. Test statistic: $t = \dfrac{b_2}{S_{b_2}} = \dfrac{-0.015}{0.001} = -16.63$. Decision: Because $t > 2.060$,

reject H_0 . The curvilinear model is better than simple linear one.

29. (a)

(b) Regression Analysis

Regression Statistics	
Multiple R	0.986
R^2	0.972
Adjusted R^2	0.966
Standard Error	3.328
Observations	12.000

ANOVA

	df	SS	MS	F	Significance F
Regression	2.000	3484.981	1742.490	157.319	9.973×10^{-8}
Residual	9.000	99.686	11.076		
Total	11.000	3584.667			

	Coefficients	Standard Error	t Stat	p–value	Lower 95%	Upper 95%
Intercept	6.643	2.133	3.115	0.012	1.818	11.468
Fertilizer	0.895	0.100	8.922	9.166×10^{-6}	0.668	1.122
Fertilizer^2	−0.004	0.001	−4.265	0.002	−0.006	−0.002

$\hat{Y}_i = 6.643 + 0.895 \times X_i - 0.004 \times X_i^2$

(c) $\hat{Y}_i = 6.643 + 0.895 \times 70 - 0.004 \times 70^2 = 49.169$

(d) $H_0 : \beta_1 = \beta_2 = 0$, $H_1 : \beta_1^2 + \beta_2^2 > 0$

Decision rule: Reject H_0 if $F > 4.26$. Test statistic: $F = \dfrac{MSR}{MSE} = \dfrac{1742.490}{11.076} = 157.318$. Decision: Because $F > 4.26$,

reject H_0 . The curvilinear relationship between mileage and speed is significant.

(e) The p-value in part (d) is 9.97×10^{-8} . This is the probability of obtaining $F \geq 157.318$ when H_0 is true.

(f) $R_{Y.12}^2 = \dfrac{\text{SSR}}{\text{SST}} = \dfrac{3484.981}{3584.667} = 0.972$, 97.2% of the variation in Y can be explained by the constructed curvilinear relationship.

(g) $R_{adj}^2 = 1 - \left[\left(1 - R_{Y.12}^2\right)\dfrac{(n-1)}{(n-p-1)}\right] = 0.966$

(h) H_0: Including the curvilinear effect does not significantly improve the model ($\beta_2 = 0$).

   H_1: Including the curvilinear effect significantly improves the model ($\beta_2 \neq 0$).

   Decision rule: Reject H_0 if $|t| > 2.262$. Test statistic: $t = \dfrac{b_2}{S_{b_2}} = \dfrac{-0.004}{0.001} = -4.265$. Decision: Because $|t| > 2.262$,

   reject H_0. The curvilinear model is better than the simple linear model.

(i) The p-value in part (h) is 0.002. This is a probability of obtaining $|t| \geq 4.265$ when H_0 is true.

(j)

Normal Probability Plot

The constructed curvilinear regression does not appear to be adequate.

31. (a) First, develop a multiple regression model using X_1 as the variable for the SAT score and X_2 as a dummy variable ($X_2 = 1$ if a student received a grade of B or higher in the introductory statistics course and $X_2 = 0$ otherwise). If we claim (say, using PHStat) that each of the two variables is making a significant contribution to the model, we still need to do one more test before we can use this model: We need to verify that the slope of the total SAT score and the grade-point average must be the same for both levels of the variable X_2. A hypothesis of equal slopes of the X_1 variable with grade-point average should be evaluated (say, using PHStat) by defining an interaction term $X_1 \times X_2$ and then testing whether this new term makes a significant contribution to the original regression model (that contains X_1 and X_2 terms only).

   (b) If a student received a grade of B or better, in the introductory statistics course, the student would be expected to have a grade-point average in computer science that is 0.30 higher than a student who had the same SAT score, but did not get a grade of B or better in the introductory statistical course.

33. Regression Analysis

Regression Statistics	
Multiple R	0.981
R^2	0.962
Adjusted R^2	0.951
Standard Error	0.010
Observations	10.000

ANOVA

	df	SS	MS	F	Significance F
Regression	2.000	0.019	0.009	88.559	1.071×10^{-5}
Residual	7.000	0.001	0.000		
Total	9.000	0.020			

	Coefficients	Standard Error	t Stat	p–value	Lower 95%	Upper 95%
Intercept	0.399	0.048	8.388	6.728×10^{-5}	0.286	0.511
Lamp Temperature	0.002	0.001	1.794	0.116	–0.001	0.005
Type	0.099	0.009	10.724	1.347×10^{-5}	0.078	0.121

(a) $\widehat{Y}_i = 0.399 + 0.002 \times X_{1i} + 0.099 \times X_{2i}$

(b) The slope equal to 0.002 represents the expected change in Y per unit change in X_1 (lamp temperature). The slope equal to 0.099 represents the expected change in Y per unit change in X_2 (type of ballast).

(c) $\widehat{Y}_i = 0.399 + 0.002 \times 40 + 0.099 \times 0 = 0.488$

(d) Due to the very small p-value 1.347×10^{-5} there is significant dependence of Y on X_2 (type of ballast). With respect to the first variable, it has a big p-value, 0.116, so there is no significant dependence of Y on X_1 (lamp temperature).

(e) $R^2_{Y.12} = 0.962$, 96.2% of the variation can be explained by the variations in the X_1 and X_2.

(f) $R^2_{adj} = 0.951$

(g)

There are some doubts about the validity of the multiple linear regression model.

(h)

	Coefficients	Standard Error	t Stat	p–value	Lower 95%	Upper 95%
Intercept	0.399	0.048	8.388	6.728×10^{-5}	0.286	0.511
Lamp Temperature	0.002	0.001	1.794	0.116	–0.001	0.005
Type	0.099	0.009	10.724	1.347×10^{-5}	0.078	0.121

There is a significant dependence of Y on X_2. Model $\widehat{Y}_i = \beta_0 + \beta_2 \times X_{2i} + \varepsilon_i$ should be used.

(i) $P(-0.001 \le \beta_1 \le 0.002) \approx 0.95$. The confidence interval contains zero, so there is no significant linear dependence of Y on X_1 for the $1 - 0.95 = 0.05$ significance level.

$P(0.078 \le \beta_2 \le 0.121) \approx 0.95$

The confidence interval does not contain zero, so there is a significant linear dependence of Y on X_2 for the $1 - 0.95 = 0.05$ significance level.

(j) Regression Analysis

Coefficients of Partial Determination			
$SSR(X_1, X_2)$	0.019		
SST	0.020		
$SSR(X_2)$	0.019	$SSR(X_1 \mid X_2)$	0.000
$SSR(X_1)$	0.007	$SSR(X_2 \mid X_1)$	0.012
$R^2_{Y1.2}$	0.315		
$R^2_{Y2.1}$	0.943		

$$R^2_{Y1.2} = \frac{SSR(X_1 \mid X_2)}{SST - SSR(X_1 \text{ and } X_2) + SSR(X_1 \mid X_2)} = 0.315, \; 3.15\% \text{ of the variation in } Y \text{ can be explained by the variation}$$

of X_1.

$$R^2_{Y2.1} = \frac{SSR(X_2 \mid X_1)}{SST - SSR(X_1 \text{ and } X_2) + SSR(X_2 \mid X_1)} = 0.943, \; 94.3\% \text{ of the variation in } Y \text{ can be explained by the variation}$$

in X_2.

(k) The slope of the temperature of the lamp with the ballast efficiency factor is the same for various types of ballast.

(l) Regression Analysis

Regression Statistics	
Multiple R	0.982
R^2	0.964
Adjusted R^2	0.946
Standard Error	0.011
Observations	10.000

ANOVA

	df	SS	MS	F	Significance F
Regression	3.000	0.019	0.006	53.348	0.000
Residual	6.000	0.001	0.000		
Total	9.000	0.020			

	Coefficients	Standard Error	t Stat	p–value	Lower 95%	Upper 95%
Intercept	0.447	0.099	4.501	0.004	0.204	0.690
Lamp Temperature	0.001	0.003	0.372	0.723	–0.005	0.007
Type	0.038	0.111	0.338	0.747	–0.234	0.310
Lamp Temperature×Type	0.002	0.003	0.559	0.596	–0.006	0.009

$H_0: \beta_3 = 0$, $H_1: \beta_3 \neq 0$, $P(-0.006 \leq \beta_3 \leq 0.009) \approx 0.95$. Zero belongs to this interval, so do not reject H_0 for the 0.05 significance level. There is no significant interaction between the lamp temperature and the type of ballast.

(m) Model $\hat{Y}_i = \beta_0 + \beta_2 \times X_{2i} + \varepsilon_i$ is appropriate.

35. Regression Analysis

Regression Statistics	
Multiple R	0.711
R^2	0.506
Adjusted R^2	0.341
Standard Error	96.656
Observations	9.000

ANOVA

	df	SS	MS	F	Significance F
Regression	2.000	57339.379	28669.689	3.069	0.121
Residual	6.000	56054.177	9342.363		
Total	8.000	113393.560			

	Coefficients	Standard Error	t Stat	p–value	Lower 95%	Upper 95%
Intercept	−572.097	405.388	−1.411	0.208	−1564.046	419.852
Diastolic	10.952	6.098	1.796	0.123	−3.970	25.875
Gender	−3.253	90.701	−0.036	0.973	−225.190	218.684

(a) $\widehat{Y}_i = -572.097 + 10.952 \times X_{1i} - 3.253 \times X_{2i}$

(b) The slope equal to 10.952 represents the expected change in Y per unit change in X_1 (diastolic blood pressure). The slope equal to 3.25 represents the expected change in Y per unit change in X_2 (gender).

(c) $\widehat{Y}_i = -572.097 + 10.952 \times 80 - 3.253 \times 0 = 304.081$

(d) $F = 3.069$. Because $F < 5.14$, do not reject H_0. There is no significant dependence Y on single variables X_1 and X_2. (This is also indicated by the large p-values: 0.123 and 0.973). Note: If gender is deleted from the model, the relationship of diastolic blood pressure and recovery is significant.

(e) $R^2_{Y.12} = 0.506$, 50.6% of the variation can be explained by the variations in the X_1 and X_2.

(f) $R^2_{adj} = 0.311$

(g)

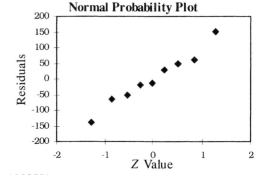

Normal Probability Plot

There are some doubts about the validity of the multiple linear regression model.

(h) ANOVA

	df	SS	MS	F	Significance F
Regression	2.000	57339.379	28669.689	3.069	0.121
Residual	6.000	56054.177	9342.363		
Total	8.000	113393.560			

	Coefficients	Standard Error	t Stat	p–value	Lower 95%	Upper 95%
Intercept	−572.097	405.388	−1.411	0.208	−1564.046	419.852
Diastolic	10.952	6.098	1.796	0.123	−3.970	25.875
Gender	−3.253	90.701	−0.036	0.973	−225.190	218.684

There is no significant dependence Y on single variables X_1 and X_2 Note: If gender is delete from the model, the relationship of diastolic blood pressure and recovery is significant.

(i) $P(-3.970 \le \beta_1 \le 25.875) \approx 0.95$. The confidence interval contains zero, so there is no significant linear dependence of Y on X_1 for the $1 - 0.95 = 0.05$ significance level.

   $P(-225.190 \le \beta_2 \le 218.684) \approx 0.95$.

   The confidence interval contains zero, so there is no significant linear dependence of Y on X_2 for the $1 - 0.95 = 0.05$ significance level.

(j) Regression Analysis

Coefficients of Partial Determination			
SSR(X_1, X_2)	57339.379		
SST	113393.556		
SSR(X_2)	27207.606	SSR$(X_1|X_2)$	30131.773
SSR(X_1)	57327.360	SSR$(X_2|X_1)$	12.019
$R^2_{Y1.2}$	0.350		
$R^2_{Y2.1}$	0.000		

$$R^2_{Y1.2} = \frac{\text{SSR}(X_1|X_2)}{\text{SST} - \text{SSR}(X_1 \text{ and } X_2) + \text{SSR}(X_1|X_2)} = 0.350\text{, }35.0\%\text{ of the variation in }Y\text{ can be explained by the variation}$$
of X_1.

$$R^2_{Y2.1} = \frac{\text{SSR}(X_2|X_1)}{\text{SST} - \text{SSR}(X_1 \text{ and } X_2) + \text{SSR}(X_2|X_1)} = 0.000\text{, }0.00\%\text{ of the variation in }Y\text{ can be explained by the variation}$$
in X_2.

(k) The slope of the diastolic blood pressure and recovery time is the same for female and male gender.

(l) Regression Analysis

Regression Statistics	
Multiple R	0.757
R^2	0.572
Adjusted R^2	0.316
Standard Error	98.471
Observations	9.000

ANOVA

	df	SS	MS	F	Significance F
Regression	3.000	64911.192	21637.064	2.231	0.203
Residual	5.000	48482.363	9696.473		
Total	8.000	113393.560			

	Coefficients	Standard Error	*t* Stat	*p*-value	Lower 95%	Upper 95%
Intercept	47.625	813.87363	0.0585165	0.9556039	−2044.500	2139.7504
Diastolic	1.5625	12.308834	0.1269414	0.9039338	−30.07831	33.203312
Gender	−868.2318	983.19322	−0.883073	0.4176262	−3395.606	1659.1427
Diastolic×Gender	12.599893	14.258499	0.8836760	0.4173302	−24.05268	49.252471

$H_0: \beta_3 = 0$, $H_1: \beta_3 \neq 0$, $P(-24.1 \leq \beta_3 \leq 49.3) \approx 0.95$. Zero belongs to this interval, so do not reject H_0 for the 0.05 significance level. There is no significant interaction between the lamp temperature and the type of ballast.

(m) Since the interaction term is not significant, and gender does not have any effect, a model that includes only diastolic blood pressure in predicting recovery time should be investigated.

37. Regression Analysis

Regression Statistics	
Multiple R	0.2565
R^2	0.0658
Adjusted R^2	0.0299
Standard Error	5.5327
Observations	28.000

ANOVA

	df	SS	MS	*F*	Significance *F*
Regression	1.000	56.098	56.098	1.833	0.187
Residual	26.000	795.900	30.612		
Total	27.000	851.999			

	Coefficients	Standard Error	*t* Stat	*p*-value	Lower 95%	Upper 95%
Intercept	9.036	4.103	2.202	0.037	0.602	17.470
SQRT(Speed)	0.852	0.629	1.354	0.187	−0.442	2.146

(a) $\hat{Y}_i = 9.036 + 0.852 \times \sqrt{X_i}$

(b) $\hat{Y} = 9.036 + 0.852 \times \sqrt{55} = 15.355$

(c)

The developed regression model is not adequate.

(d) $H_0: \beta_1 = 0$, $H_1: \beta_1 \neq 0$

Decision rule: Reject H_0 if $|t| > 2.056$. Test statistic: t=1.3537. Decision: Because $|t| > 2.056$, do not reject H_0.

There is no significant dependence of Y on $\sqrt{X}$ for the 0.05 significance level.

(e) $R^2 = 0.066$, 6.6% of the variation can be explained by the variation in the $\sqrt{X}$.

(f) $R_{adj}^2 = 0.030$

(g) The curvilinear model $\widehat{Y_i} = -7.556 + 1.272 \times X_i - 0.015 \times X_i^2$ is better than the square root model. It is significant, adequate and has a large r^2.

39. Regression Analysis

Regression Statistics	
Multiple R	0.888
R^2	0.789
Adjusted R^2	0.768
Standard Error	0.359
Observations	12.000

ANOVA

	df	SS	MS	F	Significance F
Regression	1.000	4.815	4.815	37.318	0.000
Residual	10.000	1.290	0.129		
Total	11.000	6.105			

	Coefficients	Standard Error	t Stat	p–value	Lower 95%	Upper 95%
Intercept	2.475	0.184	13.463	9.832×10^{-8}	2.065	2.885
Fertilizer	0.019	0.003	6.109	0.000	0.012	0.025

(a) $\ln \widehat{Y_i} = 2.475 + 0.019 \times X_i$

(b) $\widehat{Y} = \exp(2.475 + 0.019 \times 55) = 32.868$

(c)

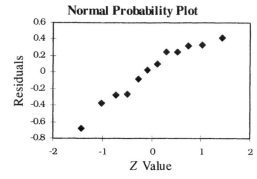

The developed regression model is not adequate

(d) $H_0: \beta_1 = 0$, $H_1: \beta_1 \neq 0$

Due to the small p-value $0.000 < 0.05$, one must reject H_0. There is significant dependence $\ln Y$ on X.

(e) $R^2 = 0.789$, 78.9% of the variation in $\ln Y$ can be explained by the variation in X.

(f) $R_{adj}^2 = 0.768$

(g) The curvilinear regression model $\widehat{Y_i} = 6.643 + 0.895 \times X_i - 0.004 \times X_i^2$ is significant and it has a greater r^2, so it is preferable.

41. Summary Output: Length and all other X

Regression Statistics	
Multiple R	0.907
R^2	0.822
Adjusted R^2	0.820
Standard Error	221.697
Observations	89.000
VIF	5.629

$VIF_1 = VIF_2 = \dfrac{1}{1-R^2} = \dfrac{1}{1-0.822} = 5.629 < 10$. There is no reason to suspect the existence of collinearity.

43. Summary Output: Lamp Temperature and all other X

Regression Statistics	
Multiple R	0.594
R^2	0.353
Adjusted R^2	0.272
Standard Error	1.123
Observations	10.000
VIF	1.546

$VIF_1 = VIF_2 = \dfrac{1}{1-R^2} = 1.546 < 10$. There is no reason to suspect the existence of collinearity.

45.

Model	Variables	$P+1$	C_p
M_1	A, B	3	4.6
M_2	A, C	3	2.4
M_3	A, B, C	4	2.7

(a) For the model that includes independent variables A and B, the values of C_p exceeds 3, the number of parameters, so this model does not meet the criterion for consideration. For the model that includes independent variables A and C, the value of C_p is less than or equal to 3, the number of parameters, so this model does meet the criterion for future consideration. For the model that includes independent variables A, B, and C the value of C_p is less than or equal to 4, the number of parameters so this model does not meet the criterion for future consideration.

(b) The inclusion of variable C in the model appears to improve the model's ability to explain variation in the dependent variable sufficiently to justify the inclusion of variable C in a model that contains only the variables A and B.

47. Stepwise Analysis: Table of Results for General Stepwise, Diastolic entered.

	df	SS	MS	F	Significance F
Regression	1.000	57327.360	57327.360	7.157	0.032
Residual	7.000	56066.195	8009.456		
Total	8.000	113393.556			

	Coefficients	Standard Error	t Stat	p-value	Lower 95%	Upper 95%
Intercept	−562.926	291.270	−1.933	0.095	−1251.668	125.817
Diastolic	10.799	4.037	2.675	0.032	1.254	20.344

No other variables can be entered into the model. Stepwise ends.

The developed regression model is: Recovery time $= -562.926 + 10.799 \times$ Diastolic

Best Subsets Analysis	
R^2T	0.510
$1 - R^2T$	0.490
n	9.000
T	5.000
$n - T$	4.000

	C_p	$p+1$	R^2	Adj. R^2	Std. Error	Consider This Model?
X_1	2.028	2.000	0.138	0.015	118.158	No
X_1X_2	2.994	3.000	0.265	0.020	117.860	Yes
$X_1X_2X_3$	4.393	4.000	0.339	−0.058	122.460	No
$X_1X_2X_3X_4$	5.000	5.000	0.510	0.019	117.918	Yes
$X_1X_2X_4$	3.016	4.000	0.508	0.212	105.677	Yes
X_1X_3	2.625	3.000	0.310	0.080	114.175	Yes
$X_1X_3X_4$	3.000	4.000	0.510	0.215	105.469	Yes
X_1X_4	1.016	3.000	0.508	0.343	96.472	Yes
X_2	1.198	2.000	0.240	0.131	110.961	Yes
X_2X_3	2.975	3.000	0.267	0.023	117.674	Yes
$X_2X_3X_4$	3.031	4.000	0.506	0.209	105.881	Yes
X_2X_4	1.031	3.000	0.506	0.341	96.656	Yes
X_3	2.353	2.000	0.098	−0.030	120.856	No
X_3X_4	1.032	3.000	0.506	0.341	96.666	Yes
X_4	−0.968	2.000	0.506	0.435	89.496	Yes

Adjusted r^2 criterion: r^2 reaches a maximum value of 0.4349269 for X_4 model (diastolic). C_p criterion: $p+1 \geq C_p$ for all models except X_1, X_3 and $X_1X_2X_3$. Summary Output: X_2

Regression Statistics	
Multiple R	0.490
R^2	0.240
Adjusted R^2	0.131
Standard Error	110.961
Observations	9.000

ANOVA

	df	SS	MS	F	Significance F
Regression	1.000	27207.610	27207.610	2.210	0.181
Residual	7.000	86185.950	12312.280		
Total	8.000	113393.600			

	Coefficients	Standard Error	t Stat	p–value	Lower 95%	Upper 95%
Intercept	150.750	55.480	2.717	0.030	19.560	281.940
Gender	110.650	74.435	1.487	0.181	−65.360	286.660

Simple linear regression of the recovery time on gender is not significant.

Summary Output: X_4

Regression Statistics	
Multiple R	0.711
R^2	0.506
Adjusted R^2	0.435
Standard Error	89.496
Observations	9.000

ANOVA

	df	SS	MS	F	Significance F
Regression	1.000	57327.360	57327.360	7.157	0.032
Residual	7.000	56066.200	8009.456		
Total	8.000	113393.600			

	Coefficients	Standard Error	t Stat	p–value	Lower 95%	Upper 95%
Intercept	−562.926	291.270	−1.933	0.095	−1251.670	125.817
Diastolic	10.799	4.037	2.675	0.032	1.254	20.344

For a 0.05 significance level simple linear regression of the recovery time on diastolic is significant.

Summary Output: $X_1 X_2$

Regression Statistics	
Multiple R	0.515
R^2	0.265
Adjusted R^2	0.0200
Standard Error	117.860
Observations	9.000

ANOVA

	df	SS	MS	F	Significance F
Regression	2.000	30047.810	15023.910	1.082	0.397
Residual	6.000	83345.740	13890.960		
Total	8.000	113393.600			

	Coefficients	Standard Error	t Stat	p–value	Lower 95%	Upper 95%
Intercept	−288.016	972.128	−0.296	0.777	−2666.730	2090.698
Age	21.403	47.334	0.452	0.667	−94.418	137.225
Gender	91.387	89.809	1.018	0.348	−128.369	311.143

The multiple regression of the recovery time on age and gender is not significant.

Summary Output: $X_1 X_3$

Regression Statistics	
Multiple R	0.557
R^2	0.310
Adjusted R^2	0.080
Standard Error	114.175
Observations	9.000

ANOVA

	df	SS	MS	F	Significance F
Regression	2.000	35177.390	17588.700	1.349	0.328
Residual	6.000	78216.160	13036.030		
Total	8.000	113393.600			

	Coefficients	Standard Error	t Stat	p–value	Lower 95%	Upper 95%
Intercept	−1925.910	1302.449	−1.479	0.190	−5112.890	1261.073
Age	56.452	41.581	1.358	0.223	−45.293	158.197
Systolic	8.135	6.649	1.223	0.267	−8.135	24.404

The multiple regression of the recovery time on age and systolic is not significant.

Summary Output: $X_1 X_4$

Regression Statistics	
Multiple R	0.712
R^2	0.508
Adjusted R^2	0.343
Standard Error	96.472
Observations	9.000

ANOVA

	df	SS	MS	F	Significance F
Regression	2.000	57552.820	28776.410	3.092	0.119
Residual	6.000	55840.740	9306.790		
Total	8.000	113393.600			

	Coefficients	Standard Error	t Stat	p–value	Lower 95%	Upper 95%
Intercept	−460.855	727.084	−0.634	0.550	−2239.970	1318.257
Age	−6.483	41.656	−0.156	0.881	−108.412	95.445
Diastolic	11.274	5.314	2.122	0.078	−1.729	24.277

The multiple regression of the recovery time on age and diastolic is not significant.

Summary Output: $X_2 X_3$

Regression Statistics	
Multiple R	0.517
R^2	0.267
Adjusted R^2	0.023
Standard Error	117.674
Observations	9.000

ANOVA

	df	SS	MS	F	Significance F
Regression	2.000	30310.300	15155.150	1.094	0.393
Residual	6.000	83083.260	13847.210		
Total	8.000	113393.600			

	Coefficients	Standard Error	*t* Stat	*p*–value	Lower 95%	Upper 95%
Intercept	−231.519	809.711	−0.286	0.785	−2212.810	1749.774
Gender	98.019	83.327	1.176	0.284	−105.875	301.912
Systolic	3.324	7.022	0.473	0.653	−13.859	20.507

The multiple regression of the recovery time on gender and systolic is not significant.

Summary Output: $X_2 X_4$

Regression Statistics	
Multiple R	0.711
R^2	0.506
Adjusted R^2	0.341
Standard Error	96.656
Observations	9.000

ANOVA

	df	SS	MS	F	Significance F
Regression	2.000	57339.380	28669.690	3.068	0.121
Residual	6.000	56054.180	9342.363		
Total	8.000	113393.600			

	Coefficients	Standard Error	*t* Stat	*p*–value	Lower 95%	Upper 95%
Intercept	−572.097	405.388	−1.411	0.208	−1564.050	419.852
Gender	−3.253	90.701	−0.036	0.973	−225.190	218.684
Diastolic	10.952	6.098	1.796	0.123	−3.970	25.875

The multiple regression of the recovery time on gender and diastolic is not significant.

Summary Output: $X_3 X_4$

Regression Statistics	
Multiple R	0.711
R^2	0.506
Adjusted R^2	0.341
Standard Error	96.666
Observations	9.000

ANOVA

	df	SS	MS	F	Significance F
Regression	2.000	57328.110	28664.050	3.068	0.121
Residual	6.000	56065.450	9344.241		
Total	8.000	113393.600			

	Coefficients	Standard Error	*t* Stat	*p*–value	Lower 95%	Upper 95%
Intercept	−557.926	641.600	−0.870	0.418	−2127.870	1012.014
Systolic	−0.055	6.100	−0.009	0.993	−14.980	14.871
Diastolic	10.819	4.867	2.223	0.068	−1.089	22.727

The multiple regression of the recovery time on systolic and diastolic is not significant.

Summary Output: $X_1 X_2 X_4$

Regression Statistics	
Multiple R	0.712
R^2	0.508
Adjusted R^2	0.212
Standard Error	105.677
Observations	9.000

ANOVA

	df	SS	MS	F	Significance F
Regression	3.000	57555.410	19185.140	1.718	0.278
Residual	5.000	55838.150	11167.630		
Total	8.000	113393.600			

	Coefficients	Standard Error	t Stat	p-value	Lower 95%	Upper 95%
Intercept	−466.518	879.031	−0.531	0.618	−2726.130	1793.098
Age	−6.396	45.989	−0.139	0.895	−124.614	111.822
Gender	−1.522	99.944	−0.015	0.988	−258.437	255.393
Diastolic	11.339	7.225	1.569	0.177	−7.233	29.912

The multiple regression of the recovery time on age, gender and diastolic is not significant.

Summary Output: $X_1 X_3 X_4$

Regression Statistics	
Multiple R	0.714
R^2	0.510
Adjusted R^2	0.215
Standard Error	105.469
Observations	9.000

ANOVA

	df	SS	MS	F	Significance F
Regression	3.000	57774.630	19258.210	1.731	0.276
Residual	5.000	55618.920	11123.780		
Total	8.000	113393.600			

	Coefficients	Standard Error	t Stat	p-value	Lower 95%	Upper 95%
Intercept	−251.612	1681.510	−0.150	0.887	−4574.060	4070.840
Age	−12.361	61.695	−0.200	0.849	−170.953	146.232
Systolic	−1.273	9.016	−0.141	0.893	−24.450	21.903
Diastolic	12.156	8.529	1.4253	0.213	−9.768	34.079

The multiple regression of the recovery time on age, systolic and diastolic is not significant.

Summary Output: $X_2 X_3 X_4$

Regression Statistics	
Multiple R	0.711
R^2	0.506
Adjusted R^2	0.209
Standard Error	105.880
Observations	9.000

ANOVA

	df	SS	MS	F	Significance F
Regression	3.000	57340.040	19113.350	1.705	0.281
Residual	5.000	56053.520	11210.700		
Total	8.000	113393.600			

	Coefficients	Standard Error	t Stat	p–value	Lower 95%	Upper 95%
Intercept	−567.365	759.988	−0.746	0.489	−2520.970	1386.242
Gender	−3.242	99.368	−0.033	0.975	−258.676	252.192
Systolic	−0.051	6.682	−0.008	0.994	−17.228	17.125
Diastolic	10.970	7.065	1.553	0.181	−7.191	29.130

The multiple regression of the recovery time on gender, systolic and diastolic is not significant.

Summary Output: $X_1 X_2 X_3 X_4$

Regression Statistics	
Multiple R	0.714
R^2	0.510
Adjusted R^2	0.019
Standard Error	117.918
Observations	9.000

ANOVA

	df	SS	MS	F	Significance F
Regression	4.000	57774.800	14443.700	1.039	0.486
Residual	4.000	55618.750	13904.690		
Total	8.000	113393.600			

	Coefficients	Standard Error	t Stat	p–value	Lower 95%	Upper 95%
Intercept	−249.379	1987.529	−0.125	0.906	−5767.660	5268.898
Age	−12.405	70.155	−0.177	0.868	−207.187	182.377
Gender	0.390	112.555	0.003	0.997	−312.114	312.893
Systolic	−1.278	10.174	−0.126	0.906	−29.525	26.9688
Diastolic	12.142	10.290	1.180	0.303	−16.426	40.7110

The multiple regression of the recovery time on age, gender, systolic and diastolic is not significant. There is only one significant regression model , X_4. Residual analysis:

Normal Probability Plot

The developed regression model is:
Recovery time $= -562.926 + 10.799 \times$ Diastolic

49. Type of school: 5 for public, 15 for private.
Stepwise Analysis: Table of Results for General Stepwise, Type of School entered.

	df	SS	MS	F	Significance F
Regression	1.000	1928.628	1928.628	184.553	2.958×10^{-22}
Residual	78.000	815.122	10.450		
Total	79.000	2743.750			

	Coefficients	Standard Error	t Stat	p-value	Lower 95%	Upper 95%
Intercept	14.160	0.590	23.992	9.46×10^{-38}	12.985	15.335
Type of School	10.142	0.747	13.585	2.958×10^{-22}	8.656	11.628

Average Total SAT entered.

	df	SS	MS	F	Significance F
Regression	2.000	2176.002	1088.001	147.559	4.557×10^{-27}
Residual	77.000	567.748	7.373		
Total	79.000	2743.750			

	Coefficients	Standard Error	t Stat	p-value	Lower 95%	Upper 95%
Intercept	−3.467	3.083	−1.124	0.264	−9.607	2.673
Type of School	8.128	0.717	11.337	4.37×10^{-18}	6.701	9.556
Average Total SAT	0.016	0.003	5.792	1.436×10^{-7}	0.011	0.022

Room and Board entered.

	df	SS	MS	F	Significance F
Regression	3.000	2276.455	758.818	123.413	3.931×10^{-29}
Residual	76.000	467.295	6.149		
Total	79.000	2743.750			

	Coefficients	Standard Error	t Stat	p-value	Lower 95%	Upper 95%
Intercept	−9.615	3.200	−3.004	0.004	−15.989	−3.241
Type of School	5.912	0.854	6.922	1.233×10^{-9}	4.211	7.613
Average Total SAT	0.017	0.003	6.578	5.406×10^{-9}	0.012	0.022
Room and Board	1.200	0.297	4.042	0.000	0.609	1.791

TOEFL Score entered.

	df	SS	MS	F	Significance F
Regression	4.000	2342.712	585.678	109.530	1.586×10^{-30}
Residual	75.000	401.038	5.347		
Total	79.000	2743.750			

	Coefficients	Standard Error	t Stat	p–value	Lower 95%	Upper 95%
Intercept	−7.786	3.029	−2.570	0.012	−13.820	−1.751
Type of School	6.096	0.798	7.637	5.836×10^{-11}	4.506	7.686
Average Total SAT	0.014	0.003	5.397	7.612×10^{-7}	0.009	0.019
Room and Board	1.134	0.277	4.086	0.000	0.581	1.686
TOEFL Score	2.519	0.716	3.520	0.001	1.093	3.945

Developed regression model is:

Annual total cost $= -7.786 + 6.096 \times$ Type of School $+ 0.014 \times$ Average Total SAT $+ 1.134$

$\times$ Room and Board $+ 2.512 \times$ TOEFL Score

Best Subsets Analysis	
$R^2 T$	0.854
$1 - R^2 T$	0.146
n	80.000
T	5.000
$n - T$	75.000

	C_p	$p+1$	R^2	Adj. R^2	Std. Error	Consider This Model?
X_1	207.397	2.000	0.448	0.441	4.408	No
$X_1 X_2$	68.480	3.000	0.722	0.715	3.146	No
$X_1 X_2 X_3$	15.391	4.000	0.830	0.823	2.480	No
$X_1 X_2 X_3 X_4$	5.000	5.000	0.854	0.846	2.312	Yes
$X_1 X_2 X_4$	61.325	4.000	0.740	0.730	3.063	No
$X_1 X_3$	32.177	3.000	0.793	0.788	2.715	No
$X_1 X_3 X_4$	19.698	4.000	0.821	0.814	2.540	No
$X_1 X_4$	197.707	3.000	0.470	0.457	4.344	No
X_2	189.124	2.000	0.483	0.477	4.263	No
$X_2 X_3$	63.153	3.000	0.733	0.726	3.086	No
$X_2 X_3 X_4$	32.132	4.000	0.797	0.789	2.707	No
$X_2 X_4$	145.979	3.000	0.571	0.560	3.908	No
X_3	76.440	2.000	0.703	0.699	3.233	No
$X_3 X_4$	43.546	3.000	0.771	0.765	2.857	No
X_4	359.373	2.000	0.152	0.141	5.463	No

Adjusted R^2 criterion: R^2 reaches a maximum value of 0.846 for the $X_1 X_2 X_3 X_4$ model. C_p criterion: $p+1 \geq C_p$ only for $X_1 X_2 X_3 X_4$ model.

Summary Output: $X_1 X_2 X_3 X_4$

Regression Statistics	
Multiple R	0.924
R^2	0.854
Adjusted R^2	0.846
Standard Error	2.312
Observations	80.000

ANOVA

	df	SS	MS	F	Significance F
Regression	4.000	2342.712	585.678	109.530	1.59×10^{-30}
Residual	75.000	401.038	5.347		
Total	79.000	2743.750			

	Coefficients	Standard Error	t Stat	p–value	Lower 95%	Upper 95%
Intercept	−7.786	3.029	−2.570	0.012	−13.820	−1.751
Average Total SAT	0.014	0.003	5.397	7.61×10^{-7}	0.009	0.019
Room and Board	1.134	0.277	4.086	0.000	0.581	1.686
Type of School	6.096	0.798	7.637	5.84×10^{-11}	4.506	7.686
TOEFL Score	2.519	0.716	3.520	0.001	1.093	3.945

The only significant model is the regression of the annual total cost on all other parameters. The same was found in the stepwise procedure.

Normal Probability Plot

The developed regression model is:

Annual total cost $= -7.786 + 6.096 \times$ Type of School

$+ 0.014 \times$ Average Total SAT $+ 1.134$

$\times$ Room and Board $+ 2.512$

$\times$ TOEFL Score

51. Testing of the entire model's significance means testing of the hypothesis that Y depends on X's at least in one term. The F test is used for testing of this hypothesis. Testing of the significant contribution of the particular variable X_k means testing of the hypothesis $H_0: \beta_k = 0$ versus $H_1: \beta_k \neq 0$. The t test is appropriate for this problem.

53. Dummy variables are used in shift regression models. The use of dummy variables permits us to consider categorical explanatory variables as part of the regression model. If a given categorical explanatory variable has two categories, then the corresponding binary dummy variable indicates that it belongs to one fixed category.

55. It makes it possible to study the common linear regression model $f(Y_i) = \beta_0 + \sum_{k=1}^{p} \beta_k g(X_{ki}) + \varepsilon_i$, where the values ε_i are independent identically distributed gaussian random values.

57. Dummy variables are used in shift regression models. The use of dummy variables is the mechanism that permits us to consider categorical explanatory variables as part of the regression model.

59. *The Stepwise regression* procedure attempts to find the "best" regression model without examining all possible regressions. Once a best model has been found, residual analysis is utilized to evaluate the aptness of the model. (At each step of the model–building process, variables are either added to or deleted from the regression model. The stepwise procedure terminates with the selection of a best-fitting model, when no variables can be added to or deleted from the last model fitted.) *The best subset approach* evaluates either all possible regression models for a given set of independent variables or at least the best subset of models for a given number of independent variables. (In this procedure, the entire set of multiple regression models is divided into two parts and the "best" models are marked for further studying.)

61. Regression Analysis

Regression Statistics	
Multiple R	0.785
R^2	0.616
Adjusted R^2	0.571
Standard Error	122.144
Observations	20.000

ANOVA

	df	SS	MS	F	Significance F
Regression	2.000	406962.030	203481.020	13.639	0.000
Residual	17.000	253626.520	14919.207		
Total	19.000	660588.550			

	Coefficients	Standard Error	t Stat	p–value	Lower 95%	Upper 95%
Intercept	−1806.474	934.749	−1.933	0.070	−3778.625	165.678
Thickness	7.921	3.658	2.165	0.045	0.202	15.639
Hardness	2.738	0.582	4.708	0.000	1.511	3.965

(a) $\hat{Y}_i = -1806.474 + 7.921 \times X_{1i} + 2.738 \times X_{2i}$

(b) The slope 7.921 represents the expected change in Y per unit change in X_1. The slope 2.738 represents the expected change in Y per unit change in X_2.

(c) $\hat{Y} = -1806.474 + 7.921 \times 275 + 2.738 \times 350 = 1330$

(d)

Normal Probability Plot

There are some doubts about the validity of the multiple linear regression model.

(e) Testing of the model's significance provides statistic $F = 13.639$, its significance level is $0.000 < 0.05$, so the developed regression model is significant.

(f) The p–value for the F test is 0.000. This is the probability of obtaining $F \geq 13.639$ when H_0 (regression model is not significant) is true.

(g) $R^2_{Y.12} = 0.616$, 61.6% of the variations can be explained by the variations in the X_1 and X_2.

(h) $R^2_{adj} = 0.571$

(i)

	Coefficients	Standard Error	t Stat	p–value	Lower 95%	Upper 95%
Intercept	−1806.474	934.749	−1.933	0.070	−3778.625	165.678
Thickness	7.921	3.658	2.165	0.045	0.202	15.639
Hardness	2.738	0.582	4.708	0.000	1.511	3.965

$P(0.202 \le \beta_1 \le 15.639) \approx 0.95$. The confidence interval does not contain zero, so there is a significant linear dependence of Y on X_1 for the $1 - 0.95 = 0.05$ significance level.

$P(1.511 \le \beta_2 \le 3.965) \approx 0.95$. The confidence interval does not contain zero, so there is significant linear dependence of Y on X_2 for the $1 - 0.95 = 0.05$ significance level.

(j) p-value 0.045 is a probability of obtaining $|t| \ge 2.165$ when H_0 (there is no significant linear dependence of Y on X_1) is true.

p-value 0.000 is a probability of obtaining $|t| \ge 4.708$ when H_0 (there is no significant linear dependence of Y on X_2) is true.

(k) $P(0.202 \le \beta_1 \le 15.639) \approx 0.95$, $P(1.511 \le \beta_2 \le 3.965) \approx 0.95$

(l) Regression Analysis

Coefficients of Partial Determination			
SSR(X_1, X_2)	406962.031		
SST	660588.550		
SSR(X_2)	337028.451	SSR(X_1|X_2)	69933.580
SSR(X_1)	76220.431	SSR(X_2|X_1)	330741.601
$R^2_{Y1.2}$	0.216		
$R^2_{Y2.1}$	0.566		

$R^2_{Y1.2} = \dfrac{\text{SSR}(X_1|X_2)}{\text{SST} - \text{SSR}(X_1 \text{ and } X_2) + \text{SSR}(X_1|X_2)} = 0.216$, 21.6% of the variation in Y can be explained by the variation

of X_1. $R^2_{Y2.1} = \dfrac{\text{SSR}(X_2|X_1)}{\text{SST} - \text{SSR}(X_1 \text{ and } X_2) + \text{SSR}(X_2|X_1)} = 0.566$, 56.6% of the variation in Y can be explained by the

variation of X_2.

63. Stepwise Analysis: Table of Results for General Stepwise, SiO_2 entered.

	df	SS	MS	F	Significance F
Regression	1.000	4774289.700	4774289.700	76.241	5.315×10^{-15}
Residual	146.000	9142718.800	62621.362		
Total	147.000	13917008.000			

	Coefficients	Standard Error	t Stat	p–value	Lower 95%	Upper 95%
Intercept	119.478	24.182	4.941	2.106×10^{-6}	71.685	167.271
SiO_2	42.880	4.911	8.732	$5.315 \times 10^{-1}5$	33.174	52.585

Type entered.

	df	SS	MS	F	Significance F
Regression	2.000	6151597.300	3075798.700	57.433	4.264×10^{-19}
Residual	145.000	7765411.200	53554.560		
Total	147.000	13917009.000			

	Coefficients	Standard Error	t Stat	p–value	Lower 95%	Upper 95%
Intercept	76.215	23.935	3.184	0.002	28.907	123.522
SiO_2	30.982	5.112	6.061	1.113×10^{-8}	20.878	41.085
Type	233.242	45.993	5.071	1.189×10^{-6}	142.339	324.145

No other variables can be entered into the model. Stepwise ends. The developed regression model is:

$ANC = 76.215 + 30.981 \times SiO_2 + 233.242 \times Type$

Best Subsets Analysis	
R^2T	0.449
$1 - R^2T$	0.551
n	148.000
T	4.000
$n - T$	144.000

	C_p	$p+1$	R^2	Adj. R^2	Std. Error	Consider This Model?
X_1	38.880	2.000	0.301	0.296	258.191	No
$X_1 X_2$	3.914	3.000	0.442	0.434	231.419	No
$X_1 X_2 X_3$	4.000	4.000	0.449	0.438	230.693	Yes
$X_1 X_3$	40.078	3.000	0.304	0.294	258.511	No
X_2	27.794	2.000	0.343	0.339	250.243	No
$X_2 X_3$	23.437	3.000	0.367	0.359	246.414	No
X_3	109.535	2.000	0.030	0.024	304.003	No

The higher adjusted R^2 corresponds to the $X_1 X_2 X_3$ model. This is the only model with $C_p \le p+1$.

Summary Output: $X_1 X_2 X_3$

Regression Statistics	
Multiple R	0.670
R^2	0.449
Adjusted R^2	0.438
Standard Error	230.693
Observations	148.000

ANOVA

	df	SS	MS	F	Significance F
Regression	3.000	6253440.000	2084480.000	39.168	1.440×10^{-18}
Residual	144.000	7663569.000	53219.230		
Total	147.000	13917009.000			

	Coefficients	Standard Error	t Stat	p–value	Lower 95%	Upper 95%
Intercept	74.435	23.895	3.115	0.002	27.205	121.665
Type	218.180	47.124	4.630	8.100×10^{-6}	125.037	311.324
SiO_2	31.544	5.112	6.171	6.530×10^{-9}	21.440	41.648
Lake Area	0.0455	0.033	1.383	0.169	–0.020	0.110

$X_1 X_2 X_3$ model does not significantly depend on X_3 (Lake Area), so it will be reasonable to delete this variable from the model.

Summary Output: $X_1 X_2$

Regression Statistics	
Multiple R	0.665
R^2	0.4420
Adjusted R^2	0.434
Standard Error	231.419
Observations	148.000

ANOVA

	df	SS	MS	F	Significance F
Regression	2.000	6151597.000	3075799.000	57.433	4.26×10^{-19}
Residual	145.000	7765411.000	53554.560		
Total	147.000	13917009.000			

	Coefficients	Standard Error	t Stat	p–value	Lower 95%	Upper 95%
Intercept	76.215	23.935	3.184	0.002	28.907	123.522
Type	233.242	45.993	5.071	1.190×10^{-6}	142.339	324.145
SiO_2	30.982	5.112	6.061	1.110×10^{-8}	20.878	41.085

This model is significant and depends on all explanatory variables.

Normal Probability Plot

Residual analysis: There are some doubts about the adequacy of the developed regression. Let us include interaction $X_1 X_2$ term into the regression equation.

Regression Analysis

Regression Statistics	
Multiple R	0.665
R^2	0.442
Adjusted R^2	0.431
Standard Error	232.186
Observations	148.000

ANOVA

	df	SS	MS	F	Significance F
Regression	3.000	6153918.400	2051306.100	38.050	3.606×10^{-18}
Residual	144.000	7763090.100	53910.348		
Total	147.000	13917009.000			

	Coefficients	Standard Error	t Stat	p–value	Lower 95%	Upper 95%
Intercept	74.417	25.529	2.915	0.004	23.958	124.877
Type	239.393	54.847	4.365	2.414×10^{-5}	130.984	347.802
SiO_2	32.388	8.500	3.810	0.000	15.587	49.189
Type $\times SiC_2$	−2.212	10.659	−0.207	0.836	−23.280	18.856

Due to the very large *p*–value 0.836 term $X_1 X_2$ does not provide a significant effect on Y. The developed regression model is: $ANC = 76.215 + 30.981 \times SiO_2 + 233.242 \times Type$

65. Stepwise Analysis: Table of Results for General Stepwise, Soil radiation entered.

	df	SS	MS	F	Significance F
Regression	1.000	2.139	2.139	7.932	0.008
Residual	38.000	10.245	0.270		
Total	39.000	12.384			

	Coefficients	Standard Error	t Stat	p–value	Lower 95%	Upper 95%
Intercept	0.611	0.100	6.128	3.794×10^{-7}	0.409	0.813
Soil Radiation	0.000	0.000	2.816	0.008	0.000	0.001

No other variables can be entered into the model. Stepwise ends. The developed regression model is:
Radon concentration = $0.641 + 0.000 \times$ Soil radiation

Best Subsets Analysis	
$R^2 T$	0.498
$1 - R^2 T$	0.502
n	40.000
T	8.000
$n - T$	32.000

	C_p	$p + 1$	R^2	Adj. R^2	Std. Error	Consider This Model?
X_1	16.739	2.000	0.173	0.151	0.519	No
$X_1 X_2$	18.651	3.000	0.174	0.129	0.526	No
$X_1 X_2 X_3$	15.427	4.000	0.256	0.194	0.506	No
$X_1 X_2 X_3 X_4$	4.970	5.000	0.451	0.389	0.441	Yes
$X_1 X_2 X_3 X_4 X_5$	6.808	6.000	0.454	0.374	0.450	No
$X_1 X_2 X_3 X_4 X_5 X_6$	8.803	7.000	0.454	0.355	0.453	No
$X_1 X_2 X_3 X_4 X_5 X_6 X_7$	8.000	8.000	0.498	0.388	0.441	Yes
$X_1 X_2 X_3 X_4 X_5 X_7$	6.004	7.000	0.498	0.407	0.434	Yes
$X_1 X_2 X_3 X_4 X_6$	6.886	6.000	0.452	0.372	0.446	No
$X_1 X_2 X_3 X_4 X_6 X_7$	6.679	7.000	0.487	0.394	0.439	Yes
$X_1 X_2 X_3 X_4 X_7$	5.476	6.000	0.475	0.398	0.437	Yes
$X_1 X_2 X_3 X_5$	17.179	5.000	0.260	0.175	0.512	No
$X_1 X_2 X_3 X_5 X_6$	19.133	6.000	0.261	0.152	0.519	No
$X_1 X_2 X_3 X_5 X_6 X_7$	20.982	7.000	0.263	0.129	0.526	No
$X_1 X_2 X_3 X_5 X_7$	19.030	6.000	0.262	0.154	0.518	No
$X_1 X_2 X_3 X_6$	17.348	5.000	0.257	0.172	0.513	No
$X_1 X_2 X_3 X_6 X_7$	19.301	6.000	0.258	0.149	0.520	No
$X_1 X_2 X_3 X_7$	17.420	5.000	0.256	0.171	0.513	No
$X_1 X_2 X_4$	5.261	4.000	0.416	0.367	0.448	No
$X_1 X_2 X_4 X_5$	6.898	5.000	0.421	0.355	0.453	No
$X_1 X_2 X_4 X_5 X_6$	6.897	6.000	0.453	0.372	0.447	No
$X_1 X_2 X_4 X_5 X_6 X_7$	6.408	7.000	0.492	0.399	0.437	Yes
$X_1 X_2 X_4 X_5 X_7$	8.892	6.000	0.421	0.336	0.459	No

(continued)	C_p	$p+1$	R^2	Adj. R^2	Std. Error	Consider This Model?
$X_1X_2X_4X_6$	4.903	5.000	0.452	0.390	0.440	Yes
$X_1X_2X_4X_6X_7$	4.680	6.000	0.487	0.412	0.432	Yes
$X_1X_2X_4X_7$	7.149	5.000	0.417	0.351	0.454	No
$X_1X_2X_5$	19.983	4.000	0.185	0.117	0.530	No
$X_1X_2X_5X_6$	17.460	5.000	0.256	0.170	0.513	No
$X_1X_2X_5X_6X_7$	19.394	6.000	0.257	0.147	0.520	No
$X_1X_2X_5X_7$	19.793	5.000	0.219	0.130	0.526	No
$X_1X_2X_6$	15.460	4.000	0.256	0.193	0.506	No
$X_1X_2X_6X_7$	17.402	5.000	0.256	0.171	0.513	No
$X_1X_2X_7$	17.804	4.000	0.219	0.154	0.518	No
X_1X_3	16.819	3.000	0.203	0.160	0.517	No
$X_1X_3X_4$	17.360	4.000	0.226	0.161	0.516	No
$X_1X_3X_4X_5$	19.346	5.000	0.226	0.137	0.523	No
$X_1X_3X_4X_5X_6$	21.323	6.000	0.226	0.113	0.531	No
$X_1X_3X_4X_5X_6X_7$	22.979	7.000	0.232	0.092	0.537	No
$X_1X_3X_4X_5X_7$	21.002	6.000	0.231	0.118	0.529	No
$X_1X_3X_4X_6$	19.360	5.000	0.226	0.137	0.523	No
$X_1X_3X_4X_6X_7$	21.113	6.000	0.230	0.116	0.530	No
$X_1X_3X_4X_7$	19.155	5.000	0.229	0.141	0.522	No
$X_1X_3X_5$	18.756	4.000	0.204	0.137	0.523	No
$X_1X_3X_5X_6$	20.718	5.000	0.204	0.113	0.531	No
$X_1X_3X_5X_6X_7$	22.616	6.000	0.206	0.089	0.538	No
$X_1X_3X_5X_7$	20.656	5.000	0.205	0.115	0.530	No
$X_1X_3X_6$	18.811	4.000	0.203	0.137	0.524	No
$X_1X_3X_6X_7$	20.770	5.000	0.204	0.113	0.531	No
$X_1X_3X_7$	18.798	4.000	0.203	0.137	0.524	No
X_1X_4	15.396	3.000	0.225	0.183	0.509	No
$X_1X_4X_5$	17.374	4.000	0.225	0.161	0.516	No
$X_1X_4X_5X_6$	19.354	5.000	0.226	0.137	0.523	No
$X_1X_4X_5X_6X_7$	21.058	6.000	0.23	0.117	0.529	No
$X_1X_4X_5X_7$	19.310	5.000	0.226	0.138	0.523	No
$X_1X_4X_6$	17.361	4.000	0.226	0.161	0.516	No
$X_1X_4X_6X_7$	19.113	5.000	0.230	0.142	0.522	No
$X_1X_4X_7$	17.371	4.000	0.226	0.161	0.516	No
X_1X_5	18.275	3.000	0.180	0.136	0.524	No
$X_1X_5X_6$	18.836	4.000	0.203	0.136	0.524	No
$X_1X_5X_6X_7$	20.779	5.000	0.203	0.112	0.531	No

(continued)

	C_p	$p+1$	R^2	Adj. R^2	Std. Error	Consider This Model?
$X_1X_5X_7$	19.464	4.000	0.193	0.125	0.527	No
X_1X_6	16.839	3.000	0.203	0.159	0.517	No
$X_1X_6X_7$	18.792	4.000	0.203	0.137	0.524	No
X_1X_7	17.478	3.000	0.192	0.149	0.520	No
X_2	27.736	2.000	0.000	−0.026	0.571	No
X_2X_3	22.458	3.000	0.114	0.066	0.544	No
$X_2X_3X_4$	18.558	4.000	0.207	0.141	0.522	No
$X_2X_3X_4X_5$	19.508	5.000	0.223	0.135	0.524	No
$X_2X_3X_4X_5X_6$	20.883	6.000	0.233	0.120	0.528	No
$X_2X_3X_4X_5X_6X_7$	10.157	7.000	0.433	0.330	0.461	No
$X_2X_3X_4X_5X_7$	8.2537	6.000	0.431	0.348	0.455	No
$X_2X_3X_4X_6$	18.887	5.000	0.233	0.145	0.521	No
$X_2X_3X_4X_6X_7$	9.339	6.000	0.414	0.328	0.462	No
$X_2X_3X_4X_7$	11.497	5.000	0.349	0.275	0.480	No
$X_2X_3X_5$	23.523	4.000	0.129	0.056	0.547	No
$X_2X_3X_5X_6$	25.271	5.000	0.133	0.034	0.554	No
$X_2X_3X_5X_6X_7$	22.807	6.000	0.203	0.086	0.539	No
$X_2X_3X_5X_7$	20.826	5.000	0.203	0.112	0.531	No
$X_2X_3X_6$	23.292	4.000	0.133	0.060	0.546	No
$X_2X_3X_6X_7$	21.478	5.000	0.192	0.100	0.535	No
$X_2X_3X_7$	21.443	4.000	0.162	0.092	0.537	No
X_2X_4	27.763	3.000	0.031	−0.021	0.569	No
$X_2X_4X_5$	28.710	4.000	0.048	−0.032	0.572	No
$X_2X_4X_5X_6$	20.111	5.000	0.214	0.124	0.527	No
$X_2X_4X_5X_6X_7$	8.253	6.000	0.431	0.348	0.455	No
$X_2X_4X_5X_7$	11.570	5.000	0.348	0.273	0.480	No
$X_2X_4X_6$	20.231	4.000	0.181	0.112	0.531	No
$X_2X_4X_6X_7$	8.525	5.000	0.396	0.327	0.462	No
$X_2X_4X_7$	12.098	4.000	0.308	0.251	0.488	No
X_2X_5	28.517	3.000	0.019	−0.034	0.573	No
$X_2X_5X_6$	23.646	4.000	0.127	0.054	0.548	No
$X_2X_5X_6X_7$	20.914	5.000	0.201	0.110	0.532	No
$X_2X_5X_7$	21.928	4.000	0.154	0.084	0.539	No
X_2X_6	22.912	3.000	0.107	0.059	0.547	No
$X_2X_6X_7$	19.912	4.000	0.186	0.118	0.529	No
X_2X_7	21.139	3.000	0.135	0.088	0.538	No
X_3	20.606	2.000	0.112	0.089	0.538	No

(continued)

	C_p	$p+1$	R^2	Adj. R^2	Std. Error	Consider This Model?
X_3X_4	18.711	3.000	0.173	0.128	0.526	No
$X_3X_4X_5$	20.315	4.000	0.179	0.111	0.531	No
$X_3X_4X_5X_6$	22.160	5.000	0.182	0.088	0.538	No
$X_3X_4X_5X_6X_7$	21.412	6.000	0.225	0.111	0.531	No
$X_3X_4X_5X_7$	19.413	5.000	0.225	0.136	0.524	No
$X_3X_4X_6$	20.160	4.000	0.182	0.114	0.531	No
$X_3X_4X_6X_7$	19.651	5.000	0.221	0.132	0.525	No
$X_3X_4X_7$	18.171	4.000	0.2123	0.147	0.520	No
X_3X_5	21.526	3.000	0.129	0.082	0.540	No
$X_3X_5X_6$	23.273	4.000	0.133	0.061	0.546	No
$X_3X_5X_6X_7$	22.029	5.000	0.184	0.091	0.537	No
$X_3X_5X_7$	20.030	4.000	0.184	0.116	0.530	No
X_3X_6	21.294	3.000	0.133	0.086	0.539	No
$X_3X_6X_7$	20.433	4.000	0.177	0.109	0.532	No
X_3X_7	19.641	3.000	0.159	0.113	0.531	No
X_4	26.171	2.000	0.025	−0.001	0.564	No
X_4X_5	26.799	3.000	0.046	−0.005	0.565	No
$X_4X_5X_6$	20.557	4.000	0.176	0.107	0.533	No
$X_4X_5X_6X_7$	19.448	5.000	0.224	0.136	0.524	No
$X_4X_5X_7$	17.928	4.000	0.217	0.152	0.519	No
X_4X_6	19.565	3.000	0.160	0.114	0.530	No
$X_4X_6X_7$	17.820	4.000	0.218	0.153	0.519	No
X_4X_7	16.484	3.000	0.208	0.165	0.515	No
X_5	26.726	2.000	0.016	−0.010	0.566	No
X_5X_6	21.651	3.000	0.127	0.080	0.541	No
$X_5X_6X_7$	20.099	4.000	0.183	0.115	0.530	No
X_5X_7	19.955	3.000	0.154	0.108	0.532	No
X_6	21.107	2.000	0.104	0.081	0.540	No
X_6X_7	18.685	3.000	0.174	0.129	0.526	No
X_7	19.177	2.000	0.134	0.112	0.531	No

List of best models: $X_1X_2X_3X_4$, $X_1X_2X_3X_4X_5X_6X_7$, $X_1X_2X_3X_4X_5X_7$, $X_1X_2X_3X_4X_6X_7$, $X_1X_2X_3X_4X_7$, $X_1X_2X_4X_5X_6X_7$, $X_1X_2X_4X_6$, $X_1X_2X_4X_6X_7$

Common subset is $X_1X_2X_4$. This will be a base model (BM).

Model	Including to the BM	*p*-value	Significantly Different From BM
$X_1X_2X_3X_4$	X_3	0.139	No
$X_1X_2X_3X_4X_5X_6X_7$	X_3	0.528	No
	X_5	0.416	No
	X_6	0.951	No
	X_7	0.104	No
$X_1X_2X_3X_4X_5X_7$	X_3	0.032	Yes
	X_5	0.227	No
	X_7	0.098	No
$X_1X_2X_3X_4X_6X_7$	X_3	0.976	No
	X_6	0.376	No
	X_7	0.145	No
$X_1X_2X_3X_4X_7$	X_3	0.062	No
	X_7	0.226	No
$X_1X_2X_4X_5X_6X_7$	X_5	0.602	No
	X_6	0.040	Yes
	X_7	0.121	No
$X_1X_2X_4X_6$	X_6	0.133	No
$X_1X_2X_4X_6X_7$	X_6	0.038	Yes
	X_7	0.138	No

Including X_3 to the BM provides a model that does not significantly differ from BM. The same is true for including X_6.
Summary Output: $X_1X_2X_4$

Regression Statistics	
Multiple R	0.645
R^2	0.416
Adjusted R^2	0.367
Standard Error	0.448
Observations	40.000

ANOVA

	df	SS	MS	F	Significance F
Regression	3.000	5.146	1.715	8.531	0.000
Residual	36.000	7.238	0.201		
Total	39.000	12.384			

	Coefficients	Standard Error	*t* Stat	*p*-value	Lower 95%	Upper 95%
Intercept	−18.201	5.566	−3.270	0.002	−29.489	−6.913
Soil radiation	0.001	0.000	4.866	2.26×10^{-5}	0.001	0.002
Soil temperature	0.287	0.084	3.424	0.002	0.117	0.458
Wind speed	−0.408	0.106	−3.856	0.000	−0.622	−0.193

Residual analysis:

The developed regression model is:

$$\text{Radon concentration} = -18.201 + 0.001 \times \text{Soil radiation}$$
$$+ 0.288 \times \text{Soil temperature} - 0.408$$
$$\times \text{Wind speed}$$

67. **There are more than 7 variables in univ&col.xls file, so PHStat cannot analyze this data.**
Below is MINITAB's solution:

```
Stepwise Regression: Average indebted versus Type of term; Location; ...


Alpha-to-Enter: 0.15  Alpha-to-Remove: 0.15
Response is Average  on  7 predictors, with N= 80
```

Step	1	2
Constant	6.869	13.239

Annual t	0.306	0.409
T-Value	4.14	4.15
P-Value	0.000	0.000

Average		-0.0072
T-Value		-1.56
P-Value		0.122

Average		-0.0072
T-Value		-1.56
P-Value		0.122

S	3.88	3.84
R-Sq	17.98	20.50
R-Sq(adj)	16.93	18.44
C-p	-0.1	-0.5
PRESS	1227.43	1248.15
R-Sq(pred)	14.12	12.67

Developed regression model is:
  Average indebtedness at graduation = $13.239 + 0.409 \times$ Annual total cost $- 0.007 \times$ Average total SAT

```
Best Subsets Regression: Average inde versus Type of term; Location; ...


Response is Average
                                            L       T R A
                                        T o T A O o n
                                        y c y v E o n
                                        p a p e F m u
                                        e t e r L   a
                                        i     a 5 a l
                                        o o o g 5 n
Vars  R-Sq   R-Sq(adj)     C-p      S   f n f e 0 d t
   1  18.0      16.9      -0.1   3.8766             X
   1  16.3      15.3       1.4   3.9152     X
   2  20.5      18.4      -0.5   3.8412         X   X
   2  18.8      16.7       1.1   3.8826     X       X
   3  21.0      17.9       1.1   3.8548         X X X
   3  20.9      17.7       1.2   3.8575         X X   X
   4  21.7      17.6       2.4   3.8619         X X X X
   4  21.3      17.1       2.8   3.8737   X       X X X
   5  22.0      16.7       4.2   3.8824   X   X X X   X
   5  21.8      16.5       4.3   3.8857         X X X X X
   6  22.1      15.7       6.0   3.9049   X   X X X X X
   6  22.0      15.6       6.1   3.9065   X X X X X   X
   7  22.2      14.6       8.0   3.9307   X X X X X X X
```

Based on the R^2 and adjusted R^2, the best multiple regression model must include the Average total SAT and Annual total variables. This is the same result as found in the stepwise regression procedure.